Print and 1

Southeast Asia

POLITICS, MEANING, AND MEMORY

Rita Smith Kipp and David Chandler

SERIES EDITORS

Print
and
Power

Confucianism, Communism, and

Buddhism in the Making

of Modern Vietnam

SHAWN FREDERICK McHALE

UNIVERSITY OF HAWAI'I PRESS   *Honolulu*

Library of Congress Cataloging-in-Publication Data

McHale, Shawn Frederick.

  Print and power: Confucianism, communism, and
Buddhism in the making of modern Vietnam / Shawn
Frederick McHale.

    p.   cm.—(Southeast Asia)

Includes bibliography references and index.

ISBN 978-0-8248-3304-6 (paperback : alk. paper)

1. Vietnam—History—1858–1945—Historiography.

2. Buddhism—Vietnam—History—20th century.

3. Confucianism—Vietnam—History—20th century.

4. Communism—Vietnam—History.   5. Printing—
Vietnam—History—20th century.   I. Title.   II. Series.

DS556.8.M387 2003

959.7'03—dc21

                                    2003007985

Illustrations credit: Archives Nationales de France,
Centre des Archives d'Outre-Mer

Designed by April Higgins, after design by Rich Hendel

Printed by The Maple-Vail Book Manufacturing Group

CONTENTS

ACKNOWLEDGMENTS

This book began to take shape years ago as a doctoral dissertation and has since been revised extensively. I would like to thank David Wyatt, Sherman Cochran, and Keith Taylor for their early counsel. For help in conducting research in France, the following persons deserve special mention: Lucette Vachier and Simone Ménager of the Centre des Archives d'Outre-Mer (Aix-en-Provence) and Professor Pierre Brocheux, Université de Paris–VII.

I would like especially to thank Professor Phan Huy Lê and Professor Đoàn Thiện Thuật, University of Hanoi, the director and vice-director of the Center for Vietnamese and Intercultural Studies, which first sponsored me in Vietnam. Nguyễn Văn Lịch, director of the Center for the Study of Southeast Asia and Vietnam, University of Ho Chi Minh City, facilitated two of my visits to Ho Chi Minh City. I would also like to thank the staffs of the Revolutionary Museum (Hanoi) and the National Archives (Hanoi and Ho Chi Minh City). For my research on Buddhism, members of the Vietnamese Institute for Buddhist Studies and monks at the Quán Sứ temple (Hanoi) and the Xá Lợi temple (Ho Chi Minh City) helped me with some rare sources.

My research abroad was made possible by a Fulbright-Hays Doctoral Dissertation Fellowship provided by the U.S. Department of Education; by a grant from the Joint Committee on Southeast Asia of the Social Science Research Council and the American Council of Learned Societies with funds provided by the Andrew W. Mellon Foundation, the Ford Foundation, and the Henry Luce Foundation; and by supplemental funding from the Cornell Department of History. Dissertation write-up was funded by a Mellon Completion Fellowship. Since then, I have also benefited from support from the George Washington University, including crucial help from the Sigur Center for Asian Studies.

Over the years, I have benefited from the advice of several individuals, including Christoph Giebel and Mike Montesano. For criticisms of various parts of the book, I would like to thank Ed McCord, Helen Chauncey, Peter Zinoman, Hue Tam Ho Tai, Keith Taylor, David Chandler, Chris Goscha, and Li Tana. I have not, I confess, always followed my critics' advice, but their criticisms have forced me to clarify my arguments. Pam Kelley and Cheri Dunn at the University of Hawai'i Press have professionally shepherded this manuscript to press. Finally, I would like to thank the members of my department at George Washington University, who have provided a pleasantly collegial environment in which to work.

This book would not have been written without the key help and support of four individuals. Over the years, Keith Taylor has provided extensive commentary on my work. Keith's combination of scholarly rigor, friendship, and support is exemplary. My spouse, Diane Kristen McHale, has been a constant source of encouragement, especially in those three stressful years before I landed a tenure-track position. To her I want to express my love and heartfelt thanks. And to my parents, Thomas and Mary McHale, my debt is incalculable. Thanks to them, I was introduced to the world of Southeast Asia. Their deep curiosity about the region sparked mine. This book is a loving tribute to them.

Ten years ago, I became captivated by the topic that forms the core of this book: the rise of a Vietnamese public sphere and the role of print therein from 1920 to 1945. While scholars have routinely commented on how "literary" the Vietnamese have been, no one had studied the economic and social history of the Vietnamese use of print. This book began, then, as a project to fill that gap.

My project was also animated by a disquieting sense that the received political narrative of Vietnamese history, in which anticolonial national-ism and revolution ultimately defined the significance of most of the twentieth century, had slighted the cultural and intellectual history of Buddhism and Confucianism while overrating the significance of com-munism. A reevaluation was, I believed, in order.

Arriving at an understanding of Vietnam's public and clandestine spheres and their print cultures was harder than I had at first imagined because of the nature of the sources at my disposal, especially archives and the pre-1945 publications themselves. I was disappointed to find that the archival sources had insufficient information on the economic and social history of publishing. These archives, product of a colonial state, overwhelmingly present a picture of the world of print in terms of its relation to politics and state power. After all, the colonial state was most interested in controlling and repressing perceived threats to its authority. This statist view of the public realm, reflected in the archives, might lead the researcher to conclude that the colonial state dominated the realm of print. It is an enormously seductive view.

Seductive? Yes, for historiographical and personal reasons. "Reading the archive," the French historian Arlette Farge states, "immediately incites a sense of the real that no printed matter, however little known, can arouse."[1] If printed texts are meant to be read by a public, the same is not true of archival documents. The fact that the archive was not meant to be open to the public leads us to believe that we are unmasking secrets: "It is in this sense that it compels reading, 'ensnares' the reader, produces in him the feeling of finally seizing hold of the real. And not of examining [the real] through *a story about, a discourse on.*"[2] It is perhaps no less important that the materiality of the archive—the yellowing paper, the dust caught on the fragile sheets—reinforces this sense of an encounter with truth.

What I found in the colonial archives was tantalizing. Reading the archives does incite a sense of finally encountering the real. Buried in the archives one can find records of embarrassing controversies in Vietnamese communist history that Party historians are loathe to mention.[3] It is a relief to find them: they seem to affirm the worth of the search. Even the best Vietnamese historians of the modern period have been hostage to shifts in the party line, and we readers hunger for unbridled access to the "secrets" that the Party wishes to conceal.

The archives do not simply provide records of Vietnamese secrets about the past. They also contain evidence of how the colonial state censored publications and thus refashioned Vietnamese discourse in the present and memories of the past. The archives can be used, in other words, to undermine the French colonial state's public transcript of its relationship with its subjects. But even with such evidence, one must always return to the question: who is writing these archives, and whose vision of reality predominates? Reading through the files of the French colonial state, I was frustrated by the partiality of the view presented. Thus, while I draw heavily on archives in Part 1, most of my book relies on other sources.

Ultimately, most of this book is based on publications printed before 1945. The ravages of war and the passage of time have conspired to destroy many copies of printed matter. Censorship and destruction of property by postcolonial states have also decimated the historical record. But many precious books and tracts remain. When I first began research into Vietnamese print culture, I was stunned by the sheer variety of material published between 1920 and 1945 that is available to the researcher— stunned because, with the exception of David Marr, no historian outside of Vietnam has extensively exploited the available collections of printed matter from this period. One of the great accomplishments of the French colonial state was to preserve collections, now available at the Bibliothèque nationale in Paris and the National Library in Hanoi, of the great majority of works published in this time period.

Starting with the Paris collection, then continuing with its Vietnamese counterparts, I became aware of a realm that I had only imperfectly known. If to Farge the archive often seems more real than stories or discourses about the past, in the case of Vietnam, this is not quite true. So many stories have not been told about this past and scholars have so rarely exploited the richness of printed texts from 1920 to 1945 that reading such (once public) material from this period can be a revelation. This book largely explores the world as viewed through such texts.

The choice of topics in this book merits a brief mention. In a very rough sense, different chapters attempt to follow the trajectory of printed matter itself: that is, from the creation and publishing of printed matter, through its control by the state, to its circulation and appropriation. To put it differently, I am not simply interested in the production of printed matter but attempt to explore how audiences made sense of such material. The first two chapters develop these points by providing an overview of the public sphere and state repression. They are followed by three topical chapters on the print cultures of Buddhism, Confucianism, and communism. The choice of these three topical chapters is not arbitrary. Although it is intrinsically interesting to explore how three beliefs with universalistic pretensions have been localized, this is not the main reason for choosing them. Two of these topics, Buddhism and Confucianism, had (with a few notable exceptions) been surprisingly neglected in works on the twentieth century. My first intent, then, was to see if this oversight was justified.

To confirm my sense that the topics of Buddhism and Confucianism retained a significance in this period, I methodically surveyed the Fonds indochinois in France's Bibliothèque nationale. While this collection cannot be said to represent what Vietnamese might have wanted to write (censors stopped many Vietnamese from publishing critiques of French political rule, for example), it is a reasonably complete collection of all publications from the 1920–1945 period. Based on my survey, I came to my first important conclusion: the writings of the avant-garde made up a small percentage of all writings. My second major realization, hardly surprising, was that tracts and books on religion and morals far outweighed those on politics. Rather than studying a topic because leading colonial or postcolonial historians deemed it important, in this book I have sought to examine what was actually important to the print culture of the 1920–1945 period. Based on the sheer numbers of books on morals and religion found in French and Vietnamese collections, it makes sense to explore the printed discourses of Buddhism and Confucianism.

Nonetheless, to exclude some topics because they are not represented in catalogs of legally published books and tracts would be a mistake: not all publications were legal. Consequently I have added a chapter on illegal communist tracts and newspapers. Communism only fitfully influenced public life between 1920 and 1945—in fact, I believe that its intellectual contribution in its early years has been overrated—but through it one can explore the ways that a public and legal realm was constituted against a persistent illegal discourse on the margins.

The three chapters in Part 2 complement the general comments about print culture and the public sphere with specific case studies. These chapters do not pretend to cover all of Vietnam: each one has a rough geographical focus. By not placing the subjects of these chapters in a national frame, this book resists the tendency of the nationalist historiography to subsume local and regional transformations to developments at the national level.

But I don't want to jump ahead of the story. Let us begin by examining the rise of a public realm of discourse and then exploring the vexed attempts of colonial administrators to control the public. It is only with such a background that one can fully grasp the character of the public realm, the limits of state power, and the inventive chaos of Vietnamese in the 1920–1945 period.

Part 1.
The State and
the Public
Sphere

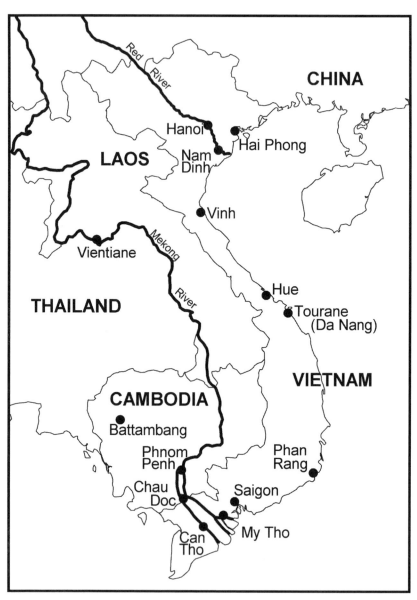

CHINA

Red River

Hanoi
Hai Phong

LAOS

Nam
Dinh

Vinh

Vientiane

Mekong

THAILAND

River

Hue

Tourane
(Da Nang)

VIETNAM

CAMBODIA

Battambang

Phnom
Penh

Phan
Rang

Chau
Doc

Saigon

Can
Tho

My Tho

By Maxwell Rucdeschel

I

Transforming Print Culture and the Public Sphere

The year is 1939. A nineteen-year-old inhabitant of the village of Hòa Hảo in the western Mekong delta, Huỳnh Phú Sổ, falls ill, then recovers. He has had a religious awakening: the Low Era is upon us, Sổ announces. The world is in turmoil and has entered a new period in cosmic history. Styling himself the "crazy monk" and drawing on the Buddhist traditions of the Mekong delta, he exhorts people to do good and follow his version of religion. He declares himself a messenger of the Jade Buddha and proclaims a message of salvation.[1]

His movement, now known as Hòa Hảo Buddhism, expands so rapidly that by 1944 it claims five million followers. In 1947, the Việt Minh attempts to crush this major rival. It kidnaps Huỳnh Phú Sổ, executes him, cuts his body into pieces, and buries them. It also proceeds to massacre other Hòa Hảo leaders and followers in the hope of extinguishing the movement. It fails: indeed, most Hòa Hảo oppose the communists from this period onward.

The story of Huỳnh Phú Sổ's rise and fall will sound vaguely familiar to students of Asian history: with its apocalyptic message of salvation, it resembles, for example, the story of the 1813 Eight Trigrams Uprising in China. The story is also familiar to those who write about southern Vietnam, even if it does not occupy a prominent place in history books. To most scholars, I suspect, the Hòa Hảo are an odd vestige of the past. The religion Sổ established, Hòa Hảo Buddhism, founded in a rural area and drawing heavily on fundamental Buddhist beliefs and oral traditions of the western Mekong delta, appears to be the antithesis of the modern, secular, and progressive movements that transformed twentieth-century Vietnam.

Yet the rise of Hòa Hảo Buddhists as well as other supposedly "traditional" movements does not symbolize the last gasp of a fading way of life. These heterodox Buddhists selectively adopted modern organizational forms, such as the political party, and embraced modern technologies of print to spread their worldviews. Print was key to spreading Hòa Hảo influence.[2] One Hòa Hảo source asserts that, from 1939 to 1965, Huỳnh Phú Sổ's oracles were reprinted more than three hundred times and with a total print run exceeding 800,000. Such proliferation of tracts would have been unthinkable one hundred years before.[3]

The Hòa Hảo use of the published word forms part of the larger topic of this book: the spread of print, the rise of northern and southern public spheres in Vietnam, and the place of Buddhism, Confucianism, and communism in this transformation. If the great majority of studies of twentieth-century Vietnam focus on the activities of political and cultural vanguards, the Hòa Hảo story is a reminder that a broad spectrum of individuals and movements used printed materials and contributed to a Vietnamese public realm. If most accounts of modern Vietnamese history center on the themes of state, nationalism, and revolution, these themes do not exhaust the potential of the past.[4] An entire world of phenomena—the world of spirits and tutelary divinities, of religious movements, mendicant monks, and Confucian reformers, to name a few—tends to be overlooked when historians tell the "main" story.

At first glance, nonetheless, the conventional story, emphasizing the dramatic political and cultural transformations of the last century, seems on target. From the 1920s, many literate Vietnamese became captivated by the rejection of the old and the embrace of the new. Between 1920 and 1945, they began to experiment with new forms of collective organization, including the political party, that would alter their country's fate in the twentieth century. Vietnamese embraced new customs: thousands of them, especially in the south, adopted Western clothes and insisted on speaking French. A modern state, seemingly powerful, extended its control over the populace. Printed matter circulated more than ever before. An iconoclastic avant-garde promoted a discourse of secular enlightenment; intellectuals displayed a chaotic inventiveness and (often) a drunken exaltation of the modern. The pace of change could be dizzying: as Vũ Ngọc Phan noted about literary life, "for us, one year is like thirty years for people from a different time."[5] These transformations seem to be telescoped in the awed words of Hoài Thanh and Hoài Chân in 1941, words that marvel over Vietnam's encounter with the West:

How many changes in roughly sixty years! Sixty years, but it seems like sixty centuries! Westernization is not simply influential. It has passed through two phases: form and thought; it shall go through one more. It has changed customs of daily life; it has changed our ways of thinking; clearly it will change our rhythms, how our emotions are moved as well....

The West today has penetrated into the deepest part of our soul. We can no longer be happy like the happiness of the past, sad like the sadness of the past, love, hate, be angry as before.[6]

The statement above is stunning. No French author has conveyed with such eloquence how the colonial encounter could strikingly transform Vietnamese sensibilities. The words are also troubling: if, as many claim, nationalism deeply shaped Vietnam in the 1920–1945 period, how does one explain this statement? If nationalists champion an indigenist point of view, this passage articulates a Westernized one. If nationalism stresses the way that a people imagines itself as a people and defines itself against an Other, this statement seems to say that to be truly Vietnamese, one had to be profoundly Westernized. One is obliquely reminded of John Fitzgerald's argument in *Awakening China* that the nationalist awakening was conceptualized first and foremost as an individual awakening; only when the individual awakened to his or her "true" self could the process of national awakening begin.[7] It seemed that only by unshackling oneself from the heritage of the past—the dead weight of Confucianism, the mindless rituals of Buddhism, the superstitions of the Hòa Hảo, and so forth—and embracing the modern could one, paradoxically, help the nation awaken to itself.

The words of Hoài Thanh and Hoài Chân may astonish postcolonial minds: no Vietnamese today would exalt the West in such innocent terms. But such sentiments are not completely foreign to us. They form but one extreme of a strand of thought found in the 1920–1945 era, the language of secular enlightenment. From Batavia in the Netherlands East Indies to Manila in the Philippines and on to Peking, this language has deeply shaped Asian views of the past and visions of the future. Twentieth-century Vietnam is no exception. The use of such language is intimately tied to the consolidation of French control, the dramatic expansion in the use of the printed word, and the search, as Alexander Woodside has put it, for new organized communities.[8]

Enlightenment discourse enthralled young intellectuals in the interwar years. Hoàng Đạo, a leading member of the Self-Strengthening Literary Group, wrote in 1937 that the past was like a never-ending dream. He advised the Vietnamese to "follow the new, completely follow the new, do not hesitate one minute." Westernize, he exhorted his audience. Others, blaming several thousand years of despotism for the poverty of Vietnamese literature, declared: "We must believe in the future, in the natural capabilities of the people. Our people cannot avoid having a brilliant future." The belief in the decadence of the old and the corresponding promise in the future found in these passages characterizes some of the most heady talk of these decades. The West loomed large in this worldview.[9]

Partisans of social change often tempered extreme versions of this forward-looking secular conviction. They came to argue that one could embrace the future without completely Westernizing and rejecting the past. Lương Đức Thiệp spoke of a "revolution in zigzags," one that saw Vietnamese embracing Confucius and Einstein, Laozi and Lenin, yin and yang, atoms and electrons.[10] The past appears part of a dialectical process in which the old is not left behind but embraced along with the new. Nguyễn Tế Mỹ adopted a similar appreciation of the past. He argued that the Trưng sisters' rebellion against the Chinese in 40 C.E. should be remembered because it prefigured the development of a Vietnamese national spirit (*tinh thần quốc gia*).[11] But if such authors moderated their embrace of the West and underlined the importance of Vietnam's heritage, their work was infused by beliefs in modernity and secular progress. They and others used "enlightenment" metaphors like "awakening" (*tỉnh ngộ*), "enlighten" (*giác ngộ*), "revival" (*chấn hưng*), "renaissance" (*phục hưng*), and "progress" (*tiến hóa*) to make sense of this contentious period. Modernity, it would seem, had triumphed.

But were all Vietnamese advocates of modernity, nationalism, and revolution? Was Vietnam "awakened" into its modern being during the 1920–1945 period? While most of the historical literature assumes or implies that this is true, the story of the Hòa Hảo that introduces this book should make us pause: only a small minority of Vietnamese, usually young, educated, and urban, held such beliefs. The heritage of the past did not disappear. One must not forget the anguish of a man who cried out in 1927 that "the hearts and minds of our country's people are in turmoil, are no longer able to distinguish orthodoxy from heresy."[12] The very language of this statement indicates that the writer occupied a perceptual world quite different from that of the young modernizers. In short, not all discourse and practice of the 1920–1945 period fits into a narrative of secular modern enlightenment.

When one examines what Vietnamese published and read between 1920 and 1945, it becomes clear that Vietnamese thought about far more than revolution and the nation. Morality tracts and lowbrow fiction circulated far more than revolutionary writings. Vietnamese argued over the nature of "tradition," women's roles, and even history. They penned love poetry and detective novels and published learned reviews and scandal-sheet newspapers. The study of print culture shows that Vietnamese engaged the past, faced the present, and wondered about the future in multiple ways, giving modern Vietnamese history a richness of texture that scholars have often overlooked.

THE MAKING OF THE VIETNAMESE PUBLIC SPHERE

Vietnam in the twentieth century saw the rise of a print culture: print increasingly supplanted oral modes of communicating information. I will argue that the development of this print culture, while occurring at the same time as the rise of nationalist and revolutionary movements, was a distinct process that should be understood on its own terms. I will also examine how the rise of this print culture was linked to the elaboration of distinct Confucian, communist, and Buddhist realms of discourse.[13] These realms were constituted, in part, as reactions to colonial practice, administration, and law. Law determined the framework of an emergent public sphere and established the grounds for censorship. By defining the nature of unacceptable discourse in legal terms, it forced anti-French writings out of public debate and into the realm of the clandestine. And, defined as it was by French and Vietnamese notions of secular and religious realms, this public sphere marginalized religious publications.

The concept of the "public sphere" refers to the space below the state and above the village in which individuals and groups engage in symbolic exchange and struggle. By the 1920s, two cities, Saigon and Hanoi, dominated this realm. These cities monopolized the production of printed matter and acted as the centers of literary, religious, and political debates. Other minor centers of intellectual production, like Huế, Vinh,

Hải Phòng, and Cần Thơ, existed in the orbit of these larger realms of debate and exchange. These realms were gendered: males heavily dominated the production and consumption of printed matter. As I will later show, this public sphere could be quite contentious, with journalists hurling accusations against each other as well as against the government. But it also contained much light-hearted fare.

While Hanoi and Saigon dominated the public sphere and its print culture, printed texts also circulated into rural areas of Tonkin, Annam, and Cochinchina. Indeed, the public realm even spilled outside of these regions. Vietnamese read books imported from China. Vietnamese in Cambodia and Laos subscribed to newspapers and journals printed in Vietnam. And Vietnamese abroad, whether in Cambodia, Siam, China, or France, published their own newspapers and books. Increasingly, print was making inroads into the highly oral society of the Vietnamese.

The public sphere was not simply defined by the production of printed matter: equally important was the reception and transformation of this material by its audiences. Not all individuals read texts in the same manner. Some Buddhists read tracts for their magical powers. Westernized intellectuals might read the newspaper for its information or its ideological debates. And Confucians linked reading to moral cultivation. In other words, Vietnamese appropriated the printed word in a plurality of ways. Since women had much lower literacy rates than men and often expressed different concerns in print, their experience of the public sphere differed radically from men's.

How successful was the state in its attempts to control the public realm? The state did shape the limits of the public sphere. Colonial law governed the initial trajectory of much printed matter, established the grounds for censorship, and determined the framework of an emergent public sphere. Because the laws allowed some important realms of freedom, especially in the south, the police resorted to extralegal and illegal means to enforce repression. While the French colonial state repressed "subversive" publications, it cared little about the vast majority. French colonial rule was selectively, not uniformly, harsh. It was political dominance without sociocultural hegemony.

To develop this last point, I will focus on Confucian, communist, and Buddhist realms of discourse in Part 2 of this book. The examination of these topics is not arbitrary. Fragments of Confucian teachings informed a wide range of Vietnamese preoccupations over the bases of action, morality, and behavior. In this sense, such arguments are of fundamental importance in understanding Vietnam from 1920 to 1945.

The chapters on communist and Buddhist fields of discourse illustrate—in radically different ways—alternative discourses outside the public sphere. By banning communist publications and cracking down on communist organizations, the French attempted to force such thought out of public debate. As a result, communists were forced to create an illegal (and thus clandestine) realm of discourse. The French colonial state, drawing on Republican ideology, marginalized religion and promoted secularization in areas like schooling. Despite these secular policies, Buddhists rarely faced overt state repression. Buddhism came, along with other religions, to constitute an autonomous realm of discourse outside the public sphere, one in which secular Western ideas had almost no impact.

In analyzing the evolving public realm, the student of Vietnamese history must address three linked issues. First, what is the origin of the concept of the "public sphere"? Second, how did a realm of public debate historically develop? Finally, to what extent was the state able to control public life? Let me begin with the first issue: the definition of the "public sphere." The question remains whether or not the concept of the public sphere, originally used to refer to developments in Europe, is "modular" and can thus be applied to non-European transformations. Does this concept describe well the rise of a distinct realm of discourse perched between village and state? I would argue that it can be used with caution, provided that one avoids imposing an exclusively Western, Japanese, or Chinese understanding of the term on the Vietnamese case.

The concept of the "public sphere" has gained currency from the work of the German social theorist Jürgen Habermas. Habermas states that the (bourgeois) public sphere of the eighteenth century "may be conceived above all as the sphere of private people come together as a public; they soon claim the public sphere regulated from above against the public authorities themselves." In the process of defining the character of this new social and intellectual space, Habermas makes an astonishing claim: that in the confrontation between the public and the state is seen, for the first time, the "people's public use of their reason."[14] Habermas, in other words, believes that people relinquish their purely private interests in order to articulate reasoned views in terms of the public as a whole.

Given the distinct European historical trajectory of state and class formation that shaped the rise of the public sphere and the critique within European studies of the Habermasian view, it would be rash to assume that such formulations neatly fit diverse Asian experiences.[15] Within European studies, for example, Robert Darnton has uncovered an eighteenth-century Republic of Letters inhabited by hacks as well as philosophers, by gentlemen amateurs as well as those who penned bawdy libels.[16] This hardly seems an empire of pure reason. Such criticisms aside, attempts to apply Habermas to Asia often miss the fact that the cultural and institutional setting of public spheres can differ so radically. David Strand, for example, points out that before the twentieth century, Chinese "had no concept of citizen to legitimize individual or group initiatives in the realm of public affairs," and they lacked "the legal rationale for municipal government and an ideological justification for expanding the compass of politically active individuals beyond scholar-officials, examination candidates, and guild leaders." It was only when such ideological and legal innovations were introduced to China that "public spaces ranging from temple grounds and brothels to public parks and theaters became available to house city politics," and political participation in politics soared.[17] But even here the apparent convergence of European and Asian public spheres masks deep differences. To Habermas, individuals used the public realm to express interests of public import, whereas to Strand, the Chinese public sphere was the stage for individuals and particularistic interests to reach a wider audience.

The discrepant understanding of the link between particularistic and public interests is not the only problem with using the concept of the public sphere. "Can a robust public sphere coexist with an authoritarian state?" Mary Elizabeth Berry asks. Focusing on Japan, she answers yes: but it is necessary to "detach the public sphere from the telos of democracy."[18] Using the interwar period in Japan as an example, she argues that if scholars jettison such a teleological view, we can make sense of Japan's boisterous public realm under authoritarian rule. The public sphere was "not ... where popular sovereignty was claimed but where leadership was scrutinized and disciplined by criticism."[19] Berry's insight is key: rather than measure such public spheres against the normative Western model and thus see them as failures, her approach allows us to chart the internal logic of their historical development. It also suggests that a strong state does not necessarily come at the expense of a vibrant public realm.

A lively public sphere developed in Vietnam during the 1920–1945 period despite French repression. Yet Habermas' notion that people abandon private interest to discuss issues of public import seems far-fetched for Vietnam. Drawing on Strand, I would argue instead that the Vietnamese public sphere is where particularistic interests contested their views. In accord with Berry, I would argue that the emergence of the Vietnamese public sphere was not linked to democratization. (Even when Vietnamese ideologues called for "democracy," one must contextualize their views: few of them appear to have meant an egalitarian, radically inclusive political culture.) In Vietnam, a relatively vibrant but hierarchical public realm of debate existed under authoritarian colonial rule.

The study of the Vietnamese public sphere benefits from comparisons to East Asian countries for a simple reason: Vietnamese appropriated many of the modern concepts relevant to the public sphere from that region. Or more accurately, it appropriated many key concepts that were Western in origin but transformed through Japanese and Chinese understandings of the Western terms. The terms for "public" (*công*) and "public opinion" (*công luận, dư luận*) are obvious examples, but numerous other terms in political and social analysis, like "politics" (*chính trị*), "society" (*xã hội*), "doctrine" (*chủ nghĩa*), and "class" (*giai cấp*), also entered the Vietnamese language via China and Japan.

While comparisons to East Asia are essential, there are clear limits to such exercises. Vietnam confounds any such approach for an elementary reason: European state institutions structured the public realm in Vietnam far more than in China or Japan. A French state imposed its construction of a public space on Indochina. Press laws and decrees ignored Vietnamese precedents and developed out of French jurisprudence. While the state apparatus made concessions to Vietnamese practices, it operated in a recognizably Western bureaucratic manner. In short, the Vietnamese public realm and its print culture incorporated competing influences from Vietnam, France, and East Asia. This sphere did not appear ex nihilo: to its historical background and transformation I now briefly turn.

HISTORY AND PRINT CULTURE TO 1920

Compared to most of Southeast Asia, Vietnamese print culture was already vibrant in the nineteenth century. Compared to East Asia, however, it was not: it did not possess the institutions, networks, and media of Japan or China to speed the circulation of Confucian teachings. There was no Vietnamese equivalent to the developments in the lower Yangzi region that transformed Qing intellectual life.[20] And Vietnam's print culture paled in comparison to that of Tokugawa Japan. Vietnam simply did not have merchant patrons subsidizing Confucian academies, nor could it boast such prolific writers and readers. One Japanese author has asserted that "it would be little exaggeration to say that by the nineteenth century, Japan was flooded with information."[21] Contrast this statement with the lament of Phan Huy Chú in the *Lịch triều hiến chượng loại chí* (Classified survey of the institutions of successive courts), written in the early nineteenth century for the Nguyễn court: "Alas! Books from past generations have been scattered about, books have been lost and are difficult to search out, those remaining are filled with errors."[22] Such statements underline the gulf between Vietnamese and Japanese use of printed matter. They also suggest that common statements about the impact of Confucianism on Vietnamese society need to be taken with a grain of salt: if that teaching had a clear impact in realms like the court or among prominent lineages, one should be cautious in extrapolating from such evidence to Vietnamese society as a whole.

It is difficult to ascertain how much Vietnamese used printed matter before the twentieth century. In 1942, the scholar Hoa Bằng noted that Vietnamese histories rarely discuss commerce and industry; consequently, "researching woodblock printing in our country is, as everyone has discovered, not easy."[23] While this statement remains true today, one can advance a few tentative observations. In the nineteenth century, Vietnamese could encounter writing through poetry, family registers, collections of mythical tales, books on medicine, Buddhist sutras, catechisms and ritual works, Confucian morality tracts, history, philosophical treatises, and geographies. The forms of written material varied as well, ranging from Chinese and demotic characters inscribed on temple pillars, steles, and amulets to printed tracts and books. Pre-1802 printed material is now extremely rare: of the 318 printers represented in the collection of the Institute for Chinese and Nôm Literature (Viện Hán-Nôm) in

Hanoi, the vast majority are from the Nguyễn dynasty. Nguyễn Thị Dương adds (ruefully?) that extremely few published works showed great literary or philosophical value: "of the individual printers, they paid the greatest attention to topics that were economically useful: they would carve the woodblock and print for whatever book sold well."[24] One can tentatively conclude that despite the plethora of genres and forms, most Vietnamese had extremely limited access to printed, written, and epigraphical materials.

The Tây Sơn wars (1771–1802), which ravaged the country, also destroyed much written and printed matter. The Nguyễn dynasty, which came to power in 1802, hesitated to promote printing and publishing. The first Nguyễn emperor (Gia Long) issued edicts for people to turn in books that they had "hidden" away and ordered that documents about the dynasty's vanquished enemies (the Tây Sơn "rebels") be burned.[25] Royal ambivalence over books appears to have continued during Minh Mạng's (1820–1841) reign. From 1820 onward, the Nguyễn court ordered that all books be printed at Huế and that officials send their own woodblocks back to the capital.[26]

Ironically, Nguyễn rulers also encouraged scholarship. The dynasty printed an impressive number of histories both to commemorate the past and to indict the Tây Sơn. Nguyễn attempts to centralize book production also appear half-hearted. Most publishing took place in temples or in urban centers. Thăng Long (present-day Hanoi), for example, was a major center for printing and selling books. The reestablishment of examinations helped in the proliferation of texts, as "many publishers competed with each other to carve woodblocks and publish books" for them. Buddhist centers (such as Liên Tông and Từ Quang temples in the north, Giác Lâm, Đại Giác, and Giác Viên temples in the south, and various temples around Huế) also printed and distributed large numbers of Buddhist texts. Indeed, Buddhist works probably formed a significant proportion of all texts printed during the nineteenth century. Not all works were published in Vietnam. Alexander Woodside notes that South Chinese traders imported books, especially to Cholon. And Chinese publishers from Foshan (Guangdong) even published many Vietnamese-language (Nôm) works.[27]

From the limited evidence, it seems that the Vietnamese printing industry had not much developed by the Nguyễn dynasty, and printed texts remained relatively rare. When the literatus Đặng Xuân Bảng complained in the nineteenth century that Vietnamese knew plenty about Chinese history but "nothing" about Vietnam's history, government, or geography, he was reflecting in part this lack of books.[28] The scarcity of books was mirrored by the apparent scarcity of libraries. Buddhist temples and the court kept books, but in the nineteenth century (and before), private libraries—such as Hải Học Đường in Hải Dương province, Chiêm Bá Đường in Thái Bình, or Thư Viện Long Cương in Nghệ An—were exceedingly rare.[29]

If printed matter was scarce, literacy was probably rather low. One cannot say for sure: no study systematically addresses how Vietnamese produced, circulated, and appropriated knowledge in precolonial times. Jean Louis de Lanessan, who served in Cochinchina in the late nineteenth century, articulated a common French view when he stated that "there is not ... an Annamite village that lacks a school. Annamites unable to read and write the characters necessary for daily tasks and for other public duties are extremely rare." In contrast, Yoshiharu Tsuboi has argued that while the literati (*văn thân*) formed an important and distinct social stratum, "traditional Vietnamese society was ... oral."[30] The truth probably lies in one's definition of "literacy." While rural society was overwhelmingly oral, a significant minority of Vietnamese probably had a restricted literacy. They could recognize a limited number of characters (such as those necessary for their trades) or sign their names but could not read or write complex texts. Some probably had memorized sections of popular primers like the *Three-Character Classic* (*Tam tự kinh*). But literacy was highly gendered: evidence suggests that men could read and write far more than women.[31]

While few Vietnamese would have had the full literacy required to understand sophisticated Chinese texts, printed matter could still have a surprising impact. Vietnamese turned many oral legends into Nôm tales. The popular tale *Thạch Sanh*, for example, existed in oral and printed versions.[32] Buddhist tales such as *Quan Âm Thị Kính* (The ode of Guanyin and Thi Kinh) have been popular among the peasantry for centuries and have developed new versions. Such popular tales, spread by literate Vietnamese, gave rise in turn to new popular oral versions. One example might suggest the importance of material written in demotic script (Nôm): Nguyễn Công Trứ, a particularly well known author, is said to have written one thousand songs and poems in Nôm.[33]

In short, it appears that most Vietnamese had limited access to the printed or written word in the nineteenth century. Location did make a difference: printed matter circulated more in urban areas like Hanoi, Saigon, or Huế than in the countryside, and some villages and particular lineages had greater access to print and manuscript culture than others. Pockets of literacy and learning existed, dotted across the countryside.[34] Printed texts, like other commodities, most probably circulated via periodic markets and itinerant hawkers, not to mention Buddhist temples.[35] The stereotype of the autonomous Vietnamese village closed unto itself often distorts the place of villages in a larger world: circuits of migration linked many areas, and one can presume that textual and printed knowledge circulated along with people. But in general, because of the limited reach of the printed word and its slow circulation, a public sphere did not really exist before the twentieth century.

This situation began to change in the second half of the nineteenth century. The creation of a robust public sphere of debate and exchange owes much to innovations in Cochinchina in the second half of the nineteenth century. The first newspaper in romanized script, *Gia Định báo* (News of Gia Định, or Saigon), dates from 1865. The first Vietnamese-owned newspaper, founded by young students, briefly appeared in 1883.[36] French notions of journalistic style began to change written Vietnamese: the editor of the early Saigon newspaper *Nam kỳ* (The south) returned a proposed article to its author with the following words: "We looked at the article you sent in but cannot publish it. It should be corrected. It is full of words (*tiếng chữ*) that only a few literary persons can understand, while most people who read this paper, and we as well, cannot fully understand it.... Our wish is that everyone who reads the newspaper will be able to read and enjoy."[37]

"Read and enjoy"—the print culture of the south was more oriented toward light reading and information than toward deep study. Southerners have recognized that Cochinchina took the lead in these early years: indeed, one scholar has argued, a bit hyperbolically, that the 1890–1920 period was the "golden age" of publishing in Saigon, thanks in part to its role in popularizing romanized Vietnamese translations of Chinese tales.[38]

The transformation of southern print culture was accompanied by shifts in social hierarchy that came to shape the emerging public sphere.

When the famous reformer Phan Châu Trinh complained in 1926 that "at times servants and cooks (*bồi bếp*) entered the ranks of the rulers and even became mandarins"[39] who oppressed the people, he voiced a common literati complaint and missed the point at the same time. Even cooks! Even servants! It was precisely the inflow of interpreters, cooks, servants and others into French service and the consequent upheavals in social hierarchies that energized the emergent public sphere in the south and fed its interest in lowbrow fiction, translated Chinese tales, and gossipy newspapers. Southern writers came from all sorts of backgrounds. In 1923, for example, the newspaper *Công luận báo* boasted one regular columnist who was a telegraph operator and another who was a fishmonger.[40] The south, in short, was hardly the center of high culture, but the dynamism of its public sphere came to surpass that of the north for much of the late colonial period.

In the north and center, in contrast, a small Confucian reformist elite defined the trajectory of print culture far more than in the south. In these areas, Chinese "new learning" began to transform literati thinking by the turn of the century. French censorship, ineffective, did not stop Chinese from importing the "new learning" in through the ports of Hải Phòng, Hanoi, Saigon, and Huế. Teachers and other members of the literati propagated these new Western, Chinese, and Japanese ideas to others. Đặng Thai Mai mentions how his father, like other "progressive literati," read Montesquieu, Voltaire, and Rousseau, not to mention works on the French revolution and on the nineteenth-century unification of Italy and Germany, in Chinese-language translations imported from China.[41] His father was probably the exception rather than the rule among literati: new currents of thought began to penetrate the Vietnamese countryside, but slowly and unevenly.

By the beginning of the twentieth century, Vietnamese print culture was changing. It is true that some Vietnamese distrusted new influences and resisted the new use of romanized materials: as several appalled literati from Nam Định province complained in 1907 or 1908, "Those who do not know characters lack moral sense (*không thông nghĩa lý*)."[42] But others did not agree. In the center, and particularly in Quảng Nam, intellectuals like Huỳnh Thúc Kháng and Trần Quý Cáp were setting up free schools, experimenting with the teaching of romanized script, and promoting a message of Vietnamese self-strengthening in the years between 1900 and 1908.[43] Vietnamese from all regions participated in the Eastern travel movement (which promoted travel abroad to Japan for study).

It was in such a climate that the Tonkin Free School opened in 1907. Its textbooks introduced the newest thought circulating in East Asia to a Vietnamese audience: for example, readers could learn about America and Japan (including the Japanese police system!). French administrators anxiously remarked that booksellers were hawking the school's books in the provinces.[44] The school's promotion of books in romanized script,[45] and its use by the French, formed part of a massive shift to the use of romanized script that occurred over the next two decades.

After literati-led challenges to its authority in 1907 and 1908, the French administration shuttered the Tonkin Free School and reasserted state control over the cities and countryside. The state cracked down on the circulation of printed matter, exercised closer scrutiny over printers and publishers, and watched the ports more closely for printed material from abroad. The example of the Tonkin Free School forced the colonial administration to take a second look at its own educational policy, which even the governor-general admitted was incoherent and a cause of the "current discontent."[46]

The beginnings of a public sphere in the south that focused on light reading and information and the example of the Tonkin Free School in the north show that the print culture of Vietnam was slowly changing. This change may have been abetted by the fact that not all Vietnamese expressed a reverence for the old learning. Đào Duy Anh notes that near Huế people sold old Chinese books in the market for cigarette paper. A friend of his bought a four-volume work by the famous nineteenth-century literatus Nguyễn Trường Tộ from such a shop.[47] Printed matter using romanized script was beginning to replace materials printed in demotic script or Chinese. But the most dramatic changes would have to wait until the period from the 1920s onward, when the production and use of printed matter would soar. It is in this latter period that there arose a lively public sphere.

THE TRANSFORMATION OF PUBLIC LIFE, 1920–1945: THE PRODUCTION OF PRINTED MATTER

In 1909, thirty-four booksellers, printers, and carvers of wood-blocks and seals served Hanoi. Only one printer was identified as a lithographer.[48] By 1920, modern print technology had replaced wood-blocks. This change in print technology did not have an immediate impact: the public realm of print languished. Subject to heavy state censorship, it suffered from the fact that few men, and even fewer women, read Vietnamese, Chinese, or French fluently. In 1918, for example, the résident supérieur in Tonkin could argue that, since the entire region already had four newspapers, he could see "no reason" to allow more to publish.[49] But his arguments were soon dated: with the growth in newspaper and book production and increasing readership, the public sphere of print grew increasingly robust by the end of the 1920s. The shift in print technology, in other words, accompanied a remarkable transformation of print culture and helped engender the rise of a public sphere of debate and exchange.

The new print technology enabled the rapid spread of information. Between 1922 and 1940 alone, French sources state that Vietnamese published 13,381 different books and tracts.[50] Vietnamese also published an impressive number of periodicals. From 1918 to 1939, at least 163 Vietnamese-language periodicals appeared in Saigon. Thirty-seven appeared in 1938 alone.[51] If Hanoi and the north initially trailed the less-populated south in numbers of periodicals, they eventually overtook it: by June 1937, the north alone boasted sixty-three periodicals.[52] Clandestine books, tracts, and newspapers, not counted by the French, would only increase such statistics.

Periodicals provided a wide range of views to their readers. Many newspapers, leery of censorship, focused on providing an array of information without delving too much into anticolonial politics. A few newspapers were overtly political in intent, and some launched blistering attacks on the French administration. Some, like *Tiểu thuyết thứ bảy* (Saturday novel) in Hanoi and *Truyện ngắn nhi đồng* (Short stories for children) in Saigon, combined literature and news. One of the earliest newspapers published in Indochina, *Nữ giới chung* (Women's bell), advocated women's education. This newspaper was followed by a variety of women's newspapers in the north, center, and south. A few publications targeted a truly small niche, such as *Ảo thuật tạp chí* (Prestidigitation review) or *Thần bí tạp chí/Mystériosa* (Mystical review). Workers, followers of the Cao Đài religious sect, Trotskyists, lawyers, afficionados of magic, Buddhists, Catholics, radio and film buffs, horse racing and sports fans, those interested in popular science, people of mixed ethnic background, and civil servants all could (at some time) find a publication that addressed their interests.[53]

The wide variety of periodical literature was complemented by an even wider variety of tracts and books. Some publishers, such as those of many Buddhist tracts, some morality books, and communist publications, did not expect to make money from printed matter. But the vast majority of publishers wanted to turn a profit or break even. They catered to popular tastes (such as the taste for adventure tales). These popular tastes shaped the literary market far more than many "cultured" Vietnamese liked.

Given the scarcity of information on the economic and technological organization of printing in Vietnam as well as on labor relations, one can only make tentative conclusions about the trade. Vũ Đình Long, who established the Tân Dân publishing house in Hanoi, managed to parlay work printing small items (such as announcements and film tickets) into a successful book-publishing business.[54] The Saigon shopkeeper Nguyễn Văn Của succeeded through luck and use of connections. His first break came when a Frenchman asked him in 1917 to help set up the newspaper *Nam Trung nhựt báo* (Daily news of the south and center). Thanks to the French connection, the Banque de l'Indochine lent him 40,000 piasters in 1918 to buy the printing presses of the Imprimerie de l'Union. "From this moment, he was established and became rich."[55] Của then benefited from the favor of Governor Maspéro, whose administration subsidized his newspaper *Lục tỉnh tân văn* (News of the six provinces). But few publishers were so lucky and competent as Nguyễn Văn Của. Nguyễn Phú Khai, one of Của's Saigon competitors and the publisher of a major newspaper (*La Tribune indigène*) was eventually overwhelmed with debts reported to total 150,000 piasters and was pursued by numerous creditors. Most other publishers struggled with much smaller operations.

Why did printers face such problems? Other than school textbooks, the printing market was initially small and somewhat segmented.[56] French, Chinese, and Vietnamese firms dominated their respective language markets, although the Chinese appear to have made inroads into the Vietnamese-language market as well. In Hanoi, the French firm Imprimerie d'Extrême-Orient dominated the high end of the market: the Vietnamese print shops "feared it most of all." In Saigon, no one shop dominated the trade.[57] The Vietnamese in particular mobilized little capital: the French and the Chinese boasted greater resources and often had more advanced presses.[58] (One source claims that Vietnamese had adequate capital: the problem was the French administration forbade them to buy foreign machinery, "forcing us to buy French [printing] apparatuses, often old presses that they [the French] were selling.")[59] With old presses, little money, and competition, few publishers lasted more than a few years.

How did publishers get the public to buy their wares? Most of them tried a variety of strategies to entice bookstores to stock their works and readers to read them. They issued catalogs and solicited agents, offering a variety of incentives (such as commissions and the right to return unsold books) to attract them.[60] They advertised new releases in newspapers and on book covers. Some readers did not live near bookstores: they could order books through the mail. Publishers sold their wares in multiple forms. They bundled catalogs with short stories: thus the Nhành Mai pharmacy interspersed advertisements for medical products with the tale of the marriage between a person and a ghost. To hook readers on novels, many publishers broke them into several slim parts and sold each one separately. They also serialized novels in newspapers and then republished them later in book form. And if prices were too high, such works could be resold: one source notes that in rural markets in the south, the "mediocre" serialized novels of Phạm Văn Thình, a southern writer, could be scooped up for one-third of the cover price.[61]

The public's desire for a cheap read sometimes came at the writer's expense. At least one individual complained about the ways that writers failed to get their just due: to avoid extra costs, publishers sometimes reprinted works without asking authors for permission. If that did not always lower the price of the final product, another practice did: on Transverse Street, Hemp Street, Huế Street, and many others in Hanoi, this writer lamented, many shops hung out signs with the words "Stories for Rent." For two *sous*—a pittance—visitors could borrow a tale for reading pleasure. If writers often ended with little money in their pockets, it is nonetheless true that such practices made the printed word more accessible to the average Vietnamese.[62]

Given the need to drive printing costs down, it is not surprising that print workers as well as publishers suffered from the ups and downs of the trade. To cut costs, printers occasionally slashed salaries or did not pay their employees. Workers complained as well of long work hours (in one case, they stated that they were forced to work fourteen hours a day;

the owner disputed this, stating that they "only" worked twelve hours). In a few cases at least, print shop owners paid a lump sum to overseers, who recruited and paid workers; this system could give rise to abuses, as when the overseers skimmed money off the top for themselves. Not surprisingly, news of strikes at print shops and publishers appears repeatedly in police reports.

At the center of this public realm were newspapers, journalists, and writers. Newspapers serving as mouthpieces of important Vietnamese figures or political groups, sometimes with contrarian attitudes, began to play an important political role beginning in the 1920s. Their politicking began slowly. At first, in the "provincial" atmosphere of Saigon and Hanoi, antagonists simply used newspapers and tracts to broadcast preexisting disputes. But in time, given that political and social organizations were strictly controlled, this space became the key site of contestation.

Speaking of Cochinchina in the early 1920s, one police report noted that, while the time of opposition through secret societies seemed to have passed, "new groups have constituted themselves, each leader having his followers (*clientèle*), with the most important groups boasting newspapers."[63] Their interests were often less in reporting the news with utmost objectivity than in jockeying for public position. The French police assiduously followed these papers, opened up files on owners and writers, inspected their mail, and harassed journalists whom it considered too anti-French. (I will discuss this surveillance and repression in greater detail in the next chapter.)

French administrators hoped that the owners of such newspapers and their journalists would create a "civilized" public realm dominated by "*les évolués,*" or the supposedly advanced members of society. They were irritated by what they got. Cao Văn Chánh, a southern journalist, became famous for a 1924 article in which he threatened violence against "those involved in activities at the people's expense."[64] If such threats were not the norm, verbal attacks were not uncommon. Furthermore, journalists sometimes ignored "civilized" topics in order to latch onto scandals. Reporters wrote about them with gusto, hoping that an appreciative public would buy their newspaper, boost their circulation, and thus keep them in business.

One administrator lamented that Vietnamese journalists would, "with a casual lack of moral scruples, practice the lowest [forms of] blackmail."[65] (French administrators, it is worth noting, made the identical complaint about some French journalists.)[66] Writing in 1923, the Sûreté complained:

> There are scarcely any serious journalists in Cochinchina. With a few rare exceptions, the young people who write in *quốc ngữ* [i.e., Vietnamese-language] newspapers are nothing but pretentious "failures," rejected by the administration and in commerce, who take refuge in journalism to meet their needs. Their circumstances, even as they confer on themselves pompous titles of "men of letters" and "educators of the people," are far from choice. Poorly paid, threatened with dismissal at the slightest opportunity and under the most frivolous pretext, they move from one management to another, selling their talent for a bowl of rice. These "journalists" only write to make a living—and in the secret hope, often crushed, to find in skillful publicity a springboard that would put them in the spotlight or provide them the means to enter into some profitable business.[67]

(If harsh and biased, the French were not completely wrong: one relatively well known journalist, Lê Hoằng Mưu, had earlier been fired from his job as a telegraph operator for embezzlement; he also spent time in prison for a different offense.)[68] Many other journalists were criticized for being "half-educated" or poorly able to digest the ideas they purported to understand.

While few newspapers had a clear ideological bent, many defied the administration and fed on the scandals that plagued colonial society. Sometimes newspapers simply reprinted tidbits already published in other papers. The Vietnamese press suffered some of the same problems as its French counterparts: inadequate press runs, poor finances, and poor training of journalists. The French police, in their reports, repeatedly despaired at the "violent" and anti-French tone of many articles, not to mention their poor quality.[69] One year, the police noted that a newspaper, the *Ère nouvelle*, was "sinking into ridicule" after the departure of its former editor, and its "schoolboy" writers had a bare command of French.

Many of these comments, first made in the early 1920s, crop up again in the late 1930s. The administration still despaired at the violent tone of the press. In Cochinchina it continued to see journalists as poorly educated failures "lacking culture." It still complained about their fondness for dishing out scandal, for printing "venomous little articles that bring joy to the reader." And it still deplored the resort to blackmail. The scandalous articles could take the form of novellas published in newspapers based on actual events; these stories exaggerated or touched up actuality to make a better story. Sometimes potential victims bought silence from "editors without scruples" so that real or imagined transgressions would not be splashed across the pages of the newspapers.

In Tonkin, the French administration echoed these complaints. Focusing on the impact of "extremists" and former political prisoners, Yves Chatel wrote: "There is no need to apply oneself to writing or even know how to write: it is enough to call oneself a 'journalist.' One tries to launch a 'newspaper,' however trifling, attend small reunions of journalists where shouts mingle with threats—engages in little acts of blackmail to gain a few piasters. Such is the way that many young see this trade."[70] One kind of criticism, however, does become less frequent: the police make fewer complaints about Vietnamese mastery of the French tongue.

The administration worried constantly about opposition from the Vietnamese. It is true that in the 1920s newspapers had little influence outside the cities, and the countryside remained quite peaceful. In 1927, the administration in Annam admitted that up to that point the masses of peasants "were little affected." It worried, however, that through tracts and newspapers "read in the smallest village ... the virus of new ideas [would] spread throughout the country."[71] In the next year, in a report on all three regions of Vietnam, the administration noted a veritable explosion in the numbers of tracts that were "appearing all over the place."[72] Illegal propaganda could be incendiary: a 1931 leaflet attacked French troops for raping women and committing other acts of repression in Nghi Lộc village, Nghệ Tĩnh, and added that "hundreds of families have had their homes set alight, thousands of people have been shot at, suffered extreme and barbaric torture, and countless people have been thrown in jail to die."[73] No legal publication could afford to express such raw anger.

In 1936, a Popular Front government, in which communists allied with socialists, came to power in France. In the Popular Front period (1936–1939), the metropolitan government under socialist prime minister Léon Blum relaxed its repression in the colonies. As a result, Vietnamese radicals increased their agitation. The local administration's fears were amply realized. In Cochinchina, the Sûreté claimed that six hundred committees had distributed 450,000 copies of tracts in the region, "conveying to the smallest villages hatred of France, calling everywhere for resistance to the authorities."[74] And in 1938, the French administration complained that "extremist elements" had set up clandestine organizations in Ninh Bình and Kiến An provinces and that, at the same time, some newspaper editors pressured local notables to circulate their newspapers in the interior.[75] Indeed, from the 1920s to 1939, printed matter, whether legal or clandestine, gradually began to penetrate the countryside.

For the 1920–1939 period, Saigon was clearly the most politically open town in Indochina. Repression of the press in Hanoi and Huế was much harsher, for legal reasons to be explored in the next chapter. Because of Saigon's openness, the south attracted journalists from the center and the north and had a relatively boisterous public realm. The south saw, for example, an on-again, off-again collaboration in the press among different Marxist groups: thus, during the 1930s, Trotskyists and Stalinists in Saigon extended their influence through their newspaper *La lutte* (Struggle). These newspapers also attracted readers from afar. Some anti-government Saigon newspapers had subscribers and correspondents in nearly every Annam province as early as the late 1920s.[76] Some of these papers even reached Hanoi: Đặng Thai Mai notes when he was attending university in Hanoi in 1924–1925, he and his fellow students often read "progressive" newspapers sent from the south.[77]

Hanoi was hardly bereft of influence. In the 1930s the Self-Strengthening Literary Group in Hanoi launched two newspapers, *Phong hóa* (Mores) and *Ngày nay* (Today), to spread its literary, social, and political ideas. Some of these papers reached the center and the south as well. But, in terms of press runs, middle-of-the-road papers dominated the Hanoi and Saigon marketplaces. Thus newspapers like *Trung Bắc tân văn* (News of the center and north), less literary and less confrontational than many other newspapers, had a wider readership and much higher press runs than their more radical counterparts.

Within this larger picture, the 1939–1945 period might appear to be a deviation: in these years, the French colonial state harshly repressed dissent at the same time that it tried to reassert control over public life. When Maréchal Pétain came to power in France in 1940 as head of the Vichy government, he promoted a "National Revolution" that exalted tradition, called for a return to the family, opposed capitalism, and supported oligarchy. Pétain's appointee as governor-general of French

Indochina, Admiral Jean Decoux, moved quickly to apply the Vichy "revolution" to the region. For too long, he asserted, the administration had monitored public opinion with the goal of controlling or suppressing it. But that was not enough:

> It also needs to be guided, to be influenced. Propaganda through inexpensive books, through newspapers that gratify one's curiosity, would not be impossible.... We would need to disseminate in various Annamite publications ideas, themes, and arguments that favor Franco-Annamite collaboration....
>
> We can accomplish this not through official articles, whose administrative origin is too easy to detect, but by keeping an eye on young writers, helping them out, publishing their works, through creating a climate favorable to the Indochina that we want to develop and transform.[78]

Decoux's new policy, combining harsh repression with cooptation and manipulation, had mixed results. Some Vietnamese were pleased, for example, when the French administration, in the guise of promoting tradition, sponsored a ritual in the south for Nguyễn Đình Chiểu, the famous nineteenth-century author of the poem "Lục văn tiên."[79] Similar events occurred in the north as well. The French attracted some writers, especially conservatives and those who had benefited from Western-style education but had not been radicalized. The new policy briefly drove a wedge between radical Vietnamese, who were forced to write for clandestine publications, and those authors who wrote for magazines such as *Tri tân* (Understand the new) and *Thanh nghị* (Refined opinion) in Hanoi.

The Japanese military launched its assault on Southeast Asia as a whole in December 1941, an event that ruptured direct connections between Indochina and France. Nonetheless, the Decoux administration worked hard to spread Vichy propaganda. It published a collection of Pétain's sayings (*Les paroles du Maréchal*) and required newspapers to print "Maréchal Pétain's thoughts" in every issue. It showed pro-Vichy films and newsreels. But this propaganda, especially heavy in 1941 and 1942, dropped off in later years. If one 1941 source indicated that the cult of Pétain was spreading among the Vietnamese and that "his words, translated into Annamese, are listened to religiously," other sources indicate that Decoux was failing to attract many Vietnamese to the cause. In

October 1941, one observer noted that, while French stores managed to put up posters of Pétain, "in the native quarters, even on the most commercial streets, posters are rare." Furthermore, by 1941 the Japanese had launched an intense propaganda effort to win the Vietnamese over to their side. The French administration believed at this early date that the Japanese effort was faltering, but it was clearly worried.[80]

French repression could be surprisingly ineffective. It is true that paper shortages meant that fewer books, tracts, and periodicals were published. But repression did not always work for an elementary reason: Vichy propaganda could be used against itself, as when Vietnamese used the Vichy phrase "National Revolution" to militate for their own national renaissance. And it proved impossible to turn the clock back to 1920. The previous two decades had seen the creation of a vibrant public sphere in which many voices clamored for attention. If these voices were quieted in the war years, they had not been forgotten.

Looking back at the evolution of the public sphere from 1920 to 1945, one is struck by how paternalistic and dismissive the French administration could be to its Vietnamese subjects. The administration repeatedly argued that, while some Vietnamese had evolved into model subjects, a minority of incompetent malcontents threatened to subvert the state. Does one write off such comments as products of French paternalism and political paranoia? Not completely: some Vietnamese did not write French well, and some probably did stoop to blackmail.

But a more sympathetic way of understanding this world of newspapers, books, and writers is to look at it in terms of market forces and popular tastes. Newspapers possessed little capital and paid reporters poorly. The rapid pace at which most newspapers went in and out of business suggests that their finances were precarious. They could not afford to be high-minded. So they helped to create a lively realm that had room for purveyors of bawdy tales as well as proper Confucians, for disreputable characters as well as upright ones.

Vietnam resembles eighteenth-century Paris or twentieth-century London and Manila in this respect. Its public realm was often defined by contrarian attitudes and a desire to appeal to the growing market of readers and listeners. Different groups of people, as I shall later discuss, had different tastes in printed matter. Although Habermas claimed that, in Europe at least, the bourgeois public sphere saw, for the first time in history, "people's public use of their reason,"[81] one not need to be hamstrung by such a view: public arenas are far more than realms of rational debate and high-minded disputation.

QUESTIONS OF AUDIENCE: READERS, LISTENERS, AND THE CLEAVAGES OF THE PUBLIC REALM

In the narrative so far, I have focused on the production of printed matter but have only touched on its audience. This is a tricky subject to broach. Scholars can only make informed guesses about the percentage of the population that could decode the printed word. Finding out who these readers and listeners were and how they responded to texts is even more difficult, as few Vietnamese wrote about such experiences.

In 1942, the Hanoi resident Hoa Bằng wrote that "the majority of city people know French, and most people already have the habit of reading books and newspapers." He added that, in the countryside, "the number of people who know romanized script is increasing greatly."[82] The first claim about city dwellers is probably exaggerated. I stated earlier that there are no reliable estimates for literacy rates before 1920. Evidence for literacy after this date is also scanty. The great majority of children did not attend school, and few who did could attend for more than a few years. By the end of 1935, for example, public and private schools enrolled only 15 to 20 percent of all children between six and twelve.[83] But individuals learned to read outside of school as well: in temples, from village elders, and so on. Given the limited available sources, it would be reasonable to assume that by the mid-1930s, 10 to 20 percent of the population was literate and that this figure was increasing.[84] This average figure, however, masks important differences. For one, men were far more likely to read and write than women. To give one example from a village in rural north Annam, 16.7 percent of the males could read Vietnamese in romanized script, while only 1.4 percent of the females could.[85] The young, some of whom attended school, had much higher literacy rates than their parents. Regions showed important differences: Annam appears to have lagged Cochinchina and Tonkin in literacy. Last but not least, urban areas had much higher literacy rates than rural ones. In short, literacy was unevenly distributed across the social landscape.

How did those fortunate enough to be able to read respond to the texts before them? Browsing through Hoài Thanh's and Hoài Chân's comments on the poetry of the 1930s, I was struck by how they overflow with emotion. On the poetry of Thế Lữ, the authors write: "But today, rereading lines that are still so familiar (*còn quen quen*), I am overwhelmingly happy. I greet these lines of poetry with the joy of a wanderer who has returned home to meet an old lover."[86] Or, as these two authors proclaim about the young man who was to become one of the twentieth century's most famous poets: "Only those young at heart like to read Xuân Diệu's poetry, and if you like it, you must passionately love it."[87]

The comments above are hardly representative: not all writing overwhelmed the emotions and transformed the reader. Some printed matter hectored. Some prescribed conduct. Some simply informed. But the words of Hoài Thanh and Hoài Chân are a reminder that, ultimately, the significance of print culture lies not simply in how texts were produced, but in how they reached their audience and how this audience responded to them.

The reading and listening public was highly diverse: it included everyone from bus drivers and "boys" (male servants) to market women, schoolchildren, and bureaucrats. Reading united Vietnamese, but it could also divide. Gender was one of the most pronounced markers of difference. The following story about the eighteenth-century poem "Phan Trần" illustrates the impact of gender on reading habits and its 1942 resolution. Nguyễn Xuân Nghị presents the story as a reflection on the saying "men should not tell the story of Phan Trần, women should not tell the Tale of Kiều."

Unexpectedly one day, while wandering aimlessly down the street, I met a man carrying two baskets of books, and he asked me:

"Do you want to buy some stories to read?"

I asked what stories he was selling, and the bookseller cordially put down [his load], opened books for me to look at, and listed the names of old stories: "Hoa Tiên," "Phạm Công," "Cúc Hoa," "Nữ tú tài," "Kim Vân Kiều," "Nhị Độ Mai," "Phan Trần." . . .

Of course, the words "Phan Trần" caught my attention the most. And the bookseller, with a calculated indifference, said to me:

"You can buy this copy of 'Phan Trần' on good paper and clearly printed."

Hesitant, I replied:

"But men aren't supposed to read 'Phan Trần'!"

The bookseller took the eyeglasses he was wearing off his downward-looking eyes, as if wanting to make me listen to reason, but then only said:

"That is what people say, but I doubt that 'Phan Trần' was a book that one should not read."

That vague reply immediately made me want to find out: should one or should one not read "Phan Trần"?

One *hào* handed over to the bookseller, and "Phan Trần" had become my own property.[88]

In the past, men were not supposed to read "Phan Trần" because Phan Sinh, the male protagonist of the poem, falls in love with Diệu Thường even though his parents had already chosen someone else to be his wife.[89] Yet the bookseller's "vague" reply excited Nguyễn Xuân Nghị's curiosity, and he bought the book anyhow. The desire for a pleasurable read surmounted the Confucian moralizing. This story makes two points: that reading was a gendered activity and that Vietnamese were quite willing to transgress notions of what was proper to enjoy a good tale.

In the colonial period, the gendering of reading took on new forms. As French increasingly became the language of (male) administrative power and of the Vietnamese elite, Vietnamese remained the language of everyday conversation and popular literature. Reminiscing about those years, the literary critic Hoàng Ngọc Hiển eloquently introduces France's impact on the world of letters:

Before the Revolution [of 1945] ... I studied in French-language schools. In my family there were two bookcases. The French-language bookcase belonged to my father, a primary school teacher. My father —who believed that only French was the key to knowledge and culture—only allowed us to read books in French. Many friends, in reading my literary criticism, have praised its clarity. Perhaps I acquired "French clarity" from my father's bookcase. The Vietnamese-language bookcase belonged to my mother and sister. But when my father was gone, I went to the Vietnamese-language bookcase and snatched the opportunity to devour all that I could read: *Ngày nay, Tao Đàn, Tiểu thuyết thứ bảy*, the prose of the Self-Strengthening Literary Group, the novels of Vũ Trọng Phụng, the stories of Nguyễn Tuân,

Nam Cao. . . . My mother's and sister's bookcase imparted to me a love of the Vietnamese language and of Vietnamese literature.[90]

As Hiền shows, French had become the language of power and prestige, while Vietnamese gained a reputation as an inferior, even womanly, tongue. This perception of linguistic inferiority shaped elite Vietnamese perceptions of their heritage and, by extension, their beliefs in proper reading habits.

Yet only a minority of the reading public believed that French was superior to Vietnamese (or Chinese, for that matter). The reading public was fragmented. By 1940, only a small fraction of Vietnamese readers preferred Chinese-language works. Of those who were literate, the great mass of readers had only completed Franco-Annamite primary schools. Most of them worked as office workers, in shops, or as low-level employees in the administration. With limited competence in French, they favored Vietnamese works. A variety of other readers—workers, other employees, younger and older women, men from the countryside— had even less access to French schooling. They also preferred works in their native tongue.[91]

The question of popular tastes became inextricably tied to the question of popular moral character. One of the constant refrains of self-appointed moral arbiters in this period is that Vietnamese craved light, frivolous, even "immoral" or "pornographic" reading, in their own words. As the police noted, parroting the views of conservative Vietnamese, the most popular publications "are those that, for a low price, flatter the base instincts."[92] Vietnamese readers could buy French and Vietnamese works that discussed homosexuality, "perversions," lesbianism, women and sex, masturbation, venereal diseases, and how to make love. Publishers catered to what they perceived to be an interest in such topics. Thus, complaining that censorship had hurt his sales, Lương Ngọc Hiển implored the mayor of Hanoi in 1940 to let his reporter write a story on the "girls" (i.e., prostitutes) who visited the municipal clinic for their regular checkups: such a story, he stated, would be "a giant hit with my readers."[93] He probably was right: the market played an important role in determining what some publishers would print.

Readers also snapped up light-hearted fictional works. As one police report stated, "the mass of readers like the supernatural and the risqué (*le grivois*) and prefer works that are moving and that arouse in them a passion or feeling for vice."[94] The report appears to be referring to the wide popularity of light-hearted love stories and adventure novels (sold in bookstores, in bus and train stations, and on the street) as well as saucier material such as sex manuals posing as tracts on "hygiene." Phạm Mạnh Phan suggested in 1941 that harmful books led young men to opium and "filthy prostitutes." No wonder he suggested that all such writings be burned.[95] In the same year, Thái Phỉ complained, without substantiating his claims, about young bullies who carried knives, swore blood oaths (and drank the blood), and liked to read cheap adventure novels (*chuyện kiếm hiệp ba xu*).[96]

Women were believed to be particularly susceptible to such light printed matter. Police once complained, for example, that women devoured the works of Lê Hoằng Mưu, a writer of light morality tales whose "dangerous" writing "bewitched the weak-minded."[97] One cultural conservative, Mrs. Lê Trung Ngọc, counseled older girls to read "philosophical" and "scientific" books. She warned against "dangerous" love novels, which provoked lust and led women toward "illicit" ways (that is, unapproved sexual relations).[98] Not all admonitions came from conservatives. A 1934 editorial in the radical newspaper *Phụ nữ tân văn* (Women's news) railed against love novels and Chinese tales: "Many young women only spend their days in a daydream, lamenting and weeping about life ... passing their days and months in the unreal world of novels, to the point that they waste away [their] lives.[99] A different article in the same paper reminded readers that some young girls had killed themselves "simply because they read excessively deceptive novels."[100] Because of such arguments, perhaps, the literary critic Thiếu Sơn struck a defensive chord when he argued that education helped women restrain their sexual desires (*dục tình*).[101]

It is ironic that French and Vietnamese moralists spilled so much ink over the depravity of publishers and readers. After all, publishers printed thousands of religious and moral tracts in the 1920–1945 period. Trần Hữu Độ, a Confucian scholar turned communist, underlined this point in 1937, lamenting that bookstores were filled with "idealist" (read: religious) books and not materialist ones. As examples, he cited, among others, Buddhist sutras and works on the Confucian sages.[102] The large number of publications on moral and religious topics suggests that such works shaped Vietnamese print culture far more than has been realized.

LANGUAGE, HIERARCHY, AND THE CONSTRUCTION OF
"PUBLIC OPINION"

Building on the narrative above, I now want to step back to note profound continuities and ruptures that characterized the public realm in the period from 1920 to 1945. Of particular interest are changes in language, in notions of community, and in the very concepts of "public" and "public opinion." The Vietnamese language was undergoing a rapid transformation, including the appropriation of key concepts that came to structure the public realm. Vietnamese enthusiastically embraced a wide variety of neologisms that were "borrowed" from Japanese, Chinese, French, or Russian. These terms transformed discourse and modes of representation, invented new meanings within the host language of Vietnamese, and shaped the Vietnamese encounter with the modern age.[103]

In 1918, many literate Vietnamese were puzzled by concepts that readers take for granted today. Words like "chính phủ" (government), "chính sách" (policy), "xã hội" (society), "thuộc địa" (colony), and "bình quyền" (equal rights) "seemed strange to the eye and ear."[104] Some of these terms had suitable Vietnamese equivalents, some introduced new aspects of meaning into the language, while others were entirely new concepts. An article in the newspaper *Women's Bell* (*Nữ giới chung*) (1918) underscored the foreignness of such words when it provided explanatory glosses for many of them. This practice was later reprised by the communists, who introduced (as I shall later describe) their new, and extremely foreign, vocabulary of Marxism and political agitation to their readers in exactly the same way.

More than the appropriation of new words was at stake: the character of public discourse itself was in question. At the beginning of the 1920s, Vietnamese could employ a variety of terms to convey the sense of a larger community. Through the use of common rhetorical conventions, texts themselves often implied their audiences. "Virtuous men and devout women," Buddhist tracts often began, implying an egalitarian world only divided by gender. Buddhism, with its emphasis on acquiring merit by propagating texts and its tradition of creating multiple styles of message so that different levels of believer could understand it, reached out to perhaps the broadest implied audience. All human beings, these texts stated, could achieve salvation.

Outside a specifically Buddhist context, members of the elite often still referred to themselves as the "higher stream" (*thượng lưu*) ruling over the lower one, dividing society into two hierarchically ranked groups of people. Quite common in printed works as well at the beginning of the 1920s was the invocation of the exclusively male Confucian hierarchy of literati, agriculturalists, artisans, and merchants (*tứ dân*). This concept, which never fit the Vietnamese context well anyhow, had fragmented Vietnamese into four corporate groups and implied that the public realm was a male preserve. It also implied that no one term could apply to all the population. Unlike Buddhists, who could gain merit by simply copying or helping to print the words of the sutras, Confucians did not exhibit a strong desire to print for mass consumption. Neither did they script their message so that the common folk could understand their works: not surprisingly, then, many Confucian texts seem to have an implied audience of literate male members of the elite.[105] When the radical journalist Trần Huy Liệu stated in 1927 that "literature is the quintessence (*tinh hoa*) of a country," he echoed this Confucian view that the world of the literate elite could represent all of Vietnam.[106]

If the texts themselves seem to imply certain kinds of audiences, what was the actuality? Did the use of the terms above indicate that Vietnamese in 1920 felt part of enduring corporate groups above the village level to which they had strong bonds of attachment or that they enjoyed other broad senses of community? It would seem not. Phan Châu Trinh, after comparing the upper classes under the French to a "gang of robbers" and lamenting that the populace did not know what people's rights (*dân quyền*) were, stated that "the people do not know a sense of collective organization and community and do not consider the public good" because of abuses by literati and past dynasties.[107] While this claim is slightly exaggerated—Vietnamese did belong to a variety of lineage and village organizations, for one—it is true that many groups had fleeting existences.

From the 1920s onward, however, Vietnamese writers began experimenting with new ways to conceptualize their wider world and the public sphere. Increasingly, they talked in terms of "society" (*xã hội*). They appealed to "citizens" (*công dân*) and justified their beliefs in terms of "public opinion" (*công luận, dư luận*). At first sight, it appears that Confucian conceptual hierarchies were breaking down and that the notion of the public was expanding far beyond the original audience of books and newspapers: intellectuals, employees of the administration, and other literate urban residents. But Vietnamese did not abandon old ways of defining community. While old rhetorical identifications in terms of Confucian ranks and corporate groups weakened and Buddhist ones seemed less used, they never lost their emotive power. Although Vietnamese intellectuals talked about "society" and "public opinion" by the 1930s, these general concepts never swept away religious, local, or ethnic notions of community. The "public," in other words, was still being formed.

Although the meaning of the "public" was indeed shifting, "public opinion" did not refer to the opinion of the masses. The term (datable to third-century Chinese texts) "had been used throughout Chinese history to describe elite opinion within the bureaucracy."[108] While both late Qing writers and Vietnamese transformed the meaning of "public opinion" to refer to a broader public outside government, clear traces of this original elitism remained in the Vietnamese conception. Vietnamese writers often belittled the common man and woman, sometimes thinking of them as "dull-witted" or lacking intelligence.[109]

In the period under study, a gulf emerged between city and countryside that deeply shaped notions of the "public": "Twenty or thirty years of Westernization has far removed us from the rural populace so that today, their language ... we are not familiar with; their dispositions, we don't understand; their customs, we don't [understand] clearly; the daily life that absorbs them, we do not know well." The author of this same quotation went on to explain that peasants were lazy, filthy, uneducated, dumb, and had a propensity to commit crimes because of their poverty (and not, one assumes, because of some innate deficiency), and that young intellectuals should realize this elementary fact.[110] Given such beliefs, it is not surprising that "public opinion" referred not to the views of the masses, but to what journalists and intellectuals believed was universally true and rational and thus what people should believe.

This new elite believed that it had the obligation to enlighten the populace. A Westernized intellectual wrote in 1944 that "we must make efforts to awaken (*giác ngộ*) those people who, up to the present, are still living in darkness, in lack, in sickness, in ignorance, and with old-fashioned customs."[111] Commenting on how public opinion had gone astray and unscrupulous people were taking advantage of the ignorant, another writer reassured his readers that "our" correct opinions (*ý kiến chính đáng*) will gradually triumph over false public opinion.[112] In a similar manner, the well-known northern mandarin Vi Văn Định stated that "mandarins have a duty to enlighten (*khai hóa*) the people": following this perceived task, he urged people to take up physical exercise as part of a general physical and intellectual uplift so that the country "could become a civilized country just like the countries of Europe and America." Peasants in particular he urged to abandon superstitions like the burning of votive paper.[113]

The sense that the elite had a duty to enlighten others was not limited to Vietnamese working for the French administration. In 1935, for example, Phan Bội Châu, while rejecting much of Confucianism, linked the Confucian emphasis on leading a life of self-cultivation (as a public example to others) to the use of the media. He believed that newspapers and their writers could improve people's morality, intellect, and benevolence (*nhân tâm*); they could "strengthen the ethical instruction of the people, taking good morals and holding them up for citizens to follow, making a shining example for people to be guided."[114] Communists, despite their egalitarian philosophy, were hardly exempt from this elitist didacticism. The Vietnamese elite, in short, saw itself as having a higher cultural level than others. This view served as justification for the elite's self-perception that it had to be the leading group in society in order to bring betterment to the society as a whole.

Despite deeply ingrained elitist attitudes, writers gradually and fitfully reached beyond elite (and increasingly urbanized) literate culture and in the processes began undermining its pretensions to universality. By the 1930s, many intellectuals began to explore popular and village culture. In the process, they began to question developments in Vietnamese society and to realize that they needed to address the growing cultural gap between village and city. In this process, a more inclusive public sphere was coming into being.

CONCLUSION

On 2 September 1945, Independence Day, the revolutionary Võ Nguyên Giáp stood before the huge crowds at Hanoi's Ba Đình square to proclaim the accomplishments of the Việt Minh. This front organization, led by the communists, had been the major force in the north opposing both the French and the Japanese during World War II. Giáp stated that the new government "had already paved the way to heighten the consciousness of the masses through propagandizing, agitation, and education so that the masses would know how to 'preserve' and know how to 'use' the rights to democratic freedom that they have won."[115] Giáp's speech had a modern tone. This was not surprising, since this former history teacher was a product both of the colonial school system and of the Indochinese Communist Party. Occasionally, however, Giáp resorted to traditional formulations to reach out to the public: "The spirit of our people today is increasingly elevated, and our power is increasingly great. The center, the south, and the north share one heart (*lòng*). Literati, farmers, artisans, merchants, and soldiers share one will. Even Buddhist and Christian priests, even King Bảo Đại have warmly responded [to the call]."[116]

It is striking that, in this fragment of his speech, Giáp, a communist, would refer to his fellow Vietnamese in terms of a modified Confucian hierarchy. He conveyed a view of the public sphere that was inclusive, hierarchically ordered, and led by an enlightened elite that believed that it had the duty and responsibility to guide others. Giáp reached out to such other traditional constituents of the public as religious communities and the monarchy. When listening to this speech, different segments of the audience could connect to different parts of the message. A communist and a mandarin, a Buddhist monk and a Catholic priest might all be satisfied. A listener might be pardoned for imagining, briefly, that the speaker was describing the public realm of 1920 and its audience.

Giáp's implied audience, the entire populace of Vietnam hierarchically differentiated yet unified, was a convenient sociological fiction. When this revolutionary stated that all the people "share one heart," he exaggerated the extent to which all individuals and groups followed the Việt Minh's lead. Indeed, the public remained divided: rather than communicating through one public sphere, Vietnamese articulated their views in multiple realms of discourse. Furthermore, in politics Vietnamese lacked any unity. In the months leading up to the August General Uprising, Việt Minh cadres and their opponents had been assassinating each other. In repeated outbursts of violence, tens of thousands of Vietnamese were killed in the years from 1945 to 1947.[117]

This violence undermines Giáp's assertion that Vietnamese were united, just as there had always been a gap between the audience implied by writers or suggested by rhetorical formulations in texts and the actual one. Authors often spoke of what "we" Vietnamese thought or believed. Intellectuals frequently wrote on "public opinion" in the colonial period. But who was "we"? Who was "the public"? One cannot assume that writers knew their audiences perfectly and that the message conveyed through their writings was the one understood by the recipients. In the ultimate analysis, the significance of the printed word lies in how audiences received, made sense of, and acted on it.

This chapter suggests that before the twentieth century, printed material played a restricted but important role in Vietnamese society. By Southeast Asian standards, Vietnamese print culture was vibrant; by East Asian ones, it was not. Printed texts were rare objects. Confucian texts competed with numerous others, like Buddhist works and practical texts, for the public attention. While Confucianism was the ideological foundation of the Nguyễn dynasty, particularly from the 1820s onward, it did not dominate public life in the nineteenth century as much as has been assumed.[118] It is true that particular lineages had impressive traditions of learning, and some areas boasted of their success in the Confucian examinations, but Confucian learning spread unevenly among the populace. Given this uneven distribution and the slow circulation of knowledge, it is safe to say that before 1920 there was no real public sphere in precolonial Vietnam.

With the arrival of the French, the character of Vietnam's print culture began to change. From the 1920s, Vietnam began to develop a lively public realm in which printed matter played a key role. This public realm did not include all publications, however. Colonial repression forced radicals and revolutionaries into the clandestine realm, where they constituted a new realm of discourse. And religious publications came to constitute their own realm.

In this process of transformation, Confucianism lost its privileged position as state ideology and began a slow process of decline. In contrast, Buddhism probably retained the same level of influence at the popular level as before. The Westernization of the elite did not sweep away either teaching. When Lương Đức Thiệp wrote of a "revolution in zigzags," in which Confucius and Laozi jostled with Einstein and electrons, he captured the diversity of belief present in the Vietnamese public sphere. Vietnamese used print for everything from blackmail to promoting Buddhist salvation and advocating communist revolution.

In studying the impact of print culture on public life, I have noted important linguistic changes from the 1920s onward. The proliferation of new terms (and even changes in style) transformed Vietnamese discourse. These changes came at a cost. When many young Westernized Vietnamese championed a "clearer" Vietnamese inspired by French and began to articulate their views using newly minted words like "society" and "class," their use of such language ironically drove a wedge between them and the populace at large. When such writers claimed to speak in the name of the "public," such claims must be taken with a grain of salt. Audiences did not always interpret the printed or spoken word in the way that cultural elites demanded.

The printed word and its audience were not spread equally throughout Vietnam. They revolved around the two poles of Hanoi and Saigon. While the colonial state worried about the spread of "subversive" publications to the countryside, it was clear that city people participated more in the emergent print culture than did rural inhabitants. Even at the height of propagandizing under the Popular Front (1936–1939), the average villager rarely encountered much reading material. Not surprisingly, public debate did not include voices representing all Vietnamese. Illiterate peasants had no voice. Women were underrepresented. And so the public realm had a contradictory character: it appeared to be both unified and divided. It was unified in the sense that writers often appealed to a new, constructed entity, "the public." They invoked "public opinion" to advance their causes. Yet religious, philosophical, gender, class, and governmental interests cut across this public realm of exchange.

2 | The Colonial State and Repression of the Printed Word

In the fall of 1945, after attending countless meetings held by a wide variety of groups in rural and urban Vietnam, the journalist Nguyễn Bách Khoa came to a stunning conclusion:

> The first impression—and also the last impression—that I had was that from the August uprising to the present, the Vietnamese masses have just begun to learn ... to speak.
>
> Indeed, under French domination, the Vietnamese masses never "spoke" at all. Outside of those cases of "matters of the home," family, village, hamlet, funerals, and weddings ... the Vietnamese masses have never spoken words that are standard, logical, based on principle, and disciplined (*có kỷ luật*).

While colonialists did not allow people to "think" and "speak," Khoa's analysis continued, the August General Uprising transformed the situation. Since that time, "countless habits, countless warped rules of 'thinking' and 'speaking' from the darkest of nights of History were chased away by the light that penetrated into the masses."[1]

In other words, Nguyễn Bách Khoa was asserting that the colonial state was thoroughly hegemonic. In his view, the August General Uprising of 1945 and revolutionary nationalism in general shattered this hegemony: after decades of repression, Vietnamese could finally "learn ... to speak." Khoa expressed common themes in revolutionary discourse: the notion that revolution marks a watershed in personal and collective consciousness, that it can overthrow a wide variety of structures of domination, and that it is inextricably intertwined with enlightenment. Such discourse is seductive and emotionally satisfying.

But was the French colonial state thoroughly repressive? Did it manage to contain all possible dissent against the regime? Given the last chapter's emphasis on the liveliness of the public realm, Nguyễn Bách Khoa's words may strike an odd, even jarring, note. Far from being muted, Vietnamese spoke and wrote with a remarkable inventiveness and diversity in this period despite repeated attempts by the colonial state to curtail freedom of expression in the public realm. This chapter will argue that, in Vietnam, the historical evidence undermines the common claim that colonial regimes institute hegemonic control over society.

It is certainly true that administrators (and particularly the police) wished for greater control over public discourse. Yet their haphazard execution of policy profoundly shaped the ability of the French state to control the public realm. Furthermore, a contradictory body of French law stymied the state's coercion of political discourse. The police chafed at these restraints and tried to evade them through legal and illegal means. But words poured from the pens of Vietnamese between 1920 and 1945. Repression was selective, not totalizing. It differed from region to region and targeted "extreme" political discourse while often leaving other realms alone. It was, in other words, political dominance without sociocultural hegemony.

The repression of the import, publication, and circulation of printed matter went through several phases. From 1908 to 1920, the French anxiously attempted to stop Chinese-language materials from entering the country. Few newspapers and publications filtered in from abroad. In these early years, the administration worried little about Vietnamese publishers: only a small number of inhabitants could read romanized script, and few Vietnamese language publications circulated. From 1920 to 1939, despite brief periods of harsh repression, the state gradually loosened restrictions on public debate. From 1936 to 1939 in particular, following policies of the Popular Front government in France, the local administration relaxed almost all controls over public discourse. Publishing flourished. This period of liberty abruptly ended with the coming of war in 1939. Imposing martial law, the administration curtailed freedom of the press. It tightened its grip in the next few years under Vichy rule.

On 9 March 1945, the Japanese military in Indochina seized power from the Vichy regime, thus ending the pretense of French rule over the region. In the months that followed, the Japanese ceded some powers to a government it had put in place, that of the Empire of Vietnam. But as the war drew to a close, no government was able to master the disarray on the ground. In mid-August, the Việt Minh leadership met to declare that the opportune moment had arrived for a "righteous uprising" (*khởi nghĩa*) against French and Japanese rule. In the following two weeks, the Việt Minh found itself scrambling to assert control over large uprisings in towns and cities throughout Vietnam. When Hồ Chí Minh declared independence on 2 September 1945, he and the Việt Minh inherited a contradictory legacy of state repression and revolutionary and nationalist opposition. All parties fighting for the future of Vietnam claimed to want freedom. All parties used violence to achieve their ends. Despite the horrific bloodletting, which became evident in the spring of 1945 and continued into 1946 and later, and despite the rhetorical violence, this early period may have been one of the freest in modern Vietnamese history.

SURVEILLANCE AND DOMINATION
UNDER THE COLONIAL STATE

In the eyes of some scholars, the last two centuries have been marked by transformations that have homogenized individuals, territories, and states. James Scott, for example, has argued that states have failed when they have embraced authoritarian means to impose a high modernist vision that simplifies reality to better dominate it.[2] He notes that, in the drive to make society and nature more "legible," colonial and revolutionary regimes have an advantage over most others: "Revolution and colonialism, however, are hospitable to high modernism for different reasons. A revolutionary regime and a colonial regime each disposes of an unusual degree of power. The revolutionary state has defeated the ancien régime, often has its partisans' mandate to remake the society after its image, *and* faces a prostrate civil society whose capacity for active resistance is limited."[3] The question that arises, in the context of this chapter, is how much the French colonial state was able to impose its modernist will on the Vietnamese, simplify perceptions of reality, transform society, and then exclude Vietnamese from the public sphere in the process.

The scholarship on colonialism proves to be a contradictory guide in orienting research on this topic. While ideologues of imperial rule once argued that colonial subjects needed guidance before they could exercise freedoms responsibly, numerous postcolonial critics have argued that colonial states failed at tutelage and excelled at repression. Crawford Young has articulated this critique with verve: the African colonial state, he states in his magnum opus, exerted brutal hegemony. "Nothing was more alien to the telos of the [African] colonial state," Young continues, "than a civil society. Sovereignty required forcible subjugation; there were few illusions that it could rest on any principle but overwhelming military power."[4] While Young argues that the African colonial state was far more dominant and repressive than most other colonial states around the world, he makes one marked exception: the French colonial state in Vietnam resembled, he declares, its African kin.[5] In seeming confirmation of such views, a revolutionary nationalist historiography on Vietnam has stressed how the systematic oppressiveness of the French regime led Vietnamese to overthrow it with force.

At first glance, this view seems persuasive. It is clear, for example, that the French colonial administration increasingly succeeded at fulfilling one of the central duties of a state: extracting revenue from its subjects. Reflecting this change, the general state budget more than doubled between 1920 and 1940.[6] Some of these revenues were plowed back into the apparatus of repression: for example, the increased revenues helped the police (Sûreté) expand their ability to gather intelligence about threats to the state.

Judicial and police repression (and regulation of public life in general) seem to have had shaped colonial Vietnam profoundly. The French administration circumscribed Vietnamese rights of association and travel, and regulated markets, land transactions, and public spaces such as temples and parks. By reading the mail, the Sûreté tracked political suspects, kept tabs on newspapers, and watched Vietnamese students in France. The police built up an impressive system to gather, classify, and share information obtained through arrests and interrogations. Agents infiltrated political parties. They attended public meetings. The police monitored the press closely and threatened reprisals against publishers who printed materials deemed politically sensitive. They produced extensive dossiers on journalists: they even compiled them on relatively pro-French ones such as Bùi Quang Chiêu. The administration bought the silence (or acquiescence) of some newspapers and publishers through subventions. It seemed to have its tentacles everywhere.

Stories about French repression of Vietnamese are legion. Hương Giang noted the sad sight of women, wearing the cangue and dirty blue vests, sweeping the streets; at the smallest sign of slacking off, an overseer would whip them. The problem, the author noted, was that, "having accustomed ourselves to this sight, we no longer see its horror." Vietnamese city council members in Saigon seemed resigned to such violence. While stating that "some brutality is necessary" when arresting notorious criminals, they added that "we should not raise to the level of a principle the right to torture the accused." This is not to mention a more common complaint: petty harassment by low-ranking police officers, as when gangs of them went from store to store in Sóc Trăng, wishing the owners a happy Vietnamese New Year and shaking them down for small contributions.[7] Clearly, repression had been routinized.

Nothing epitomizes the colonial encounter better than conflicts between individual Vietnamese and Frenchmen. The French, from their positions of prestige, routinely engaged in petty acts of racial discrimination. They infantilized their male house servants by calling them "boys." They frequently referred to young women as "*congaie*"—from the Vietnamese "*con gái*"—which simply means "girl" in Vietnamese but which the French commonly used in a pejorative sense to refer to their concubines. French settlers belittled Vietnamese in numerous other ways, such as by the use of the personal pronoun "*tu*" generally used with intimates and inferiors. This latter practice was only forbidden (by official decree) under the Vichy regime in 1941.[8]

Sometimes, racial domination could be more brutal. In one instance, a Legionnaire grabbed a Vietnamese woman at a hotel and tried to kiss her. The man's Vietnamese husband intervened; the Legionnaire rebuffed him. "You, you're a slave. Me, French citizen. Me, go to war: look, I had all my teeth bashed in by the Huns. Me, have the right to take [here he used a different word] all Annamite women, all, you understand!" He broke a bottle over the young journalist's head. Another soldier ripped up the communist newspaper *Le travail*. When the hawker complained, the soldier kicked him in the rear. A police officer yelled at a Vietnamese car driver: "You bastard ... you dumb bugger (*bougre de c ...*)." A Frenchman at the journalist Andrée Viollis' hotel in Huế shouted at his *boy*, or young male servant, every morning: "Come here, you animal, you dumb bugger.... How often do I have to call you?

Come on, you bastard, [or] I'll kick you." On 19 December 1936, the Vietnamese delegate of the Hà Tiên provincial assembly sat on a hotel veranda, drinking beer, while two Frenchmen hit the coolie Lý Văn Bình. The delegate even saw the Frenchmen force a lit candle into the coolie's nostrils and ears. Only when one of the men, Bernard, pointed a rifle at Bình did the delegate ask them to stop the brutality.[9] Lý Văn Bình eventually died from his beating; Mr. Bernard protested that he was innocent and indeed never went to jail.

The unfairness of this racial domination was underlined by the unequal punishments meted out to French and "natives" who violated the law. Two contemporaneous incidents in 1929 illustrate this point. After slapping a plainclothes police officer by mistake—the officer had grabbed his identity papers, and he tried to grab them back—the erudite radical Phan Văn Hùm was hauled off for questioning (and eventually jailed). When Nguyễn An Ninh came to the defense of Hùm, he too was punished with a jail term. In contrast, when a Frenchman in Sóc Trăng shot dead his foreman Ninh and invoked the right to self-defense, he was cleared of any wrong. The writer concluded bitterly: French public opinion let the Frenchman get off free, accepting the argument that it was an act in self-defense, while Hùm's and Ninh's "yellow skin" meant that they would go to prison for a far less significant offense.[10] The story illustrates an important point: what the French saw as implementation of the law came across to many Vietnamese as utter hypocrisy.

While such examples of French repression are legion, anecdotal evidence cannot hide the fact that, to borrow a phrase from Robert Cribb, the colonial state exhibited a "puzzling weakness."[11] It failed at hegemony. It relied heavily on collaboration to accomplish its will and allowed colonial subjects to stake out zones of autonomy from state rule.[12] Contesting the rationality of the French colonial state in Vietnam, Hue Tam Ho Tai has noted the "haphazard fashion that characterized the whole colonial enterprise."[13] Jürgen Osterhammel has noted that, in the realm of law, "despite its reputation for strict centralization, the imperial French Republic was an even more chaotic legal hodgepodge than the British Empire, which was well known for its piecemeal arrangements."[14] The repressive apparatus and the legal framework undergirding French colonial rule were poorly organized and often ineffective. As Peter Zinoman has argued, even the heart of this repressive apparatus, the prison system, was in "perpetual disorder."[15]

Thus the French colonial state never lived up to its self-image of rationality. Although French colonials could be utterly racist, a nuanced view of French rule is still in order. The obvious examples of brutality cannot prove that Vietnamese were cowed into silence and submission. The print culture of Vietnam remained lively, and one reason lies in the limits of the law and of police repression.

POLICE, THE LAW, AND THE PUBLIC REALM

Up until 1917, French repression of dissent was carried out on an ad hoc basis. It relied on police services that were chaotically organized: separate police units with very different functions rarely established regular and effective liaison among themselves.[16] Faced with this disorganization, Governor-General Sarraut overhauled and centralized the Sûreté in 1917. This year marks a turning point: within the country, the police services moved from reacting to perceived threats to French authority to collecting information in order to preempt such threats.[17] The administration increased the Sûreté's intelligence-gathering powers and tightened liaison among police forces in Indochina and other European colonies.[18] Police branches in Cambodia, Laos, and throughout Vietnam regularly exchanged information with one another. A special section in France, the Service de liaison des originaires des Territoires d'Outre-Mer (SLOTFOM), kept a close watch on Asian, African, and Arab immigrants. It detected much of the first evidence of anarchist and communist activity among Vietnamese.

The administration now aimed its surveillance more effectively. The police targeted intellectuals, journalists, and political figures. They searched out potential suspects, read their mail, and infiltrated their organizations to collect information and sow discord. Combined with increasingly vigilant censorship, this surveillance helped to moderate the tone of printed debate. The administration then used the information gathered to compile dossiers on suspects. This activity, carried out by the Section des informations politiques, proved especially important. The results are evident in the archives: police dossiers from the early 1920s on suspects are sketchy, but documents improve in analytic depth, comprehensiveness, and accuracy from the mid-1920s onward. The relentless acquisition of information over time also meant that the police became increasingly skilled at forecasting threats to French authority.

But how total was police control over the public realm? The colonial administration invoked codes, regulations, decrees, and laws, and used courts and a prison system to give an orderly face to its domination. But the police rarely exercised unfettered power. If in the chaotic prison system, hidden from public view, the administration seems to have repeatedly violated its own laws,[19] in the public sphere, legal and political concerns tempered the arbitrary exercise of state will. Indeed, French law was key in shaping the public sphere: it defined the "rules" of printed discourse and of social and political association.[20] In sharp contrast to its laws on marriage and the family, the administration based this press and publication law completely on French precedent.[21] The French fully intended to refine the parameters of free speech and printed expression. Law shaped the parameters of repression while allowing Vietnamese limited means to use the system for their own ends. As the Nationalist Party activist Nhượng Tống wrote about his experience in Tonkin:

> Our books were sold for very low prices: only one or two *hào*. The reason was that at that time [1927?], book publishing was still free, there was no prepublication censorship as there was for newspapers. Essays that were deleted from newspapers could be printed up as books. Of course they could be banned. But, because of the "administrative tardiness" of the French, when they issued the decree to forbid, our books had sold out already![22]

It was precisely such experiences that allowed writers a margin of freedom.

The French legal and administrative approach to the public sphere developed out of a contentious tradition of censorship and a shorter history of press freedom. In France, state censorship was radically curtailed in 1881, when the government promulgated a remarkable law on publishing and the press. With limited exceptions, French citizens gained the right to print freely.[23] They no longer had to submit printed matter to authorities for prepublication censorship. While vendors had to register with the authorities, they could sell and distribute printed matter without government approval.[24]

Drawing on this French model as well as on the longer history of censorship and ignoring Nguyễn dynasty precedents, the French government exported the preexisting 1881 law to Indochina to regulate the realm of print.[25] French bureaucrats then modified this law to suit the colonial situation. The French administration extended the law on the press and publications, initially promulgated in Cochinchina, to Tonkin and Annam after 1884. In Tonkin and Annam, which the French government considered to be "protectorates," however, the 1881 law only had the force of a decree. Over time, the "Indochinese" legal realm took on a life of its own, creating a corpus of colonial law that drew on French precedents while growing increasingly distinct from them.

French jurisprudence combined with the difference in the legal statuses of protectorates and colonies shaped laws on publications. In legal terms, France was the undisputed sovereign authority in its one colony in Indochina (Cochinchina), where it ruled directly. But this expansion of authority brought with it restraints as well. In Cochinchina, the local French administration could not issue decrees that contradicted existing French laws. Thus, French laws designed to protect the rights of inhabitants of France often gave residents of colonies theoretical protections as well.

The legal situation in Annam and Tonkin differed. In these protectorates, France was supposed to "consult" with the de jure sovereign power, the Nguyễn court, which issued all laws. This court selectively refused (with the active encouragement of the French administration) to adopt French laws that curbed its power. It overrode, for example, the liberal provisions in the 1881 law on publications and the press. Not surprisingly, the French repressed most severely in their protectorates of Tonkin and Annam, while they had the hardest time stifling dissent in their colony of Cochinchina.

The legal restriction of Vietnamese opinion began when the French administration supplemented the 1881 law with the 30 December 1898 decree. This decree declared that "publication in Indochina of every newspaper or periodical written in Annamite, Chinese, or any other foreign language cannot take place without the previous authorization of the Governor General."[26] While in Cochinchina French-language newspapers retained their freedom, in Tonkin and Annam all newspapers now had to request permission to publish. A 1908 decree in Cochinchina, copied elsewhere, instituted prepublication censorship on newspapers. These laws and decrees shaped the public sphere of print.

From such clear beginnings, the laws on publications in Indochina evolved in a disorganized, ad hoc manner. The administration responded to threats to state control by adding a wide variety of laws, decrees, and rulings. This evolution continued to differ in the colony of Cochinchina and the protectorates of Tonkin and Annam. A 1927 report described the result: "In Indochina, the regulation of the press is contained in scattered, fragmentary, even contradictory measures that vary according to region and which give rise to great difficulties of interpretation for the judges charged with their application."[27]

Despite the proliferation of regulations, decrees, and laws, important loopholes remained. For example, owners of French-language newspapers did not need to request permission to publish or to submit page proofs to the censors. Publishers of nonperiodical matter (such as books) did not have to submit texts to the censors for prepublication review: according to the law, these works could only be seized when the police had examined the work after publication. Taking advantage of such loopholes, Vietnamese were able to voice numerous criticisms of the colonial state.

FROM EVERYDAY REPRESSION TO CONTROL OF THE
PRINTED WORD, 1920–1939

There is abundant evidence that the French administration could be brutally repressive. In daily life, Vietnamese occasionally encountered violence at the hands of fellow Vietnamese (including agents of the state) as well as from French citizens. But the emergent print culture was not hostage to such everyday repression. Press law provided limited protection against the arbitrary imposition of French will on publishers and printers. In many ways, it was against the foil of everyday racism that Vietnamese created a public sphere of debate in which French authors rarely participated.

By the 1920s, the public sphere was beginning to heat up. Remarking on the increasing self-assertiveness of the Vietnamese press, a police administrator reflected in 1921 that "it is good that a democratic government [*sic*] has, facing it, to counterbalance, to stimulate, to keep it in check, an opposition." He anxiously added, however, that too large an opposition could lead to problems: "If heretics are necessary, there should not be too many of them. The favor with which nationalism has been welcomed by all educated Annamites ... makes the situation serious because every day their newspapers, their propaganda, well, because we ourselves, by the improvements that we are bringing to their lot, we are working for them, to attract in a French sense these young minds."[28] Some Vietnamese confirmed the truth of this assertion. The southern journalist Cao Chánh stated in 1924 that "despite the severity of censorship, readers can always find in the Annamite language press material to strengthen this feeling [patriotism], which is spreading in a truly remarkable manner."[29]

From the 1920s onward, Vietnamese writers and editors sparred with French administrators over the character of the public realm. The French worried that the colonial state might lose its grip on public discourse and thus over the Vietnamese. From the early 1920s, police reports repeatedly warn of the dangers of nationalism. French censors feared that articles about the unity of the Vietnamese race, love of one's native place, or the loss of the Vietnamese soul might indicate nationalist dissent. In Tonkin, the censor Vinay complained in 1922 that Vietnamese rarely expressed such sentiments directly: "They tend to try to slip past [the censors] vague articles in which Annamites are invited to wake up from their long sleep, to blot out their shame."[30] Indeed, the themes of loss, shame, frustration, and lament were quite common in the teens and early twenties. But they were less a sign of nationalism than of a sense of defeat and a xenophobic anticolonialism. Anticolonial nationalism, in contrast, would join such sentiments of loss to a positive vision of the future, a future in which people perceived that they could transcend fragmentation to create affective bonds linking them together. This vision was soon to arise.

From the censor's point of view, the French state faced a clear dilemma: how to accommodate dissenters without allowing them to "awaken" to nationalism and revolution and undermine French rule.[31] What if Vietnamese rejected the French vision of the nation and developed an alternative one? In 1925, a French administrator could claim that "until now ... Indochina does not seem to have [come under] the slightest influence of Bolshevik propaganda."[32] From the late 1920s, however, the tenor of official reports changes. In the following years, an increasing number of Vietnamese, particularly of the younger generation, began to articulate nationalist, radical, and communist opinions.

To repress such views, the colonial state adopted a variety of tactics. The police extensively censored Vietnamese-language newspapers before publication. They sometimes stretched their definition of "dissent" to absurd limits: in 1927, for example, a censor deleted an "enigmatic" article in *Đông Pháp thời báo* (Indochina times) on the coming celebration of Bastille Day. He admitted that the article lacked "any disagreeable allusions," but he nonetheless concluded that it was "tendentious" and aimed to keep Vietnamese away from scheduled festivities.[33] The administration also banned publications for violations of the penal code or of administrative rulings. But banning was a cumbersome process: to take a book or newspaper out of circulation, the governor-general or the governor of the region had to issue a formal stay (*arrêté*) after its publication and then track down copies. As such, it was a poor weapon.

The administration also resorted to other tactics, like intimidation, to stop the circulation of "subversive" ideas. In the 1920s, when newspapers were few and many of their readers worked for the administration, the governor of Cochinchina is reputed to have pressured employees not to subscribe to antigovernment newspapers.[34] A writer in *L'écho annamite* complained in 1924 that police detectives followed his newspaper's subscribers, then threatened them. He claimed that the administration slapped disciplinary sanctions on its employees while warning them that their names were being put on secret lists.[35]

Strong-arm tactics were not limited to readers and subscribers. The radical Nguyễn An Ninh asserted in 1924 that the Cochinchinese administration tried to crush his newspaper by strong-arming printers to refuse to print the paper, threatening to put him on trial, and forcing subscribers to renounce their subscriptions. "The street urchins who sold *La cloche fêlée* often came in for a roughing up as well."[36] *La cloche fêlée* was not the only target of French police wrath. When the French authorities closed *Pháp Việt nhựt gia* (Franco-Vietnamese daily) and banned its final issue, police stood guard outside the Saigon print shop to ensure that no copy left the premises.[37] Similarly, Monin, the French director of the newspaper *Indochine*, complained that his Chinese and Vietnamese clients were repeatedly threatened by the police and forbidden to have relations with him. He also charged that the police intercepted and read his correspondence and that the post office did not deliver his newspaper to its mail subscribers, all because he had dared criticized the governor of Cochinchina. His complaint rings true: I had the pleasure of finding a copy of his intercepted letter in the police files.[38]

The police also targeted publishers. Nguyễn An Ninh stated that publishers threatened by the administration often shied away from printing controversial materials simply to curry favor with the administration. Police sometimes stood guard at the doors of printers to seize books and newspapers as they left the building. They also found excuses to search premises for subversive materials. In 1926, Saigon police raided the home and newspaper office of Phạm Văn Duyệt, editor of *Le nha que* (The peasant), confiscating documents, printed matter, and correspondence, and then questioned and arrested suspects.[39] From the above litany of practices, it is clear that the administration was willing to bend the law or find extralegal ways to enforce its will.

As time passed, the police found themselves increasingly hobbled by laws and rulings imposed by the Colonial Ministry or the governor-general of Indochina. The police grew increasingly frustrated with their administrative superiors over liberalization of the public sphere. The governor-general took an early step to relax restrictions on publishing on 30 December 1927, when he issued a new decree for Tonkin and Annam to supersede the 1898 decree on the control of printed matter. By allowing individuals in those two regions to publish French-language periodicals without the permission of the administration, the government slightly liberalized the public sphere there.[40] Yet as time passed, Tonkin and Annam tended to lag behind Cochinchina. As southern Vietnamese successfully launched legal challenges to press restrictions in Cochinchina, the south became far more open than the center and the north.

Local administrations accepted such liberalization grudgingly. By 1929, Governor Krautheimer of Cochinchina warned that "we can foresee, given the increasing spread of suspect literature, the real danger that it could become one day if the public authorities do not have sufficient weapons to combat and annihilate its influence."[41] Krautheimer was right: he had few legal weapons to stop the spread of "subversion." To seize materials, he had to be able to show that publications presented a danger to state security or that they violated the *dépôt légal*, or "legal deposit," which stated that all publications had to list the name and address of the printer.[42] Given the weak legal basis for repression of the printed word, the Cochinchinese administration advanced the flimsiest of pretexts to justify the seizure of disliked materials. A case in point is the 1929 seizure of the brochure *Anh hùng yêu nước* (Patriotic hero), which extolled the exploits of the English admiral Lord Nelson against the French. A Saigon bureaucrat argued that, "in this tract, the author, in narrating the exploits of the English admiral, brings out the bravery, selflessness, and patriotism of this warrior, whom he cites as an example to his compatriots."[43] One assumes that the problem lay not with these virtues, but in the fact that Lord Nelson drew on them to defeat the French.

In Tonkin and Annam, the police seized printed matter far more often than in Cochinchina. Many publications banned in Tonkin and Annam circulated freely in Cochinchina. The administration also reserved the right to ban publications printed outside of Indochina. Ironically, very few of these publications could reach a broad public. Most of the books that were forbidden, for example, had print runs of under a thousand copies. A glance at Table 1 is eye-opening: some of the most important political agitators in the south (such as Trần Huy Liệu) show up on the list of authors.

Seizures of printed matter cost authors and publishers dearly. Sometimes the police threw writers in jail. Raids could force a newspaper to close temporarily or compel the publisher to raise prices to recoup lost income. In 1938, for example, the Tư Tưởng Mới (New Thought) publishing house of Tourane explained that it had suffered a large loss when the government seized two of its books, *Ngục Kontum* (Kontum prison) and *Giai cấp* (Classes). "We do not have enough money to continue publishing further books ... if we do not set a high price for this volume."[44] It is doubtful that the publisher recouped his losses, as the volume that contained these words was soon banned in Tonkin and Annam.[45]

When banning or seizing brochures did not work, the government resorted to extreme tactics. It reserved the right to expel journalists back to their "country" of origin (that is, any of the five "*pays*" of French Indochina). These expulsions proved useful in the south, since many prominent journalists had moved there from the north or the center. For example, the governor-general of Cochinchina expelled Bùi Thế Mỹ and Diệp Văn Kỳ back to the center because of their newspaper articles.[46]

The administration relied on two other means, searches of mail and of imported goods, to control the circulation of the printed word and track down suspects. Initially, surveillance of the mails produced few results. In 1921, the Tonkin administration admitted that, despite reading a great number of letters, it had discovered little about Vietnamese political leanings.[47] Nonetheless, this method of political surveillance soon bore

TABLE 1. A Sample of Publications Banned in Vietnam, 1927–1936

Publication	Year Banned	Where Banned
Trần Hữu Độ, *Hồn độc lập* (Soul of independence) (Saigon: Xưa Nay, 1926)	1927	Tonkin
Trần Huy Liệu, *Một bầu tâm sự* (A heartfelt concern) (Saigon: Bảo Tôn, 1927)	1927	Tonkin
Diệp Văn Kỳ, *Sự cách mệnh* (Revolution) (Saigon: Bảo Tôn, 1927)	1927	Tonkin
Phan Bội Châu, *Sách thuốc chữa dân nghèo* (Medical remedies to cure the poor) (Saigon: Imp. Cô Mu [?], n.d.)	1928	Tonkin
Nhượng Tống, *Dân tộc chủ nghĩa* (Nationalism) (Hanoi: Long Quang, n.d.)	1927	Tonkin
Việt Nam học sanh báo (Vietnamese students' newspaper) (printed outside of Indochina)	1928	Indochina
La nation annamite (printed outside of Indochina)	1928	Indochina
Phan Bội Châu, *Lời hỏi* (Questions) (Saigon: Xưa Nay, 1928)	1928	Tonkin
Loi kinh cao cung dong bao cua Dang Viet Nam doc lap (printed outside of Indochina, n.d.)	1928	Indochina
Trần Huy Liệu and Đào Khắc Hưng, *Tân quốc dân* (New citizens) (Saigon: Tam Thanh, 1928)	1928	Tonkin
Nguyễn An Ninh, *Hai bà Trưng* (The Trung sisters) (Saigon: Bảo Tôn, 1928)	1928	Tonkin
Rabindranath Tagore, *Đông phương tây phương* (East and West)	1929	Tonkin
Anh hùng yêu nước (Patriotic heroes)	1929	Tonkin
Tịch tà qui chánh (Abandon heresy, return to righteousness) (Hanoi: Imprimerie Évangelique, 1931)	1931	Tonkin
Nguyễn Tử Siêu, *Lịch sử tiểu thuyết Mai Hắc Đế* (Mai Hắc Đế: a historical novel) (Hanoi, 1930 [?])	1930	Tonkin

Continued on next page

TABLE 1—*Continued*

Publication	Year Banned	Where Banned
Nguyễn Tử Siêu, *Lịch sử tiểu thuyết Lý Nam Đế* (Lý Nam Đế: a historical novel) (Hanoi: Nhật Nam Thư Quán, n.d.)	1930	Tonkin
Lý Mai, *Vần quốc ngữ* (The quốc ngữ alphabet) (Saigon: Thiet Hanh [?], n.d.)	1930	Tonkin
Phú Đức (Pharmacy), *Tiểu anh hùng Võ Kiệt* (The young hero Võ Kiệt) (Saigon: Tin Đức Thư Xã, 1929)	1930	Tonkin
Lương Văn Can, *Tri thức phổ thông mới* (New popular learning) (Hanoi: Thuy Ky, n.d.)	1932	Tonkin
Nguyễn An Ninh, *Tôn giáo* (Religion) (Saigon: Bảo Tôn, 1932)	1932	Tonkin
Cao Hải Để, *Tư tưởng xã hội* (Thought and society) (Bến Tre: Bùi Văn Nhẫn, 1933)	1933	Tonkin
Nguyễn Văn Liễn, *Esquisses et opinions annamites* (Saigon: Đức Lưu Phương, 1933)	1934	Tonkin
Ngô Tất Tố, *Vua Hàm Nghi* (King Hàm Nghi) (Hanoi: Nhật Nam Thư Quán, 1935)	1935	Tonkin
Ngô Tất Tố, *Những trận đổ máu hồi Pháp mới sang ta đến ngày nay* (Bloody battles from the time the French arrived to the present) (Hanoi: Nhật Nam Thư Quán, 1935)	1935	Tonkin
Trần Huy Liệu and Nguyen Thanh Lam, *Hội kín* (Secret societies) (Hanoi: Đông Dương, 1936)	1936	Tonkin
Nguyễn Văn Tạo, *Mặt trận bình dân Pháp với nguyện vọng của dân chúng Đông dương* (The French Popular Front and the aspirations of the Indochinese masses) (Saigon: La lutte, 1936)	1936	Tonkin

Sources: National Archives Center–I, Hanoi, Residence Supérieure au Tonkin, d. 74.197; *Bulletin administratif du Tonkin*, various issues; *Journal officiel de l'Indochine française*, various issues. Publication information given when available.

fruit. By 1927, the French Sûreté in Cochinchina was stating that postal surveillance had become "the main and most effective means of [gathering] information for the Service." It added that such monitoring

> allowed [us] to identify most of the newspaper correspondents, who were then brought to the attention of the administrative authorities of their province or country of origin; to be aware of the undertakings of suspects, all carefully watched by the service; to keep up to date on the undertakings of students in France, of which a certain number, infected by communist pamphlets, plan or propose to travel in Russia or China. Surveillance allowed us to figure out the organization of the Kuomintang, to keep track of propaganda carried out in Cochinchina and in Cambodia by the overseas department of the Kuomintang's Central Committee and to identify delegates of the latter in the colony.[48]

The post office focused its attention on newspapers and previously identified suspects. It paid particular attention to mail from China and from overseas Vietnamese. It examined letters and packages sent from abroad to seize "tendentious" newspapers (such as *Le paria* and *Việt Nam Hồn* [Soul of Vietnam]).[49] Within Indochina, Vietnamese used the mail to send tracts that, while free to circulate in the south, were banned in other parts of the colony.[50] The administration followed the movements of the leaders of the *La lutte* group by reading the mail of its major political figures (Tạ Thu Thâu, Trần Văn Thạch, Nguyễn Văn Tạo, Dương Bạch Mai, Phan Văn Hùm, and Nguyễn An Ninh).[51] *La lutte* was a well-known French-language newspaper in Saigon around which much opposition to the French centered. The newspaper tended to be Trotskyist but included, at various times, Stalinists and independent radicals.

The shift of tactic by the French administration over time from reacting to perceived threats to attempting to prevent them kept most opposition parties in check. It ensured that, if the urban print culture was lively, the urban areas would not be the locus of armed resistance to French rule. Nonetheless, this strategy had its limits. In 1930, the Việt Nam Quốc Dân Đảng, a party inspired in part by China's Guomindang, launched the Yên Báy uprising in northern Vietnam to seize power from the French. And later that year and into 1931, communists and peasants in the central provinces of Nghệ An and Hà Tĩnh also rebelled, setting up autonomous local "soviets." Both of these challenges to French rule shook the French administration profoundly.

By the 1930s, the Sûreté had increased the sophistication of its analysis of anti-French forces. As it perceived the communist threat to increase, however, its aims and those of Paris began to diverge. By early 1934, the Sûreté was complaining that judicial and governmental authorities failed to provide it with the orders to carry out repression; thus, "the Sûreté watches helplessly at the birth and growth of danger. It can do no more than give the alarm."[52] Focused on repression, the police had little faith that other methods, such as the expansion of educational opportunities, would bring youth into the French fold and thus stifle dissent.

On 1 January 1935, Governor-General Robin overrode police protests and abolished prepublication censorship in Indochina. When the Popular Front government came to power (1936–1939), the local administration, under strong pressure from the Ministry of Colonies, abandoned remaining press restrictions in the south. In publishing, Cochinchina became as free as France itself. Tonkin and Annam eventually followed suit. Court rulings determined that any decree that contradicted the 1881 French law on the press was null and void, a decision that called into question the legal basis of repression in those regions.[53] Vietnamese and others could freely publish without precensorship, although until 1938 the administration reserved the right to authorize or rescind newspapers in those two regions.[54] It was forced to fall back on other powers: for example, when Trần Huy Liệu and Nguyễn Đức Kinh began publishing fiction in 1935 about Vietnamese heroes from the past, the governor-general forced them to stop, because their actions posed a "danger to public opinion."[55]

Throughout the three Vietnamese regions of French Indochina, and especially in Cochinchina, the loosening of repression led to predictable results. The Sûreté stated that in Cochinchina six hundred committees had held 150 public meetings and distributed 450,000 copies of tracts.[56] There is no way to confirm that Vietnamese radicals and revolutionaries distributed this number of tracts in two months of 1936; suffice it to say that propagandizing was extensive. The governor-general of Indochina also warned that the very bases of French sovereignty were being challenged by a newly assertive press: it was "one of the instruments, if not the instrument, that will contribute the most to the breakdown of the spirit of Cochinchinese society."[57] The new helplessness of the Sûreté indicates that Vietnamese print culture, and especially political culture, had come a long way since the early 1920s. It also shows that tensions between the colonial Sûreté in Vietnam and the French government in Paris had grown immensely.

POLICING THE WORD: MARTIAL LAW, VICHY, AND WORLD WAR II

Under the Popular Front (1936–1939), Vietnamese enjoyed more freedom of expression than at any previous time under colonial rule. This freedom abruptly ended it in 1939. With war imminent in Europe and Japan expanding its war in China, the French government feared destabilization in its colonies. It banned all political parties in Indochina, cracked down on the communists, and issued five decrees on the censorship and control of printed matter.[58]

At the beginning of October 1939, the police raided then shut down the Association of Annamite Journalists of Cochinchina. On October 12 alone, the Saigon-Cholon police carried out seventy-seven raids on suspected communists and seized almost three thousand tracts and brochures. In that month, the French administration shut down nineteen "communist" newspapers and raided bookstores, printing presses, and other stores to seize communist writings.[59] These measures severely curtailed what little press freedom remained. After being freed on 3 March 1939, Nguyễn An Ninh, the famous anti-French agitator, was rearrested on 5 October 1939 for "illegal association" and "subversive activities."[60] Other suspected subversives were rounded up as well.

On 23 November 1940, communists in Cochinchina rose up in revolt. French troops and police crushed the uprising, arrested over five thousand communists, and seized or shut down communist newspapers as well.[61] Communists in the south were hit hard, while those in the north and center of Vietnam fell on the defensive. The French had severely weakened the Vietnamese opposition, and they turned their attention to meeting the Japanese challenge. Under the new Franco-Japanese "alliance," the Japanese military occupied Vietnam and promoted the Greater East Asian Co-Prosperity Sphere ("Asia for the Asians"). It allowed the French to remain as nominal authorities of Indochina.

The Vichy government in French Indochina combined repression with systematic attempts to mold public opinion. Between 1939 and 1942, the governor-general closed down at least nineteen noncommunist magazines or newspapers, thirteen of them in 1942.[62] The government also forbade the importation of many books and magazines, especially Chinese communist publications. It returned to the prepublication review of all printed matter, radio scripts, and films. Vichy censors did not simply target political writings. As a southern police censor put it, the problem with the Vietnamese was that they liked to read publications that "pandered to their base instincts." Even the Vietnamese bourgeoisie despaired that such material was so popular. By rigorously censoring "pornographic, libertine, or immoral publications," the censors averred, they were helping to stamp out such vice.[63] Indeed, one of the marks of the Vichy period was the return of the police to the role of moral arbiter of Vietnamese literary tastes.

The Vichy administration adopted policies to support friendly newspapers and magazines and punish others. For friendly newspapers, it inserted official notices and advertising, bought administrative subscriptions, gave subsidies, and provided advance notice of news as well as interviews. It withheld such benefits from others. In at least one case in 1940, the governor-general secretly paid a Mr. Michel, the owner of the newspaper *Bạn dân* (Friend of the people), to stop a negative campaign against government fiscal policies.[64] Such generous treatment of government critics was rare. In general, Governor-General Decoux stressed that he did not "want there to be equal treatment between those who collaborate effectively with the work of the National Revolution and those who show no interest or those who discredit it openly or in an underhand manner."[65]

The newly created Information, Propaganda, and Press Service laid down detailed guidelines for censorship. It banned criticism of France, of Maréchal Pétain, and of Pétain's "National Revolution." It specified certain guidelines for its "Indochinese" publications. Anything that gave Indochinese the sense that the French disdained them was banned. For example, the Information, Propaganda, and Press Service stressed that it would censor any text that made Indochinese think that they were oppressed and that pushed them to join with the "Asian or yellow race" rather than with the French. It also forbade any writings that left readers with the impression that France was "decadent" or "that sooner or later Indochina will be separated from France, that it is not an essential part of

Empire."[66] This service no longer applied strictly political criteria to censor material, but cut anything that might put the French government in an unflattering light. For example, on 2 February 1942, censors deleted an article from the Saigon newspaper *La dépêche* in which a French planter complained that it was difficult to buy potatoes.

The French administration instructed censors to take particular measures for German, Japanese, Italian, Chinese, "Indochinese," and French readers. While the French were titular rulers of Indochina, its Information, Propaganda, and Press Service obeyed Japanese wishes for censorship.[67] On 20 March 1942, the administration deleted an article in *La dépêche* on Japanese military attachés in Malaysia with the simple explanation: "Censored at the request of the Japanese."[68]

In addition to censoring texts, Governor-General Decoux ordered that librarians purge public libraries of "harmful" books. He pointed out that given their attempts to suppress "literature that is morally and politically harmful (*pernicieuse*) ... it would be a paradox if our libraries remained a resource for those who want to thwart our actions."[69] Finally, the French administration adopted a systematic approach to postal censorship. Rather than simply open the mail of suspects, the postal service went a step further, attempting to analyze mail to determine "mass opinion" as well as the views of specific categories of Vietnamese (bureaucrats, peasants, and so forth).[70] Through such measures, the French administration reasserted tight control over the written and printed word, a control that had slipped away in the late 1930s.

Despite the reassertion of the state against its opposition, Vietnamese pioneered two forms of dissent in the 1941–1945 period. On the one hand, Vietnamese legally used the Vichy ideology of "National Revolution" to promote their own views of radical social change. On the other hand, the Việt Minh sharpened a message of opposition to French and Japanese domination and attempted to spread it in rural areas. Both the legal and illegal forms of dissent showed the burgeoning consciousness of rural Vietnam and its people, heralding the beginning of a new stage in the development of a Vietnamese public sphere.

"The first ten days of July 1945 could be called the time of all freedoms," the newspaper *Thanh nghị* announced. The emperor Bảo Đại had issued edicts granting the rights to freedom of assembly and freedom to form unions.[71] In the chaotic summer of 1945, after northern and central Vietnam had suffered heavily from famine and while the government was losing its grip on the people, the Vietnamese were nonetheless gaining limited new liberties. The change was underlined in the August 1945 General Uprising, since renamed the August Revolution. In its first communiqué, the Việt Minh called on Vietnamese to realize "the rights of democratic freedom, of assembly, of organization, of religious beliefs, of thought, of free speech, of travel, [and] of universal suffrage."[72] It is hardly a surprise that Vietnamese took up these freedoms enthusiastically. But if the years from 1945 to 1947 were characterized in part by experimentation with freedom, they were also marked by widespread bloodshed and repression. The contradictory legacy of the colonial period lived on.

CONCLUSION: CENSORSHIP AND THE PUBLIC SPHERE

When one initially examines Vietnam from 1920 to 1945, it seems to make little sense to contest the notion that French repression was brutal. The historian can find numerous incidents that indicate that French rule could be harsh, racist, and capricious. Law and police practice structured the public sphere of print and affected the production and circulation of knowledge. But the French colonial state was not all-powerful. Its laws gave a limited amount of freedom to book and newspaper publishers. Its police did not always operate effectively. In short, the French colonial state failed at hegemony.

When one examines the kinds of material that the French administration censored, it becomes clear that it cared little about the vast majority of morality tracts, Buddhist tracts, novels, or popular songs. It focused the vast majority of its attention on "subversive" political publications. Even after spending millions of piasters on its repressive apparatus, however, this same state had an ambiguous impact on political dissent. Given this mixed success and the state's lack of interest in other realms of print culture, Vietnamese were able to stake out zones of autonomy from the colonial state.

Part 2.
Three Realms
of Print

In the first part of this book, I have sketched an overview of the public sphere and the role of the state in controlling the developing print culture in the period from 1920 to 1945. The French colonial state, more powerful than any other Vietnamese state in history, shaped the parameters of the public realm. Through the implementation of laws, the development of a school system, and the construction of Vietnamese historical and cultural memory, the state affected the ways that Vietnamese saw the world. Colonial discourse (with all its talk of civilization, progress, and systematizing reason) could have insidious effects, as when Vietnamese measured themselves against Western ideals and practices and found themselves wanting.

But, as earlier chapters have suggested, the French colonial state failed to exercise a hegemonic grip over the minds of the Vietnamese. Legal constraints over the extent of repression, especially in Cochinchina, meant that Vietnamese were able to carve out pockets of autonomy from the state. With the exception of politics, a realm watched closely by the French Sûreté, the Vietnamese often managed to pursue their interests unmolested by the colonial administration. It is thus time to leave behind a state-centered view of the colonial period and to explore the print culture of the period to find out what Vietnamese themselves found important.

The chapters that follow examine Confucian, communist, and Buddhist realms of discourse. Each one of them had a different relation to the colonial state. The French administration affected the world of Buddhism the least: indeed, this world seems to have been impenetrable to them. Although the French had a limited impact on Confucian

discourse, which it promoted at times as a bulwark against communism, most of the discourse in this realm developed independently of
administration interests. The French clashed directly with communists.
Ironically, the examination of communist discourse and the way that
the French forced it into the clandestine realm shows the limits of the
public sphere and the need to go beyond it to understand Vietnamese
print culture of the period.

Historians cannot escape the retrospective reconstruction of the past.
But they can mitigate its abuses. If we try to set aside a post-1945 or even
a post-1954 view, in which all events are fated to lead inexorably to the
triumph of revolutionary nationalist forces, what do we see? Looking forward from 1920 or 1935, the future trajectory of "Indochina"
or "Vietnam" was not at all clear to most Vietnamese. Revolution and
nationalism were but two options open to the populace. Not surprisingly, then, only one of the three chapters that follows centers on these
themes. Each of the chapters that follow has a rough geographical focus:
those on Confucianism and communism discuss writers from the center
and north, while the one on Buddhism centers on developments in the
south. That said, it can be notoriously difficult to contextualize the reach
of the printed word. One of the lessons from the study of print culture
is that frontiers can inhibit but not stop the circulation of ideas and
practices.

In examining Confucianism, communism, and Buddhism in successive chapters, this book advances a variety of arguments about the precolonial past and its relationship to the 1920–1945 period and beyond.
I assert that modern ideologies were nowhere near as successful as they
often claimed to be in displacing so-called traditional ones. What, then,
is this "tradition"? Many scholars argue that Confucianism defined the
Vietnamese past. Others point out that Vietnamese adhered to the *tam
giáo*, the combination of the three teachings of Confucianism, Buddhism,
and Daoism. But ultimately, scholars fall back on the view that the
modern ideologies of nationalism and revolution pushed aside Confucianism, while Buddhism, they assume, had lost influence even earlier.
This view is problematic: for one, the precolonial past was far more
heterogeneous and Confucianism less dominant than much of the
scholarship implies.[1]

Two examples will drive this point home. Trần Cao, who led a massive
rebellion in 1516, claimed to be an offspring of the old Trần ruling

family; he also claimed to be Indra reborn, wore black, shaved his head, and launched his rebellion from the famous Quỳnh Lâm temple in the district of Đông Triều. The unlettered vagabond Phan Bá Vành, on the omen of a comet, styled himself king and launched a rebellion against the Nguyễn court in the mid-1820s.[2] The two examples show that Vietnamese combined, to use a Vietnamese locution, different "cultural streams" (*dòng văn hóa*). Sometimes these streams intersected; sometimes they flowed their own ways. While I have adopted the historian's conceit of breaking these streams into clearly demarcated realms like "Buddhism," "Confucianism," and communism, this is only a provisional attempt to impose order on a fluid reality. It is not, however, completely arbitrary: if the actual boundaries between these realms can easily be disputed, it is no less true that Vietnamese constantly argued over such boundaries and their relevance.

Envisioning this transformation with attention to gender drives this point home. Buddhism, which appealed greatly to women, persisted in part because of female patronage. Confucianism once appealed to the male ruling elite but gave way when a new male elite embraced ideologies ranging from nationalism to communism. But as histories have, so far, focused on the heavily male realms of statecraft and war, and taken them to represent the entirety of the Vietnamese experience, realms like Buddhism, where women play a greater role, have been slighted.

3 | Confucianism and Vietnamese Culture

During a 1992 stay in Paris, a Vietnamese scholar urged me to go to Huế. "It is the most Vietnamese city of Vietnam," he said, presumably because the former capital of the Confucian Nguyễn dynasty was less Westernized than Hanoi or Saigon. At the time, I thought that the notion that Huế (the seat of a monarchy that adapted the outward forms of Chinese civilization) could be more Vietnamese than any other part of Vietnam betrayed an anxiety about the authenticity of the country's culture. I wondered if to this scholar the Nguyễn monarchy had receded far enough into the past that its capital—which the French once considered the most Sinic and most Confucian part of Vietnam—could be resurrected as authentic Vietnamese tradition.[1]

After visiting Huế, however, I have come to wonder if a different, unexpected, and startling truth is contained in this scholar's words. The Huế area is quintessentially Vietnamese because, paradoxically, it draws on multiple streams of Vietnamese and non-Vietnamese influences. This region, once a frontier, where Nguyễn rulers drew on Vietnamese, Chinese, highlander, and Cham cultural streams, shows that the search for an essential Vietnamese culture is doomed to failure.[2]

But the search for such a cultural core continues. On the one hand, modern Vietnamese repeatedly claim that "Confucianism" has profoundly fashioned Vietnamese identity. Nguyen Khac Vien is representative of this view when he writes that "for ten centuries Confucianism was the intellectual and ideological backbone of Vietnam."[3] But was it? Such claims lack conviction, for many scholars also state that inhabitants of the country manifested a shallow, faulty, and incomplete grasp of its teachings. This paradox is compounded by another. In this age of nationalism, many modern Vietnamese have celebrated the uniqueness of Vietnam's cultural heritage while accepting that an imported set of teachings and beliefs, Confucianism, have largely defined premodern beliefs and institutions. Contrary to the conventional wisdom, this chapter argues that Confucianism's impact on Vietnam has been exaggerated and misconceived. By the 1920s, with bureaucratic examinations abandoned, this teaching fell on increasingly hard times.

Given the sweep of such claims, let me clarify these views. I believe that the "teachings of the scholars" (*nho học*) had a deep impact in certain areas of human thought and behavior. In arguing that Confucianism's impact has been exaggerated, however, I am asserting that the vast majority of Vietnamese did not understand "Confucianism" as a coherent and structured doctrine, sharply distinguishable from other teachings and of such power that it fundamentally transformed daily practices and beliefs. My argument here is definitional. Indeed, most Vietnamese appropriated Confucian teachings not as a sharply bounded and internally consistent doctrine, but as related fragments in a mix of Confucian, Buddhist, Daoist, and other teachings combined with local customs and even Western ideas.

One can find evidence that suggests that, historically, Vietnam fits clearly within the East Asian Confucian world. Nineteenth-century Nguyễn kings compared their Confucian institutions favorably with Qing ones. Vietnamese Confucian reformers at the turn of the twentieth century, like Phan Bội Châu and Lương Văn Can, drew inspiration from their Chinese counterparts. Further afield, marked similarities seem to connect Vietnam and Korea. In both of the latter countries, progressives and conservatives have deployed Confucianism in arguments over resistance to foreign aggression, colonialism, and nationalism.[4] Such surface similarities among modern Vietnamese, Chinese, and Korean historical debates might lead one to read these convergences back onto the pre-twentieth-century past. That would be, as this chapter argues, a mistake.

For all the obvious similarities, numerous authors have mentioned clear difficulties with such comparisons. While there is clear evidence of Confucian influence, it is also true that a variety of Vietnamese in the colonial and postcolonial periods have lamented that Vietnamese manifested a poor and fragmented understanding of the teaching.[5] Phan Đại Doãn, putting a more positive spin on the matter, argues that when Vietnamese appropriated Confucianism from China, they "simplified" it and focused on its practical applications, not its philosophical ones.[6] One indirect proof of this claim is that Vietnamese seem rarely to have participated in East Asian debates in Song and Ming learning. Such writers imply that the appropriation of Confucianism in Vietnam did not follow the same trajectory as in other East Asian countries. Indeed, the historical evidence does not demonstrate that these teachings have been the key influence on Vietnamese society for the past one thousand years. At best—and even this common argument faces problems—one can date the dominance of Confucianism from the fifteenth century.

In exploring the influence of Confucianism on Vietnamese discourse, I focus on debates over Confucianism that took place between 1920 and 1945. To contextualize these debates, I will sketch out the place of Confucianism in Vietnamese society from precolonial times to the 1940s. By examining three sharply different accounts of Confucianism's role in Vietnamese history—by Trần Trọng Kim, Đào Duy Anh, and Trương Tửu—I will pull apart a common narrative of Vietnamese history as a tale of a transition from Confucianism to modernity. These writers deployed a wide range of incompatible arguments: that Vietnamese identity was rooted in an ancient, pre-Confucian oral culture; that it developed out of the Chinese legacy of Confucianism; that it should be rooted in Western notions of culture; and that Vietnamese should find their identity in the present but be aware of their past.

What is striking about the works of these authors, taken together, is that their political views do not correlate neatly with their perspectives on Confucianism. Trần Trọng Kim, an inspector for the French colonial school system, has often been typed as a "conservative." Đào Duy Anh was an idiosyncratic Marxist with a healthy appreciation for Confucianism. Trương Tửu was an independent radical journalist, but his views are hard to pigeonhole. Rather than reducing their work to expressions of political views, I will focus instead on what others have overlooked: the major rhetorical tension in these individuals' writings between essentialist and constructivist readings of the Vietnamese past.

The essentialist argument, as found in writings that searched for Vietnam's "national essence" in Confucianism, aimed to uncover eternal truths about Vietnamese identity. The constructivist argument stressed that Vietnamese determined their identity historically through participation in social processes (Westernization, progress, class struggle, and so forth). All writers used both kinds of arguments and occasionally deployed similar rhetorical strategies.

These essentialist and constructivist arguments were deployed in a rapidly changing intellectual field. As Vietnamese writers appropriated a new social and political vocabulary and applied it to a newly invented object, "society," they reconceptualized social hierarchy, gender relations, the common people, and the nature of the Vietnamese past. They shifted from language that placed Vietnamese in Confucian hierarchies and orders (e.g., *tứ dân*, or four social ranks, and *quốc gia*, nation [literally "nation-family"]) to terminology that encompassed both equality and economic class; they used race (*chủng tộc*) and lineage (*dòng dõi*) less and less in conceptions of identity, while experimenting with ones that were more inclusive (like *dân tộc*, "the nation" or "the people").

This transformation took place so quickly that the discursive field saw many voices contradicting each other, appealing to different conceptual language, making reference to different intellectual masters. To understand this intellectual shift, I preface my discussion of Trần Trọng Kim's and Đào Duy Anh's work with an examination of the contested legacy of Confucianism to Vietnam before the twentieth century.

THE PLACE OF CONFUCIANISM
IN VIETNAMESE HISTORY

"For two thousand years or more," Alexander Woodside argued in 1971, "Vietnam, like Korea, Japan, and China, was a member of what appropriately might be called the East Asian classical civilization."[7] This classical influence was not restricted to the court: even the "lower levels of the socio-cultural system" became sinicized.[8] Woodside's early work, undergirded by an impact-response model of Chinese-Vietnamese interactions framed in terms of "borrowing," "importing," and "siniciza-tion," contributed to a view of Vietnam as a variant on the Chinese Confucian model. Vietnam did not selectively appropriate Chinese practices: "In Vietnamese eyes, the Chinese institutional tradition was not a haphazard accumulation of innovations by individual courts. Instead it was believed to represent a complex of parts which were all specifically interrelated, which had proven their utility as a system in China, and which would be fundamentally modified by a people who had not created them only at great peril."[9]

For many Western scholars of East Asia, Woodside's erudite work, based heavily on his study of the nineteenth-century court, has defined the classical character of Vietnamese history. Yet Oliver Wolters, focusing on the Trần period (1225–1400), soon presented a radically different argument about the Vietnamese and their engagement with Confucianism: that Vietnamese selectively appropriated from the Confucian canon to make "local statements" about themselves. But even such appropriations of Confucianism did not diffuse evenly through society. Wolters has since revealed that the Trần rulers were seen by one key Lê historian, Ngô Sĩ Liên, as exemplars of how *not* to govern.[10] They did not, in other words, manifest Confucian virtues.

One cannot assume that Confucianism made no inroads after the Trần period, and Woodside has modified his 1971 position. Woodside now argues, for example, that if Vietnam was more a part of an East Asian "Confucian commonwealth" by the eighteenth and nineteenth centuries than he had earlier thought, "it was also more dominated by its own medieval past, and by the many pockets of that past that survived."[11] Compared to many other East Asian states, the Vietnamese one was weak, and thus the state could not always act as an effective agent of Confucianization.[12]

This chapter pushes such revisionist arguments even further, suggesting that, before the twentieth century, Confucian influence was remarkably uneven. The earlier notion that the Trần period was a time of great Confucianization now seems suspect. Consider, for example, a 1351 account in which a doctor saved King Trần Dụ Tông "from the greatest dereliction of Confucian morality, that of not having a child."[13] According to the main dynastic history for this period, however, the doctor advised the king to kill a young boy and have sex with his sister in order to cure his impotence.[14] The king followed this advice. Not only does this example show a lack of Confucian influence, but numerous other actions of the ruling families during the Trần period (like taking a brother's wife) show how rulers casually disregarded Confucian norms.[15] There is little reason to assume that the populace at large was any different.

It is easier to claim that Vietnam became clearly Confucian between the Lê and independent Nguyễn dynasties (1428–1883).[16] The Ming occupation of Vietnam in the early fifteenth century, followed by the Lê dynasty, is often portrayed as a watershed event in Vietnamese history. From this point on, ruling groups definitively put forth the claim that

Confucianism was the main teaching of the country. By the nineteenth century, this claim made some sense: with the resumption of the examination system and the spread of Confucian teachings in government and among the literati, Confucianism made deep inroads into parts of Vietnam. Many Vietnamese suppose that this process culminated in the nineteenth-century reign of the extremely orthodox Confucian emperor Tự Đức. But how accurate is this story?

First of all, repeated unrest in the sixteenth through eighteenth centuries calls into question the extent to which the "state" (if one can even call it that) could propagate Confucianism effectively, let alone exemplify it institutionally. For much of this period, northern Trịnh lords struggled with the upstart southern Nguyễn. In this conflict, warriors continued to have great prestige. Furthermore, as Li Tana has recently argued, the early Nguyễn lords led what was, in many ways, a militarized Mahayana Buddhist state where Confucian influence was weak.[17] This argument calls into question the notion of the universal spread of Confucianism in Vietnam.

Second, if one moves beyond literati self-representations to examine the place of Confucianism in a larger social and political context, it becomes harder to assert that Confucianism was ubiquitous. In the Mekong delta at the beginning of the eighteenth century, Cao Tự Thanh has argued, a recognizable stratum of Confucian intellectuals could only be found in the Chinese enclave of Hà Tiên. In the north, according to the missionary de la Bissachère, while the "mass of the populace" adopted a range of practices ranging from ancestor worship and veneration of tutelary divinities to Buddhist practices, it was only the "chief members of the state, and above all the literati," who followed Confucian teachings.[18] Even the literati (*nho sĩ, nhà nho*) can be hard to characterize: while they gradually deepened their knowledge of Confucian texts, it is hard to generalize about this highly eclectic and constantly shifting assemblage of people. One can be sure, however, that they did not abandon all other worldviews.

There is a third reason to question the primacy of Confucianism: the nature of Vietnamese print culture. I have discussed this issue briefly at the beginning of this book: let me simply reiterate that comparisons to China, Japan, or Korea can be misleading, given that Vietnamese did not possess the same density of institutions, networks, and media as these other countries. Few Vietnamese had access to books, and publishers were relatively rare. Scattered evidence suggests that Vietnamese appropriation of the classics was often shallow. For all the references in dynastic histories to moral exemplars (like chaste widows), one can find counterexamples of a pervasive lack of interest in the teaching of the scholars.

A 1711 entry in a Lê dynasty chronicle, the *Đại Việt sử ký tục biên* (Complete historical annals of Đại Việt, continuation), suggests that few Vietnamese really had a good grasp of Confucian teachings. Discussing reform of the examinations, the entry states that, under the old system, "of the people passing the examinations, the majority had no talent." The reasons: examinations changed little, so examination candidates memorized answers from books compiled by previous test takers and regurgitated these answers on examinations, furtively brought books into the examinations, and cheated by having others take the examinations for them.[19] At the highest levels, then, Confucianism was (at times) in a sorry state.

It is true that significant institutional and intellectual changes were under way in Vietnam from the fifteenth century onward. By the nineteenth century, the court was drawing heavily on Confucian texts and developing its bureaucratic system. Nonetheless, it is safe to say that careful attention to the variegated spatial reach of Confucianism, appreciation of other discourses, and recognition of the apparent lack of robust networks of Confucian academies and publishers calls into question some of the more expansive notions of Confucian influence on the past.

When twentieth-century writers have looked back on their past, however, the highly Confucian representations of Nguyễn dynasty historians combined with an essentialized notion of Confucianism developed by East Asian scholars and activists have colored their perceptions of Vietnamese history. Writers have mixed together such scholarly arguments with accounts based on personal experience: after all, many members of the literate elite followed an apparently Confucian education when young. Like numerous other children, Trần Huy Liệu writes, the first primer he used was the *Three-Character Classic*.[20] Echoing the Song scholar Wang Bohou's comments on this book, Trần Huy Liệu wrote that "with the phrase 'At birth, a person's nature is fundamentally good; close by nature, people grow distant through habit' . . . we were taught a natural philosophy of conceptions of human life and of society."[21] Other writers mention the importance of the *Minh đạo gia huấn*, which is, like the *Three-Character Classic*, an introduction to Confucian teachings and morality. Nguyễn Đôn Phục (b. 1878) mentioned that from age ten to twenty he read the Four Books and the Five Classics, the core of Confucianism.[22] Phục appears to have had a broader introduction to Confucianism than the great majority of his contemporaries. But what is striking in these lists of books is the Vietnamese absence of engagement with Confucian scholarship produced in China from the fourteenth century through the mid-nineteenth century.

Despite this apparent lack of deep knowledge of a broad array of Confucian texts and the apparent reliance on (introductory) primers to convey the Confucian message, modern scholars have made striking claims about the Vietnamese past. One of the most famous was penned in 1924 by the anti-French literatus Ngô Đức Kế:

> In our country of Vietnam, for several thousand years, we have studied Chinese characters and followed Confucianism. Chinese literature is the national literature: although the rivers and the mountains change, dynasties change several tens of times, dangerous rebellions have been many, this current of orthodox learning still has not declined. The benevolence (*nhân tâm*) of the people, the customs, the morality, politics all derive from it. Government and lineage, in a similar manner, find stability in it.[23]

Ngô Đức Kế insisted that the essence of Vietnamese culture lay in its Chinese and Confucian heritage, a heritage that had penetrated deep into the thought and practice of the Vietnamese people.

As the precolonial past receded into memory, Vietnamese writers like Ngô Đức Kế simplified and Confucianized their past. Influenced by the Chinese New Learning and the works of intellectuals like Kang Youwei (1858–1927) and Liang Qichao (1873–1929), Vietnamese applied Chinese critiques of the Qing dynasty to their country. These writers were aided, ironically, by the actions of the French colonial government. The French administration set about putting its imprint on the accepted understanding of the Vietnamese past. It censored tracts and historical novels on anticolonial heroes like Hàm Nghi, who reigned from 1884 to 1885 before participating in an anti-French uprising. It exalted emperors like Gia Long (reigned 1802–1820), the first emperor in the Nguyễn dynasty, but not his opponent, the "rebel" Tây Sơn. French scholars wrote books that emphasized the common Confucian lineage of China and Vietnam. A result of such French endeavors was both to re-Confucianize the past and to strip Confucianism of any subversive content.[24]

Neil Jamieson has asserted that, to the majority of educated Vietnamese living in the first half of this century, it was "not really debatable" that they had a strongly neo-Confucian heritage.[25] It is one of the ironies of modern Vietnamese history that Jamieson is right: writers have exaggerated the significance and coherence of a "Confucian tradition."

CONFUCIANISM AND CULTURE, 1920–1945

As the quotation from Ngô Đức Kế above suggests, Confucianism has loomed large in modern representations of the Vietnamese past. At one extreme, some "progressive" writers in the interwar period saw Confucianism as a pillar of the past but irrelevant to the present. At the other extreme, more cautious and conservative Vietnamese intellectuals, resigned to colonial rule, countered that Confucianism was central to the past and could still contribute to a new culture that blended the East and the West. And many intellectuals staked out positions somewhere between these two positions. The historian and revolutionary Trần Huy Liệu (1901–1969) had been schooled through Confucian primers when young and intellectually rejected many of these teachings when older. Despite this rejection on the political and intellectual level, he seemed unable to shake an emotional attachment to the world of his youth. And if this was true of revolutionaries like Trần Huy Liệu or even Hồ Chí Minh, it was even more so for many other members of the elite who did not share such revolutionary sentiments.

By the beginning of the twentieth century, many Confucians perceived their teaching to be under siege. The decline of state Confucianism began in the south (Cochinchina) immediately after the French asserted control of the region in 1862. That process culminated in 1919, the date of the last Confucian examination. In 1924, partly to preempt radicals, the French agreed to include the study of morality and etiquette (*politesse*) at the primary level. But this was a hybrid moral instruction, combining elements of French moral teachings with Vietnamese ones; it could not be called purely Confucian.

One cannot reduce Confucianism in Vietnam to its state version.

Outside of state control, the situation of Confucianism is at first puzzling. In some ways it seems to have flourished in the 1920s and 1930s; in other ways it appears moribund. Discussion of Confucianism crops up everywhere. Vietnamese Confucian reformers at the turn of the twentieth century drew inspiration from their Chinese counterparts. Women's newspapers in the 1920s and 1930s ran articles on marriage and family life that discussed topics like the Confucian Three Obediences (*tam tòng*). "In the past, who did women live for? They only lived for their fathers and mothers, for their husbands, and for their sons."[26] Communists and Westernizers attacked Confucian strictures. "Confucianism" had gone beyond a specialized realm of discourse to become a commonly shared idiom of intellectual life.

In this same period, writers perpetuated a broad (and often idiosyncratic) discourse on morality, customs, and culture. Vietnamese printed numerous small morality books to inculcate virtuous behavior in girls and boys as well as adults. Even reading primers often had moral teachings tucked in. The French administration taught morality and civics in its schools, and topics such as the virtues of collaboration were frequently broached. David Marr notes, for example, how one French morality primer "led off with the assertion that 'Franco-Vietnamese collaboration is the road to a paradise of advantages.'"[27] In one of the odder combinations of French and Vietnamese thought, advocates of the Vichy regime tried to marry Maréchal Pétain's celebration of the "National Revolution" and its emphasis on the importance of resurrecting tradition to Vietnamese reverence for traditional Confucian values.

Most discussion of morality, however, took place outside the orbit of the state. Vietnamese themselves were obsessed with the nature of Vietnamese customs and their transformation. One reformist tract, for example, suggested abandoning the custom whereby men of sixty married seventeen-year-old girls or where fifteen-year-old males married girls a year younger. Believing that such practices sapped the "life force" (*nguyên khí*) of the race, the author hoped that such practices would decrease and that the race would strengthen.[28] This last example underlines an important point: while young intellectuals often saw such practices as vestiges of the Confucian order, their Confucian origins are often dubious at best.

As the examples above suggest, there were different audiences for

Confucianism. Women's newspapers, for example, had discussions of women's duties to their husbands. Primers inculcated in young children a respect for their teachers. But the audience of the more sophisticated debates over the Confucian canon was overwhelmingly restricted to male members of the elite. The message directed at this audience focused on the intensive reading of core Confucian texts, counseling the need to read and reread in order to understand fully the meaning of the Way.[29] It focused on making the reader into a "superior man" (*quân tử*). Given this message, focused on a small male elite, it is not surprising that "high" Confucianism gradually lost its influence in Vietnam at the same time that a popularized version of the teaching endured.

The more that one reads, then, the more one understands that Confucianism occupied a peculiar place in the Vietnamese mental universe. It is stunning to realize, for example, that Vietnamese penned extremely little scholarship on Confucianism between 1920 and 1945: the main outlet for the few widely read scholars like Huỳnh Thúc Kháng or Phan Khôi was the newspaper article. Few institutional supports for Confucian learning existed after 1920: there were no Confucian academies to train young scholars, no bureaucratic examinations, and few links to Confucian scholars outside of Vietnam. The vast majority of Confucian scholars in Vietnam lacked a wide appreciation of the Confucian classics and the vast commentarial literature. (Few Vietnamese in the nineteenth century, let alone the twentieth century, had mastered such canonical writings.)

In short, the claim that Vietnamese had a deep scholarly appreciation of the classics in the period from 1920 to 1945 rings hollow. What does seem true, however, is that Vietnamese deeply understood a few key Confucian notions like *tứ đức* (Four Virtues) and *tam tòng* (Three Submissions), and spoke frequently about virtues like filial piety and loyalty. To call Vietnamese society "Confucian," therefore, is to use the term in a loose sense to refer to a cluster of practices and ideas that appear to have some recognizable coherence. "Confucianism" (or *Nho giáo*, as it is usually called in modern Vietnam) has indeed become an omnibus concept covering a bewildering array of historical practices and beliefs.[30] It is a problematic usage of the term.

With such thoughts in mind, the remainder of this chapter addresses key debates over Confucianism between 1920 and 1945. The most important participants in these debates came from either the north

(Trần Trọng Kim, Ngô Tất Tố, Nguyễn Văn Tố, Phạm Quỳnh, Trương Tửu, Trần Văn Giáp) or the center (Huỳnh Thúc Kháng, Phan Bội Châu, Phan Khôi, Đào Duy Anh). No southerners of any prominence participated in these debates, nor were there any prominent women scholars of Confucianism.[31] The works of Trần Trọng Kim and Đào Duy Anh are exemplary, both because of their perceived importance at the time and for the ways that they helped frame the modern understanding of Confucianism.

TRẦN TRỌNG KIM: MAPPING A "FORGOTTEN" CONFUCIAN ANTIQUITY

Trần Trọng Kim (1882–1953) is best know to posterity as a writer, educator, and political figure. Two of his books, *Việt Nam sử lược* (Brief history of Vietnam; 1920) and *Nho giáo* (Confucianism; 1929–1933), established him as a leading intellectual in the 1920s and 1930s. He also pursued a career as a teacher, inspector of schools, and school principal. Trần Trọng Kim also had a brief political career. He served as the prime minister of the Empire of Vietnam, which ruled (under Japanese authority) from March to August 1945. To many, Kim's collaboration with the French and Japanese tarnished his reputation. I bring up these biographical details with some hesitation, for reducing the meaning of texts to extensions of biographies is absurd. Suffice it to say that, in the post-1945 period, most writers have typed Trần Trọng Kim as a "conservative."

The single most important book on Confucianism to appear during colonial rule was Trần Trọng Kim's *Nho giáo*. This book, devoted almost exclusively to Confucianism in China, defined these teachings for thousands of Vietnamese. It also asserted that Confucianism had been central to Vietnamese identity in the past. One of the best histories of modern Vietnamese literature, that by Phạm Thế Ngữ, gives this book a prominent place.[32] Ngô Tất Tố, lamenting the state of Vietnamese Confucian scholarship, gave the work a backhanded compliment: he complained in 1940 that readers relied so much on its faulty interpretations that he feared "Confucianism would become 'Trần Trọng Kim–ism.'"[33] Such complaints indicate that the book had become a key work in Vietnamese intellectual history.

In one sense, *Nho giáo* is a logical successor to Trần Trọng Kim's 1920 work, *Việt Nam sử lược* (Brief history of Vietnam). In the first book, Kim stated that Chinese civilization's "influence, over a long time, became our national essence (*quốc túy*)."[34] *Nho giáo* amplified Kim's interest in Chinese civilization and notions of "essence" to its logical extreme. While the book concentrates on Chinese Confucianism, Trần Trọng Kim takes pains to underline that the Way "truly prospered" in Vietnam during the Trần, Lê, Mạc, Later Lê, and Nguyễn dynasties.[35] Indeed, it is clear that to Kim Chinese Confucianism was the original source of Vietnamese culture: "In the past, our country of Vietnam honored Confucianism, holding it to be the unrivaled and correct way (*chính đạo độc tôn*). Philosophy, customs, politics, everything took Confucianism as its essence (*lấy Nho giáo làm cốt*)."[36]

This is a sweeping statement. But Kim believed that, of all Asian countries besides China, Vietnam had "the most intimate contact of all" with Confucianism. Given what I have asserted about Confucianism's exaggerated impact on Vietnam, this view may come as a surprise. Kim put forth two main reasons for the supposed depth of Confucianism's impact. First, China had ruled Vietnam for more than a thousand years; "our country, from Nghệ An and Hà Tĩnh [provinces] north, formed part of the map of the Chinese people." Second, Kim argues that most Vietnamese were descended from Chinese who had settled in Vietnam and become Vietnamese.[37] Through such ethnospatial logic (not through historical evidence), he claims primacy for Vietnam over Korea and Japan as the most Confucianized state outside of China.

Trần Trọng Kim takes for granted that Confucianism is deeply important to Vietnam. Yet his certainty jars his reader, for Kim is also puzzled by the demise of Confucianism. This sense of unease helps make sense of the author's professed aims. On the first page of his introduction, Trần Trọng Kim states that he is driven to write to ensure that Vietnamese don't forget their past:

An old, very beautiful house, which no one has repaired for ages, reaches the point that a storm could knock it over flat. Up to now, people were still living in that house, helpless, not knowing what to do. Although they wanted to rebuild it, they could not, for if people were lacking [to help], they also lacked wealth. Furthermore, circumstances had evolved, times were changing, and people in the country were eager to throw away the old and embrace the new, and no one thought about the old house any more. But in itself that old house was a priceless object; it was senseless to let it fall into ruin and not find a way to preserve the historical relic (*di tích*). Neither had anyone sketched a map for future generations to know that this house, once beautiful, had fallen into its current ruin. Thus, the cultural situation of Confucianism today is like that of the old house.

The fashioning of this book that discusses Confucianism is the drawing of a map of Confucianism.[38]

Thus began a book that inaugurated a long debate about Confucianism, its study, and its relevance to Vietnam. The fashioning of this work took place at a key point in Vietnamese history. As Trần Trọng Kim was researching and writing his work in the 1920s, some Vietnamese began flirting with approaches to modernity ranging from rejection to bourgeois assimilationism to radical iconoclasm.

This decade was marked by the development, among educated youth, of a virulent disdain for the past. To them, the past was a problem, the source of Vietnamese weakness, or (as Hoàng Đạo would later put it) an "endless dream" (*giấc mơ vô cùng*) from which they needed to wake up.[39] These youth preferred the promise of the present and the future. The end of the decade culminated in a surge of activism. Strikes broke out in 1929. The next year, radicals at the head of the Vietnamese Nationalist Party led the Yên Báy uprising to overthrow the French. It was soon crushed. The same year, 1930, saw peasants and communists briefly establish soviets in the Nghệ An–Hà Tĩnh region. It was also (and this is a point conveniently overlooked in the revolutionary nationalist historiography) a time in which many elite youth fervently embraced Western ideas and practices, devoured Lamartine and romantic novels, and outfitted themselves in Western garb.

Trần Trọng Kim saw a break developing between his generation and Vietnamese youth. He presented his book as a map to a cherished place—the Vietnamese past—now fading from memory. Seeing his work as the fruit of a collective engagement with the past, Kim wrote that his book was "the work of people who grew up in a Confucian atmosphere, who were imbued with a Confucian sensibility." With this atmosphere gone forever, he said, the book "is a work to preserve its traces for the future."[40] Faced with a disorderly present, Kim tried to map an epistemological order onto the past and to "remember" the past before it was forgotten. Only, the past that Trần Trọng Kim was interested in "remembering" was more a projection onto the past than a chronicle of it. Trần Trọng Kim, a hybrid intellectual trained in French schools yet curious about China's and Vietnam's heritage, can be forgiven for arrogating to himself the right to speak of a past that he had never really experienced. Nostalgia, after all, contains within it an element of fiction.

Trần Trọng Kim tends to provide a static picture of Confucianism. He says that he is drawing a "map": in other words, fixing Confucianism in space and time. He talks about "preserving traces" of a (Confucian) "house." With such words, Trần Trọng Kim ignores Confucianism as an actual philosophy for self-transformation: it has died, he implies, and it needs a monument to commemorate its passing. Inexorably, such language leads to an essentialization of Confucianism. But I will return to this point in due course, for Trần Trọng Kim combines essentialist language with flashes of a more dynamic interpretation of the Way.

Trần Trọng Kim explains why Vietnamese readers needed to know more about Confucianism. "Every people (*dân tộc*) has its own particular spirit, just as every tree has roots that reach deep into the soil."[41] Comparing the Vietnamese people to a plant, he argues that Vietnamese needed to take in nutrients for nourishment: "The spirit of a people is similar.... A people is strong and prosperous because it knows how to keep its spirit vital, a people grows weak because its spirit has decayed and cannot find a way to renourish it. Now if we want to know why the West is prosperous and powerful while the East is weak, then we must clearly understand how the Confucian spirit and the Western spirit differ from one another."[42] Linking his project back to the destiny of the Vietnamese, Kim adds that, for a people to evolve, it must use such study "to create a new spirit that is suitable to its situation, suitable with its level and nature. That is my hope."[43]

Trần Trọng Kim confronted a difficult problem. If Vietnam was indeed the most Confucianized country outside of China, how could its influence vanish so quickly? Kim gives a variety of answers. He admits that, for much of Vietnamese history, communications were poor and books were "insufficient for study."[44] As if to show that Vietnamese Confucianism was less open to change than its East Asian cousins, Kim points out that Wang Yangming studies, which spread throughout China and into Japan, had no impact on Vietnam.[45]

The central reason for Confucianism's demise was, however, spiritual. Ideally, Kim argues, the "inner" and the "outer" (or "spirit" and "form," as he sometimes puts it) should be in accord with and complement one another.[46] "But because people who adhered to Confucian studies in the past usually paid excessive attention to outward appearances, they reached the point that they were spiritually in error and missed a lot. The method of study of these people ... concentrated on examinations to climb the ladder of fame. As a result, the doctrines of Confucius and Mencius increasingly fell into disrepute, so that they had a renown but [one] with no authentic reality."[47] Vietnamese, in other words, simply mimicked true Confucianism.

Evaluating Trần Trọng Kim's comments, a reader is confronted with two incompatible views of Confucianism in Vietnam. In some places, Kim argues that Confucianism is an essential cultural core: everything, including customs and politics, derives from it. In other places, he admits that such a core may not have existed. Vietnamese, he states, adopted shallow versions of Confucianism rather than internalizing it. Such contradictions run through discourses of Vietnamese identity from the 1920s through 1940s. They have affected debates up to the present.

In many ways, Trần Trọng Kim seems confined by his focus on the past and its achievements. Skeptical of modernity, he criticizes Vietnamese who are quick to abandon old ways and passionately embrace anything new.[48] Using a familiar phrase, Trần Trọng Kim states that it is through such haste that the Vietnamese are losing "the essence (*tinh túy*) that had kept our society enduring for several thousand years."[49]

Does Kim simply champion the glories of the past? His reference to the concept of "intuition" (*trực giác*) appears to move away from an essentialist notion of a deeply Confucian past to a constructivist concept of identity that stresses a reader's engagement with the texts in the construction of self-knowledge. He shifts from a description of Vietnam in the past to explain the need for a dynamic mode of appropriation—intuition—to grasp the intellectual truths of Confucianism.

In the introduction to *Nho giáo* (Confucianism), Trần Trọng Kim invokes the use of "intuition" to counter criticisms that Confucianism lacks structure: "Confucianism is a teaching that has a system (*thống hệ*) and a method.... But we must recognize that our learning frequently attaches great importance to the use of intuition. Cognition in learning is like method in aesthetics: one must use intuition to see the totality; only then can one perceive [its] spirit."[50]

The coherence of Confucianism, in other words, is evident not in the form of an overall argument, but in the intuitive apprehension of the whole. Trần Trọng Kim derived his understanding of "intuition" from the French philosopher Henri Bergson.[51] According to Bergson, intuition "refers above all to inner duration (*la durée intérieure*)" in which the past is not marked off from the present or future. Key here is the notion of unmediated consciousness (*conscience immédiate*): in intuition, "nothing more comes between; no more refraction through the prism whose one face is space and other is language."[52]

Trần Trọng Kim's use of Bergson may at first appear problematic, for Kim veers between general claims about the incompatibility of East and West and the notion that one could draw on the Western heritage. (This problem is compounded by the fact that he does not have a consistent notion of "the West.") "The two cultures [of East and West] contradict each other," he wrote. Kim told his readers that Western culture was characterized by fierce competition, a way of life with many troublesome aspects, and much hardship.[53] When it came to morality and the practice of everyday life, Kim believed that the two "civilizations" diverged radically. At the same time, he admired much about the West and showed that not all modern Western thinkers shared the same views of modernity, cognition, and science. He was willing to draw on a peculiar galaxy of Western philosophers (the "pantheists" Spinoza, Fichte, and Hegel, and the positivist Comte, all culminating in Bergson) to shed light on Confucianism. Trần Trọng Kim ignores the central philosopher of the European Enlightenment, Immanuel Kant, presumably because Kant argues that moral laws are universals and rejects any notion of unmediated consciousness. Besides Bergson, he does not engage any Western writers of the past sixty years on modernity. The use of Bergsonian "intuition" allowed Trần Trọng Kim to ignore history when he wanted, to assert radical social differences between East and West, but then to build limited bridges between East and West at the level of epistemology.

I have stated that the reference to "intuition" represented a move toward a constructivist notion of identity in which the reader acted as the agent of self-awareness. Through intuition, Vietnamese could understand the natural reason (*thiên lý*) of Confucianism, break down barriers of understanding, and link themselves to a larger whole. But Trần Trọng Kim's use of the term was fraught with problems. First, as the scholar Phan Khôi pointed out, the neologism "intuition" did not exist in Confucius' time. Consequently, how was it possible to understand the original thought of Confucius through such an alien concept?

A second problem, admitted by Trần Trọng Kim, was that Confucianism was a "relic" more than a living philosophy. It was unclear how intuition could help the reader actualize the dynamism of this teaching. Furthermore, the shift from an authorial description of the past to the reader's construction of Confucianism held within it an essentializing impulse. The action of intuition would appear to be dynamic, but in claiming that Confucianism's "essence [resides] in the spirit of the totality,"[54] and in nesting this comment in his version of Confucian history, Trần Trọng Kim forced readers back on a totalizing and static vision of the world.

Alexander Woodside has suggested that Trần Trọng Kim's work is an "anticolonial orientalism." He has further argued that, for Trần, "China is a device to decolonize the Vietnamese identity."[55] This interpretation is intriguing: for one, it rescues Kim from the ghetto of colonialist collaborators and underlines his commonalities with Vietnamese of radically different ideological persuasions. It suggests that a notion of "resistance" could be enlarged to include thinkers like Kim. While Kim did not attack the French, he did argue that the Vietnamese rush to embrace Western culture was often mindless and dangerous. If in the end I do not completely embrace this view, it is for two reasons. First, it is impossible to divine the authorial intentions behind Trần Trọng Kim's words. Second, if at times Kim does exhibit an anticolonial orientalism, at other times he does not. Kim turns out to be a classic case of the colonial intellectual caught between competing visions of the world. In its entirety, his work, characterized by its ambivalence, by its competing essentialist and constructivist discourses, flirts with a coded anticolonialism but then retreats.

One comes away from Trần Trọng Kim feeling that he infuses his work with nostalgia for a constructed past. He clearly laments the passing of a Vietnamese Confucian world. And yet, reading Trần Trọng Kim's work, the reader senses that the author has hastened Confucianism's demise: he has constructed a philosophical discourse of scant relevance to the problems facing Vietnamese in the present.

DÀO DUY ANH: SOCIAL HISTORY MEETS PHILOSOPHY

At first glance, Trần Trọng Kim and Đào Duy Anh (1905–1988) appear sharply different. Đào Duy Anh was one of the Vietnamese who introduced Marxism into Vietnam. After he became involved in the New Viet Revolutionary Party (Tân Việt Cách Mệnh Đảng) in 1927, the French police arrested him; the courts gave him a suspended prison sentence. Đào Duy Anh kept out of political trouble in the 1930s. He published his most widely known book, *Việt Nam văn hóa sử cương* (Brief history of Vietnamese culture), in 1938. The same year his *Khổng giáo phê bình tiểu luận* (Short critique of Confucianism) also came out.[56] I shall discuss both works below.

Đào Duy Anh's biography and his post-1945 collaboration with communist historians suggest that he was a radical. Indeed, the conventional view is that his writings (and those of his generation in general) challenge the conservative writings on Franco-Vietnamese harmony of an earlier generation of writers like Phạm Quỳnh and Trần Trọng Kim. The earlier writers tended to defend Confucianism; Đào Duy Anh's generation sharply attacked it.

However, it is not necessary to treat a person's or a generation's work as a bounded whole. Both Trần Trọng Kim and Đào Duy Anh are alike in deploying essentialist and constructivist arguments, arguments that spill beyond the particular books in which they are found to link up, intertextually, with similar arguments by authors who preceded them. The two authors shared the belief that Confucianism shaped the Vietnamese past. Furthermore, Đào Duy Anh differed sharply from many radical intellectuals of his generation. He censured the many modernizing Vietnamese who wanted to rush headlong into Westernization and in the process abandon any knowledge of Vietnam's past: "Outwardly, it seems as if everyone in society is turning to modern studies (*tân học*); of the young intellectuals, almost none know what Confucianism is, to the point that the elderly who were born and raised in the Confucian tradition (*của Khổng sân Trình*) also would like their children to take up Western learning and are not the least concerned with Confucianism's fate."[57]

Đào Duy Anh clearly champions change. But he is of two minds about it: while he wholeheartedly believes in the promise of the modern age, he is clearly irked that many (elite?) Vietnamese denigrated the past as they willfully entered a cultural and historical amnesia. These Vietnamese had forgotten, in Đào Duy Anh's eyes, the deeds of their ancestors.

Đào Duy Anh's books address a slightly different audience than Trần Trọng Kim's: while the latter author's works assume some familiarity with philosophy, Dao Duy Anh's books require none. In *Việt Nam văn hóa sử cương* (Outline history of Vietnamese culture), for example, Đào Duy Anh states that his book had "a popular character, but pupils and teachers can use it as a reference book." He mentions, perhaps disingenuously, that he was inspired to write the latter book when the French administration added a new program on Vietnamese culture to the curriculum of primary schools. Written in an accessible style, the book quickly gained a reputation throughout Vietnam.[58]

Đào Duy Anh's writings show a greater tension between constructivist and essentialist views of the past than Trần Trọng Kim's. *Việt Nam văn hóa sử cương* in particular draws on an array of Marxist arguments, beginning with a discussion of the economic basis of Vietnamese society. In fact, the first question that he asks in this book is an extremely broad one: what is culture? His answer is suitably broad: "culture is livelihood."[59] Following the lead of the French scholar Félix Sartiaux (whom he cites), Anh divides his analysis of Vietnamese culture into three categories: economic, social, and intellectual livelihood. He places this view of culture in world-historical context: "Culture is livelihood, [and] ... peoples who are civilized or barbarian possess their own cultures that only differ in their level of development. For example, the culture of Western peoples is high, but the culture of savages (*mọi rợ*) in Africa or Australia, like that of the Man or Mường savages in our country, is low."[60]

Developing a materialist argument of culture, the author stresses how nature shapes lived experience. "Natural factors have a decisive influence on the livelihood of people," he states, "for livelihood is nothing more that the use of material and spiritual forces that fit with and make use of nature." He notes as well that geography has influenced Vietnamese livelihood and by extension shaped its culture.[61]

By breaking Vietnamese culture into the realms of economic, social, and intellectual livelihood, Đào Duy Anh restricts the extent to which he can make totalizing claims. This intellectual division of the past sharply contrasts with Trần Trọng Kim's approach, which sees identity arising from the encounter with philosophical writings. If Đào Duy Anh places economics first in his narration, it does not follow that he gives this category ontological primacy.

Up to this point, Đào Duy Anh contradicts Trần Trọng Kim. He shows promise of developing constructivist arguments about Vietnamese society that would foreground the historicity of the Vietnamese. This promise is soon broken. The reader soon encounters essentializing strands that undermine the book's rhetoric of transformation. The book comprehensively surveys Vietnamese culture by organizing it according to ahistorical categories like "Buddhism" or "merchants." Although Đào Duy Anh gives examples ranging across time, the reader gets the clear impression that this past is collapsed and thus has little temporal depth: it is but a mirror to shed light on the present. It is not surprising, then, that the book does not show how class relations develop over time. Instead, the author uncritically borrows the Confucian ranking of literati, peasants, artisans, and merchants to organize his discussion of economic classes. The past becomes homogenized; these social rankings are presumed to fit the entire history of Vietnam. In short, the constructivist spirit of his vaguely Marxist analysis is often negated by the simultaneous use of ahistorical and essentializing categories. Such is the dilemma of Đào Duy Anh's writings.

The turn to essentialism is most marked in Đào Duy Anh's discussion of Confucianism. While the author discuses the centrality of Confucianism to Vietnamese culture in *Việt Nam văn hóa sử cương*, he reserves his most extensive comments on the issue for *Khổng giáo phê bình tiểu luận* (Short critique of Confucianism). In the latter book, Anh states that

> for more than two thousand years, Confucianism has existed in China and in our society without changing, and thus from the past to now, all through society, not only the ranks of Confucian scholars, but the common people ... as well became imbued with the Confucian spirit. We can say that throughout one's life, a person in Chinese society and Vietnamese society breathed a Confucian atmosphere, fed on the milk of Confucianism, ate Confucianism, and even died with Confucian rites. From thought, language, and the actions of individuals to learning and the social system, nothing escaped the control of Confucian philosophy and ritual teachings.[62]

In *Việt Nam văn hóa sử cương*, Đào Duy Anh also makes broad statements that imply that Confucianism pervaded all realms of life. For example, he asserts that historically in the Vietnamese family "women had no power (*quyền*) at all." To support his claim, he quotes from the *Book of Rites.*[63] Chinese texts are drawn into the narration to justify a statement that is historically false. He also claims that the Vietnamese monarchical system was one in which the king "had absolute power."[64] Others, such as bureaucrats, only exercised power on the king's behalf.[65] (This neat account is contradicted by the fact that court intrigue plagued Vietnamese history.)

As the reader might gather, the picture of Vietnamese society that Đào Duy Anh draws is built on careful research interspersed with conjecture. Given that so much was still unknown about Vietnamese history, the author based many of his vague and sweeping statements on preconceptions. For the last two thousand years, he states, Confucianism was unchanging, as if standing outside of history. In his book critiquing Confucianism, Anh argues that we do not really know what the impact of Confucianism during Chinese rule was, "but we can surmise that throughout this time period ... our people followed only Confucianism."[66] In *Việt Nam văn hóa sử cương*, Đào Duy Anh pulls back slightly from such essentialist claims. He presents a picture familiar to scholars of Vietnam, one in which Confucianism gradually pushed aside its rivals: by the Trần period (1225–1400) it "had already begun to triumph over Buddhism," and by the fifteenth century, it had seized an unassailable position that it would not relinquish until the French seized power.[67]

As another example of essentialism, one could point to the fact that Đào Duy Anh does not question the category of "Vietnamese." He assumes that "Vietnamese" have existed throughout history and avoids the question of how their interactions with other ethnic groups formed who they are. Unlike postcolonial scholars, who tried to portray Vietnamese identity as the amalgamation of many peoples' identities, Đào Duy Anh assumes that the story of the ethnic Vietnamese defines all relationships worth discussing within the borders of Vietnam.

Despite the obvious essentialist pitfalls, these writings show a tension between essentialist and constructivist arguments. It is true that in many sections of *Việt Nam văn hóa sử cương*, as in his discussion of agriculture, Đào Duy Anh can show little change over time. In other sections, however, he emphasizes transformations and even subverts earlier essentialist claims. For example, he pays some attention to class differences and gender. In his discussion of the situation of women, the author claims that women had no rights at all. But soon after making that claim, he undermines his own point by showing that the Gia Long code, promulgated under the Nguyễn dynasty, allowed women some rights.[68]

Đào Duy Anh's work, unlike Trần Trọng Kim's, is centered on history. He cites facts and dates, and charts the transformation of Vietnamese society over time. But despite his historical bent, a philosophically timeless Confucianism often becomes the essentialized part of the past that comes to stand for the whole. As the importance of Confucianism expands in some parts of his narration and comes to explain more and more of the past, the narration of that past is reduced from its once-certain plurality to a timeless unity. Such acts of intellectual legerdemain are common in Đào Duy Anh's work. But if in Trần Trọng Kim's work the essentialist arguments overwhelm the narration, there is more tension in Đào Duy Anh's writings between essentialist and constructivist arguments.

Whereas Trần Trọng Kim saw the cultural elite's amnesia as a tragedy, Đào Duy Anh is more nuanced in his judgments. The elite's abandonment of Confucianism did not mean the end of Confucianism in Vietnam: "It is said that we venerate Confucianism, but one has to enter the peasantry to see clearly what the feeling of filial piety and loyalty truly is. It is not in the class of mandarins and literati, where we only see [them] taking advantage of the sages to secure personal honor. It is said that we venerate Buddhism, but one also must go into the populace to see people who actualize the way of compassion."[69]

To conclude the discussion of Đào Duy Anh's work, I would like to point out how concerns of the day infuse it with some dynamism. Trần Trọng Kim ultimately embalms Confucianism in nostalgia; Đào Duy Anh uses his discussion of Vietnam's long past to frame a message of change in the present. After accepting that families lent stability to societies in the past, Anh notes that institutions, including that of the family, have been weakening. Unlike Kim, he does not despair at this development: he even suggests that in the uncertain modern era Vietnamese should turn to a Western-inspired individualism to help solve Vietnam's weakness. These final observations, which emphasize the multiple possibilities of the future, overwhelm much of the earlier essentialist writing and give the book a constructivist stamp.

TRƯƠNG TỬU AND THE NEGATION OF CONFUCIANISM

The early 1940s saw a reconfiguration of the intellectual field. The debates over culture and the place of Confucianism therein continued from the 1930s, but the context differed radically. The French administration practiced strict censorship in this period, particularly before French power collapsed in 1945. The Vichy government in Hanoi, following the lead of Maréchal Pétain in France, exalted the role of tradition, the folk, and regionalism, including attention to traditional East Asian culture. At the same time, the Japanese occupation forces promoted the revival of Confucianism and Buddhism. In such a context, it is not surprising that some Vietnamese tried to revive Confucianism; it is equally unsurprising that leftists like Trương Tửu attempted to subvert the Vichy message on the folk and their traditions.[70]

After years on the defensive, some Vietnamese took clear pleasure at the supposed "revival" of Confucianism. A small number of Vietnamese writers acted to "restore" old morality and aesthetics and oppose recent tendencies in Vietnamese literature. Many of these cultural conservatives believed that they had returned their views to center stage during the 1940–1945 period after years of neglect. In 1944, for example, Từ Lâm noted,

> If we go back approximately three years, a person who stood up and spoke the word "*hiếu*" [filial piety], who appealed to the family, how could he avoid a group of youth who, believing themselves to be progressive, would react with slogans like "overthrow the oppressive family system," "leave behind the family," "love conquers all," "individual freedom."
>
> Now it is different: after three years of National Revolution, the slogans "Labor, Family, Fatherland" of Maréchal Pétain have reached our Vietnam, have borne results, especially in reestablishing Confucianism.[71]

Phạm Thế Ngũ refers to this period as a "renaissance" (*phục sinh*),"[72] when Vietnamese literature "gave the appearance of fresh and bustling creativity." This creativity drew much of its inspiration from a return to problems discussed earlier by the writers of *Nam phong* (Southern wind; 1917–1934) and subsequent publications on Chinese and Vietnamese culture and literature, without the influence of Japanese ideology.[73]

Phạm Thế Ngữ adds: "But there were, as well, other persons who wanted to turn toward a more unfamiliar horizon, to find the bases of thought, the course of action in a Western internationalism."[74] The debates over culture, including Trương Tửu's, took place at this intersection of a "revival" in interest in the past and an upsurge of interest in Western thought.[75]

Trương Tửu's *Kinh thi Việt Nam* (Vietnamese classical odes) is the most radical reconceptualization up to that point of Confucianism's place in Vietnamese history. Trương Tửu argues the unthinkable: that Confucianism had not deeply influenced Vietnamese society. He argues that the essence (*tinh túy*) of the Vietnamese people is found not in (written) elite culture, which he agrees was heavily influenced by Confucianism, but in folk songs. This folk legacy is linked to the period predating the Confucian impact on Vietnam. Contradicting Đào Duy Anh, he asserts that Confucianism "stimulated Vietnamese to develop their character" in opposition to its teachings but that it was not the basis of this character.[76]

Trương Tửu commits another radical act: in naming his book *Kinh thi Việt Nam*, he argues that the Vietnamese treasury of songs is as important as the Chinese *Classic of Odes* (*Shijing*).[77] Trương Tửu is no longer content to see these songs as mere folk literature; he wants to form a canon of songs and underline their importance to Vietnamese identity:

> In short, we [Vietnamese] also have precious canonical Odes (*Kinh thi*) that are no less worthy than the Odes of the Chinese. Our duty today is to write them down, ensure their accuracy, and annotate them, as the Duke of Zhou wrote down, Confucius ensured the accuracy, and Zhu Xi annotated the Odes of China.
>
> This task, we can do it today. We already have enough bricks, mortar, and tiles; we only lack the architectural forms to build the palace, our own palace.[78]

If Trần Trọng Kim had lamented that Vietnam's old house of Confucianism was falling into ruin, Trương Tửu saw the situation radically differently: he was reconstructing a Vietnamese "palace."[79] Then he appropriated a metaphor once used by Trần Trọng Kim: while Kim said his book was intended as a "map" or "plan" (*bản đồ*) of Confucianism, Trương Tửu said that he had "tried to sketch an architectural plan (*bản đồ*) that roughly approximates the map of antiquity we have un-thinkingly misplaced."[80]

Trương Tửu skillfully constructs his argument, even if his empirical historical basis is highly speculative. He asserts his position with what one can call "negative" and "positive" arguments. On the one hand, he contests the notion that many practices and beliefs that appear Con-fucian actually are. Vietnamese culture is not descended from Chinese culture, he claims. "Both are descended from the same lineage, have the same root. This root is the agricultural economy."[81] For example, many popular concerns of the Vietnamese, like those of the Chinese, revolve around the agricultural cycle.

If many Vietnamese scholars had located identity and national essence in patriarchal Confucianism, Trương Tửu did not. Citing Louis Finot, he argued that Vietnamese society was originally matriarchal,[82] and thus at odds with the Confucian view of proper gender roles. In an interesting twist on this matriarchal argument, invoking Freud, Trương Tửu argues that, while Confucianism "repressed people's instincts and emotions,"[83] it was precisely the strength of the Vietnamese that they tended to follow their instincts and emotions "more than follow the philosophy and laws of Confucian scholars."[84]

Trương Tửu argues that popular culture shows the traces of popular opposition to Confucian rule. Confucianism was a force in Vietnamese society, but it was one that stimulated a strong cultural reaction: "Thanks to the unusual efforts [of our ancestors], now we can take pride in having preserved in the realm of consciousness a Vietnamese essence, an essence that Chinese culture only crystallized but was never able to overwhelm."[85]

This assertion begs the question: how did these ancestors resist the power of Confucian ideology? For it was precisely the contention of a wide range of Vietnamese thinkers (Trần Huy Liệu, Trần Hữu Độ, Ngô Đức Kế, Phan Bội Châu, Đào Duy Anh, Phan Khôi, Hoàng Đạo, and many more) that Vietnamese had not resisted the influence of Confucian-ism.

Trương Tửu, although a Marxist, comes up with a novel argument: Vietnamese ancestors resisted the power of Confucian ideology through a Vietnamese "soul force": "We Vietnamese, for several thousand years, have always had a rich and strong soul force (*linh hồn*). That soul force connected to one another, on this territory, more than twenty million people who know how to live, to struggle for forty centuries. That soul force, that struggle, has left its traces in Vietnamese folk songs."[86]

This statement sounds idealist, even mystical. It combines a belief that the Vietnamese have constituted themselves historically through struggle with an appeal to a timeless "soul force." Trương Tửu occasionally refers to this "soul force" as the "essence" (*tinh túy*) of the Vietnamese people. This way of approaching Vietnamese identity shows a layering of language: the older approach to national identity that focused on essences is combined with the new approach that focuses on the way that identities are constructed through life and struggle.

Trương Tửu has often been referred to as a "Trotskyist."[87] But he refused to reduce Vietnamese identity to labor. He refused to relegate consciousness to an epiphenomenon, to say that it was secondary to socioeconomic activity. Consciousness and material life interpenetrate and influence each other. Furthermore, Trương Tửu's notion of consciousness was rather idiosyncratic: he argued that Vietnamese had resisted Confucianism through their instincts and through their emotions, not through the conscious articulation of interests.

Like many intellectuals of his generation, Trương Tửu tried to combine an East Asian language and a Western one in his historical analysis. He was able to reconcile, to his own satisfaction, the apparent contradictions between an essentialist and a constructivist world view. He could argue at the same time that Vietnamese constituted themselves in struggle and through allowing their instincts to oppose attempts to rein in personal freedom. In so arguing, he changed the framework of debate on Confucianism.

Trương Tửu's major contribution was not in discovering this folk culture. Nguyễn Văn Ngọc, Phạm Quỳnh, and Léopold Cadière, for example, had collected many examples of popular culture. Trương Tửu, who also gathered examples of folk ways, interpreted them in a novel way and asserted their importance in intellectual discourse. This work inspired further studies of popular culture from the 1940s onward. Trương Tửu challenged the view that the Vietnamese city or elite culture could define a new Vietnamese identity, that politics was the preferred realm of discourse, and that "culture" had to be defined in terms of printed literature.

CONCLUSION

Trương Tửu's attack on Confucianism and his embrace of popular culture represent one variant of the encounter with the past in the inter-war period. Faced with the traumatic impact of French colonization, Vietnamese intellectuals in the 1920s and 1930s searched for what they believed must have held Vietnam together in the past. French repression of political discussions and writings meant that, in the search backward, Vietnamese were pressed to find cultural explanations for Vietnam's strength in the far past as well as its more recent failure to stand up to the West. Searching for their origins, some Vietnamese came up with Confucianism and all its "strengths" and "weaknesses." Others suggested that the fundamental bases of Vietnamese identity were to be found in peasant culture.

As I have noted, the modern Vietnamese discourse on Confucianism is striking in its surface similarities to those of Korea and China. Chinese debates over the relationship between a "Confucian" past and the modern age shaped twentieth-century Vietnamese discourses on this topic. Korea and Vietnam both combine a discourse on Confucianism with a nationalist and anticolonial narrative of resistance to foreign aggression. Confucianism has then been implicated in this nationalist reading of the past, as progressives and conservatives pillory or champion the teaching to make their points. But if the two countries have converged in the twentieth century in their styles of approaching Confucianism, they do so from different historical paths.

The persons studied in this chapter put forth incompatible arguments: that an essential Vietnamese identity (*quốc túy, tinh túy, tinh hoa*) was rooted in Confucianism (Trần Trọng Kim), that it was based on "livelihood" and influenced by Confucianism (Đào Duy Anh), or that Confucianism had never been the basis of Vietnamese action and belief (Trương Tửu). They shifted their attention from conceptions of identity and culture that stressed the centrality of written and printed learning to ones that underlined the importance of folkic knowledge. Indeed, Trương Tửu went so far as to argue that textual knowledge was, at some level, the bearer of foreignness and artificiality, a conduit of contamination into the purity of an oral realm. Ironically, despite their differences, all three authors used Confucianism as the foil against which Vietnamese defined themselves. Trần Trọng Kim's metaphor of a map is most instructive. He, Đào Duy Anh, and Trương Tửu all wanted to establish epistemological control over the past through the deployment of essentialist and constructivist arguments. Their arguments have come to shape the ways that Vietnamese intellectuals, and even the party-state, now think about the Vietnamese and East Asian pasts. In this sense, Trương Tửu's comments are proven right: Chinese culture "crystallized" a previously inchoate Vietnamese identity.

Where did the debate go from there? Despite Trương Tửu's argument that Confucianism was a relic of the past, many contested such extreme views. Vietnamese writers argued both that Confucianism was key to Vietnam's past and present and that it was irrelevant. Both sides seem right: fragments of Confucian discourse were ubiquitous, indicating that the teaching had indeed penetrated deeply into Vietnamese life. These fragments sometimes showed up in the most unexpected places. Confucian ideas mixed with those of Herbert Spencer, with French-sponsored morality tracts calling for better hygiene, and in appeals for the Buddhist Revival. In short, the semiotic field of Confucian thought was changing.

While traces of Confucian discourse can be found everywhere, it is remarkable to find so few institutional and intellectual supports for a culture of Confucianism. Networks of scholars and schools, libraries of Confucian classics, and books discussing in depth the contributions of Vietnamese, Ming, and Qing scholars were rare. One is left concluding that, in a few areas of human existence, Vietnamese manifested some longstanding familiarity with Confucian teachings but that the impact was far less extensive than in either Korea or China. Confucianism as a systematic and coherent body of beliefs had faded in importance by midcentury, and very few institutions specifically aimed at the propagation of its teachings remained. But if one forgoes a search for a coherently organized set of beliefs and searches instead for concepts (like loyalty or filial piety) with clear Confucian origins, then Confucianism remained quite common.

Faced with the impact of modernity, some writers in the 1920 to 1945 period chose to argue that Vietnam was undergoing a clash of the old and the new, of the East and the West, and that Vietnamese needed to achieve some sort of synthesis. "[In] whatever [social] class we examine in Vietnam today, we see a spiritual crisis" arising from the clash of

Western and Eastern civilizations, one author argued. The solution was to renovate Confucianism. The writer Lương Đức Thiệp put a different spin on this clash of the old and the new. Addressing the contradictions of modernization, he spoke of a "revolution in zigzags" in which Vietnamese simultaneously could embrace Confucius and Einstein, Laozi and Lenin, yin and yang, atoms and electrons.[88] But the fate of Confucianism was still an open question. Would it serve as the basis for a new hybrid culture, or would it be embraced only to be transcended on the path to modernity?

By the late 1930s and into the 1940s, Vietnamese intellectual life had become quite lively and even polarized. At the same time that the French Vichy regime and some Vietnamese called for a revival of Confucian teachings, others attacked them. Young radicals, for example, called on their fellow writers to become interested in the history of daily life and the subaltern classes and stressed the importance of the countryside in preserving a popular culture. With the reconceptualization of the place of the common people in the Vietnamese worldview, a new problem arose that would animate literary life in northern Vietnam for the next fifty years. Were the common people the subject of study who would themselves define a new Vietnamese culture? Or were the common people the raw data for intellectuals to use in constructing a new folkic identity? In this new debate, Vietnamese authors struggled with essentialist and constructivist approaches to the problem of cultural identity that they had developed in the interwar years. They also, as the next chapter argues, articulated new views in an intellectual field transformed by the slow and difficult appropriation of communist ideas and practices.

A staged portrait of a well-to-do family from Annam. The males read while the females look on.

While female literacy lagged that of males, some girls did learn to read. Here, a Buddhist nun teaches a novice to read.

Pictures magnified the appeal of printed matter. Here is a poster from
the Cao Đài, a religious group from southern Vietnam.

To hawk their wares, newspapers put out broadsheets. A few phrases grab the attention of passersby: "Read in *Annam* July 18: China and Annam—A Lesson for the Strong Sex—Our National Holidays?— The Natives' Struggle for Independence Continues—Slaves of Rubber."

Pictures combined with the text could reach a broad audience. Here, a poster recruits employees for the police.

Printed matter was distributed in a variety of ways. Here, a woman sells paper money and other printed matter in the market before Tết.

4 | Printing Revolution, Spreading Communism

The vast majority of post-1945 accounts of Vietnamese history take the eventual rise and triumph of Marxism-Leninism as a given. They pass over the difficult first encounters of Vietnamese with the doctrine or stylize these experiences as part of a process of revolutionary enlightenment. The individuality of each event is lost in a sea of rhetoric. But some passages suggest a different understanding of the Vietnamese revolution, such as the following words about a minor event in 1930 or 1931 when a man hears the communist message for the first time.

> Then one day, and I'm not sure from where, a stranger appeared suddenly at the home looking for father. He explained to father that our village had a *"movement"* (*phong trào*). He talked politics with father. He declared that he also was an *"exploited"* person (*người bị áp bức*). He explained: at this time it was essential to oppose *imperialists*, oppose *feudalists*, to carry out a *revolution* against *imperialism*, against *feudalism* ... and so forth. Father was pleased, but hearing these words rattled his brain. The ideas he understood, but the [particular] words he couldn't figure out (*những lời chẳng hiểu ra làm sao*). He [the stranger] instructed father that if he opposed taxes, how he should oppose them; if he opposed forced labor, how he should oppose it; if individuals redistributed the village-owned communal lands, then what it should be like, what should be done for the poor people in the village to be in accord, and so forth....
>
> He left and then returned. Father was increasingly troubled (*thắc mắc*). Could he really be one of us?[1]

Chánh Thi's reminiscences of his father, who was speaking of his experiences during the Nghệ Tĩnh soviets (1930–1931), show that a giant gap separated the development of revolutionary theory from the lived experience of rural peasants. Hearing the communist cadre speak, Chánh Thi wrote: "Father was increasingly troubled (*thắc mắc*)." The word "*thắc mắc*," with a wide range of meanings in Vietnamese from troubled, unsettled, and worried to having a vague discomfort, conveys a key point: the history of the introduction of communism to the Vietnamese is the history of an encounter with alien concepts and practices. It is an account of misunderstandings and creative transformations. It is the story of the creation of a new audience for the printed word.

Until now, interpretations by communist historians and French bureaucrats have served as the starting point for discussions of the rise of communism in Vietnam. Drawing on these sources and on archival materials and memoirs, Vietnamese and overseas historians have discussed the Indochinese Communist Party and its successors more than any other topic in modern Vietnamese history. Their deep interest seems quite reasonable: after all, the communist struggles against colonial rule to 1945, followed by a succession of wars against the French, Americans, and Chinese, have played a key role in modern Vietnamese history. In their narrations, historians often portray the communist success as a skillful combination of revolutionary and nationalist ideologies with astute organizing. Despite initial difficulties, communist success often comes to be presented as inevitable. Huỳnh Kim Khánh, for example, ultimately concludes his analysis of the communist rise to power by invoking the "indomitable spirit of the Vietnamese people" and Hồ Chí Minh.[2]

The scholarship mentioned above has been supplemented by memoirs of the revolutionary experience. These memoirs have played a crucial role for the Party and its followers, as they have linked the lived experience to the Party line and thus reinforced its perceived legitimacy. Leading cadres of the revolution such as Trần Văn Giàu and Trần Huy Liệu have written about their participation in politics and then used this work as a basis for their historical analyses. The party-state has promoted these acts of remembrance: since the 1950s, it has churned out an impressive array of texts, such as communist memoirs, novels, and histories, that re-present the past in state-approved ways. Communist memoirs and novels uphold socialist virtues and disparage noncommunists. Unpalatable episodes from the past and losers in interparty struggles drop from view. The catholicity of Vietnamese engagements with Marxism from 1925 to 1945, a period that saw "Trotskyists" such as

Tạ Thu Thâu collaborating with "Stalinists" such as Trần Văn Giàu or the polymath Marxist Phan Văn Hùm advising the Buddhist millenarian Hòa Hảo sect, is suppressed. The "triumph" of communism turns out to be a highly selective retelling of history, purged of feuds, crimes, treason, and cowardice.

This version of history has led to surprising results. For example, a once antitraditional communism has been recuperated as a part of Vietnamese tradition. To be sure, scholars and Party activists have linked communism to a heroic popular tradition of resistance; however, this recuperation has gone further. Trần Đình Hượu, for example, has stated that in the period from 1926 to 1930, "Confucianism did not attack but on the contrary was sympathetic to communism, and it can be said that it created the conditions for Marxism to enter our thought."[3] While the last phrase in this explanation may have some merit, the first part of the quotation is puzzling at best. It marks an attempt to link communism to Vietnamese tradition and thus, in nativist fashion, to mask communism's European (and thus alien) origins.

As time passes, it becomes increasingly clear that the standard accounts of Vietnamese communism, from Huỳnh Kim Khánh's *Vietnamese Communism, 1925–1945*, to the numerous memoirs of events, need to be updated.[4] As Hue Tam Ho Tai has pointed out, their retrospective vision has shaped the story of communism as one of inevitable triumph and masked the early diversity of radicalism.[5] In line with the most recent scholarship, from David Marr's study of the events of 1945 to Christopher Goscha's study on the Southeast Asian contexts of the Vietnamese revolution, this chapter argues for a more open-ended approach.[6] Vietnamese communism emerged out of competing, highly autonomous groups, often defined by friendships as well as lineage, village, and regional ties. Initially, these groups had little sense that they should all adhere to a common Party center, follow similar organizational policies, or even stress the same ideology. Early Vietnamese communism, in its diversity and lack of Leninist organization, resembles the early Chinese communism described by Hans Van de Ven.[7]

What follows is an examination of the links among communism, language, and print culture in the Nghệ Tĩnh uprisings of 1930–1931 and the resurrection of Vietnamese communism in Việt Bắc in 1941–1945.[8] I look at the spread of communist texts as the rise of a discursive formation, affected by legal restrictions and police repression, and shaped by the stunningly rapid linguistic changes of the 1920–1940 period. I then link the evolution of discourse to a discussion of the audience of the printed word and how this audience's reception of communism led, fitfully, to changes in communist practices. To accomplish this task, I rely on a broad range of documents from revolutionary writings to French police records. Two groups of materials stand out: communist memoirs and a collection of communist and Việt Minh tracts and newspapers dating from 1929–1931 and 1940–1945 from central and northern Vietnam.[9]

The 1920–1945 period as a whole is marked by many important transformations. The Vietnamese language changed remarkably rapidly in the 1920s and 1930s: a mass of neologisms surged into the language, especially in the realms of social and political analysis. By distinguishing between "fertile" and "institutional" language, the phenomenologist Merleau-Ponty has suggested a way to understand this transformation of understanding. Fertile language, such as the language of poetry (used in unfamiliar ways), is open to multiple interpretations. Stereotypic or institutional language, in contrast, is utterly familiar to its adepts. In *Phenomenology of Perception*, Merleau-Ponty states that "for all these many commonplace utterances, we possess within ourselves ready-made meanings. They arouse in us only second-order thoughts; these in turn are translated into other words which demand from us no real effort of expression and will demand from our hearers no effort of comprehension ... and it is within a world already spoken and speaking that we speak."[10] In the Vietnamese case, Comintern ideologues hoped, perhaps, that communism could be exported as a ready-made ideology—an institutionalized language that could be applied to the world. Yet it first appeared in the minds of many as a "fertile" language, open to a bewildering number of interpretations.

The transformation in language is linked to a major change in the nature of audience. An audience for the communist message had to be created. The heterogeneity of the Vietnamese populace had to be mastered: out of this diversity of Vietnamese, a new entity, "the masses" (*quần chúng*) came into being. The story of the next few decades is in part the institutionalizing of a new language: of ensuring that the audience gave "ready-made" interpretations to individual concepts, nested these concepts within a structured ideology, and then linked this mental world back to practice.

Today, the Vietnamese vocabulary for social, political, and literary analysis is saturated with neologisms. Many of them entered the language between 1920 and 1945. Lydia Liu's careful work on tracking down neologisms and their routes of diffusion into the Chinese language is relevant here: many of the same missionary, Japanese, or Chinese neologisms that flooded into modern Chinese, such as "class" (*giai cấp*) and "society" (*xã hội*), also made their way into Vietnamese. Furthermore, Vietnamese texts from the 1920s through 1940s occasionally contain transliterations of French words or Vietnamese words followed (in parentheses) by their French "equivalents." But I must emphasize that the transformation of the meanings of concepts and their place in a larger structured ideology cannot be understood apart from the lived experience of Vietnamese encountering communism.

Two of the most important "communist" events of the colonial period defy the Marxist-Leninist logic that is so often imputed to them. The uprisings in Nghệ Tĩnh and the growth of the Việt Minh in the Việt Bắc region took place in areas that were the least developed economically in Vietnam. The struggle between capital and labor there rarely reached the intensity that it did in southern Vietnam. For this reason, analysts like Nguyen Khac Vien have felt compelled to highlight the importance of regional, national, and revolutionary "traditions" (such as a history of literati-led peasant uprisings) to explain the rise of Vietnamese communism. As such "traditions" are invoked, any orthodox Marxist-Leninist interpretation becomes problematic. It becomes clear that the audience of revolutionary propagandizing could not have understood Marxism merely in terms of Marxist ideology.

The incongruity between the revolutionary language used by revolutionaries and the situation on the ground is of compelling interest. No writers have centered their analyses on widely circulated propaganda texts and extrapolated from these simple texts to communism as a whole. Instead, they have tended to pursue the opposite strategy: after determining the party line of the moment and the interpretive strategy to be used, they have slotted the interpretation of poems and writings into this larger interpretation.[11]

Such approaches have clear limits. In particular, they do not provide an adequate understanding of the question of audience. A gap exists between revolutionary language and its implicit conception of the world and that of the life-world of many Vietnamese. This gap turns out to have key importance in the study of the importation and appropriation of the communist message.

Historians have paid little attention to the problem of the appropriation of the communist message: Is the message sent by the cadres the same as the message received by the peasant or the worker? How does the worldview of the reader or listener play a role in understanding the meaning of the communist text? It strains credulity to believe that all people interpret texts in identical ways, yet this assumption undergirds much writing on Vietnamese communism.

Understanding audience was a key problem for communists. Studying for Confucian exams had created an audience conversant with Confucian writings; attending temple and Buddhist festivals introduced many Vietnamese to Buddhism; study in colonial schools was creating a generation of young Vietnamese who had been initiated into French culture. In contrast, no institutions or shared cultural practices were creating a communist audience in the 1920s. It was up to communists and their sympathizers to develop new cultural practices that would allow them to spread a message that could be shared by revolutionary members of the Vietnamese intelligentsia and by Vietnamese peasants and workers. This task was extremely difficult.

As I have explained, Vietnam's public realm was divided between religious and secular publications and between legal and illegal ones. The discursive formation of communism operated in the sharply defined realm of illegality, bursting out into the legal realm only in the 1936–1939 period. While the legal realm was most open to competing views in the latter period, illegal publications never disappeared.

Below I look at two periods when repression of printed matter was harsh, 1929–1931 and 1940–1945. In the world of secret publishing, language, readership, and geography differed from the public realm, and dissidents experimented with alternative discourses. For these reasons alone, this world commands attention.

THE CREATION OF A COMMUNIST IDENTITY: FINDING REVOLUTION, MASTERING THE PROBLEM OF LANGUAGE

Among other changes, the twentieth century gave birth to the communist cadre and follower. Given the difficulties of meeting one another in large meetings, communists forged their collective identity through multiple strategies. Some traveled to Siam, France, China, or the Soviet Union to become politicized. In Vietnam, family members sometimes introduced kin to the new ideology. Cadres and followers bonded together intimately in small cells (whether in prisons, factories, or villages) and through meetings of front organizations. But they also met others and encountered the thoughts of others through the seemingly impersonal act of reading.

Vietnamese communism is often dated from 1925, when Hồ Tùng Mậu, Nguyễn Ái Quốc (later known as Hồ Chí Minh), and others founded the Việt Nam Thanh Niên Cách Mạng Đồng Chí Hội (usually referred to as Thanh Niên) in Guangzhou, China. Alternatively, it is dated from 1930, when three rival communist factions met in Hong Kong to unite as the Indochinese Communist Party. These particular events, not to mention the importance of Siamese and Chinese bases to the early revolution, show that Vietnamese communism was born in an international arena and that international orientation marked its early years. This communism grafted onto noncommunist networks in Siam and China, such as the Đông Du (Eastern Travels) revolutionary network.[12]

By the end of the 1920s, Vietnamese could boast an array of small and loosely organized radical groups ranging from the Việt Nam Quốc Dân Đảng (Nationalist Party) and the Tân Việt Cách Mạng Đảng (New Viet Revolutionary Party) to a variety of communist organizations.[13] Competition among groups could be nasty and petulant: in a memorandum about the Annam Communist Party "clique," the Indochinese Communist Party complained that "they are not communists ..., they do not have a Bolshevik mentality and can't have a Bolshevik mentality."[14] Exiles played a key role in these groups, particularly communists in Guangzhou and Siam. Thanh Niên activists, for example, gained some converts in the north and south of Vietnam. The same appears to be true of Vietnamese émigrés such as Nguyễn Ái Quốc and Hoàng Văn Hoan in Siam.

By the late 1920s, Marxist-oriented organizations were gaining influence among a small group of intellectuals and anticolonial activists. Through a 1929 "proletarianization" campaign, Marxists deepened the impact of internationalist and class thinking on the small number of communists in Vietnam. Communists (frequently intellectuals or persons with some schooling) were encouraged to "proletarianize in order to agitate for the proletariat" (*vô sản hóa để vận động vô sản*): that is, they entered the proletariat by taking on jobs in mines, printing plants, textile mills, and similar venues. One of these early communists, Khuất Duy Tiến, states: "Guided by that slogan [of proletarianization] of the Party, I abandoned my studies and asked to become a worker. At the time, I was studying in the College of Commerce in Hanoi." He went to work in the textile mill in Nam Định.[15]

The proletarianization campaign trained cadres for the Nghệ Tĩnh soviets. The impetus for the campaign came not from heavily agricultural Vietnam but from the Sixth Comintern congress of 1928.[16] Trần Văn Cung, who had attended Whampoa Academy in China and participated in the Guangzhou "proletarian" uprising of 1927, cited three major examples for the movement: the October Revolution in Russia, the "resounding influence" of the Canton commune, and the international workers movement, "especially that of France."[17]

In the early years, cadres trained abroad shaped the communist movement. The example of the peripatetic Nguyễn Ái Quốc is well known. He and other "internationalists" put a strong mark on Vietnamese communism. Quốc himself met Zhou Enlai, Liu Shaoqi, Peng Pai, and other early prominent Chinese communists in the 1920s when he served as a Comintern representative; he spoke before labor rallies in Guangzhou; and (notably) he encouraged the early Chinese communist Peng Pai in his attempts to organize peasants for revolutionary action.[18] In addition to Nguyễn Ái Quốc, approximately sixty Vietnamese, including early activists such as Trần Văn Giàu, received training from the Comintern in Moscow.[19] It is important to note that the influence of those trained abroad reached down into the communist apparatus. One French report on the communists working in Thanh Chuông, Nam Đàn, and Anh Sơn villages during the Nghệ Tĩnh uprisings mentions the leading role of "émigrés" in spreading communist tracts to villagers.[20] One should not assume that the ideological message in and of itself converted others. I strongly suspect that these émigrés tapped friends and kin networks in the village to spread their message. For example, the Nguyễn Sinh lineage of the Kim Liên–Nam Đàn area of Nghệ An province (to which Nguyễn Sinh Cung, also known as Nguyễn Ái Quốc and Hồ Chí Minh, belonged) contributed numerous members to the revolution. One of them, Nguyễn Sinh Diên, was active with Vietnamese communists in Guangzhou province, China, attended the University of the East (the so-called Stalin School) in Moscow, and died fighting against Germans in the defense of Moscow. The Nguyễn Năng lineage of Nghi Trường, Nghi Lộc, Nghệ An province contributed eight members to the Nghệ Tĩnh soviet movement, including two women who were the first members of the Nghị Lộc party branch.[21]

The question still remains: how, at an individual level, did Vietnamese come to revolution? The answer is surprisingly difficult to give for two main reasons. First, most memoirs are written by relatively educated communists and not by the peasants and workers who were the target of the revolutionary message. Second, accounts of the road to enlightenment and revolution often are formulaic. In *Giọt nước trong biển cả: hồi ký* (A drop in the ocean: a memoir), Hoàng Văn Hoan lays out an architectural logic common to many discussions of revolutionary politicization. He first discusses his youth, which "speaks of the process of revolutionary awakening (*giác ngộ cách mạng*)," then turns to the "process of finding the revolution," and finally discusses the "road to revolution," or "beginning to participate in the revolutionary ranks."[22] The book is organized around the metaphor of the "road" (*đường*), a powerful metaphor because it conveyed the idea of the long physical route that Hoàng Văn Hoan and many other revolutionaries had to trek and the notion of the psychological distance he had to travel to "find" and understand communism.

Not the least of the distances Hoàng Văn Hoan had to travel was that from, as he characterizes it, an oppressive Confucian learning to a liberating communist one. With a second metaphor of "awakening" (*giác ngộ*), this tale has great emotive power indeed. It plots experience in a clear linear path: the path from darkness to light, from ignorance to knowledge, from lack of political action to politicization. Seen from the present, such a notion of revolutionary enlightenment may seem unproblematic. Seen from a Vietnamese viewpoint in 1925, 1929, or 1931, this concept was remarkably unfamiliar. The same could be said of related concepts such as "cadre" (*cán bộ*), "worker" (*công nhân*), "class struggle" (*đấu tranh giai cấp*), and even of a "communist party" (*đảng cộng sản*), all of which had to be explained to their audience.

During Hoàng Văn Hoan's youth, Vietnamese grasped the Confucian concept of *tứ dân* (the four social orders of scholars, agriculturalists, craft workers, and merchants) far more easily than the modern notion of class. While most were aware of the Buddhist notion that life is a sea of suffering, few grasped the Marxist idea that class exploitation leads to misery. Even more important in daily life, however, was the network of social relations through which they practiced a set of moral obligations. These relationships found root in local customs and canonical writings about gender and hierarchy. Seen in this context, Marxist categories of social analysis were quite strange and obscure.

In contrast to Hoàng Văn Hoan, most Vietnamese did not find a clear path to revolutionary enlightenment. Early radical discourse confused many of them. Nguyễn Ái Quốc understood this problem acutely; in 1925 he wrote: "Our language is poor. When we speak, we must borrow many words from foreign languages, and especially [from] Chinese. I think that the excessive use of Chinese, except for common words, known by everybody, such as Bolshevism [and] finance ... makes the understanding of a text difficult.... If your writing aims to propagandize, it must be understood by all."[23]

Nguyễn Ái Quốc was optimistic: in 1925, words such as "finance" and "Bolshevik" would puzzle most Vietnamese. Some of these words tripped up communist cadres themselves, who sometimes seemed more facile using foreign terms. A 1929 internal party memorandum of the Indochinese Communist Party, for example, was sprinkled with French words such as *"bureaucratique," "enthousiasme," "cache,"* and *"discipliner."*[24] A 1928 document from a precursor of the unified Indochinese Party, the Tân Việt Cách Mạng Đảng, imported terms from Chinese: it spoke of Mã Khắc Tư (Marx) and Liệt Ninh (Lenin), transliterations that were soon abandoned in favor of more phonetically accurate versions.[25] In 1938, key communist terms had become more familiar, but readers and listeners still were bedeviled by abstruse vocabulary. In that year the Marxist Sơn Trà noted that, although he tried to write simply, readers with little education complained that his books were still "exceedingly difficult to understand." Sơn Trà admitted that this criticism might have merit; he counseled his readers not to get discouraged. "Perhaps it is also that [you] friends have not yet read many books on politics, so that you are not used to hearing and understanding political vocabulary."[26] In 1944 and 1945, cadres made similar laments about wrong interpretations of communist ideas by the populace. In short, the populace had only a faint idea of the party line. This observation should hardly be surprising, but it has repeatedly been ignored in secondary accounts on Vietnamese communism.

At this early stage, communist Vietnamese struggled to define their identities. Trần Huy Liệu, a famous Vietnamese revolutionary and intellectual, described the trajectory that many early communists took when he said: "I came to the party not by the easy road but by a twisting and bumpy one."[27] The road was difficult not only because radicals faced constant police surveillance, but because their key readings did not directly address their problems. There is no mention in the literature of Vietnamese communists reading agrarian radical tracts. On the contrary, many of them understood communism by reading Nikolai Bukharin and Evgenii Preobrazhenskii's *The ABC of Communism* (1919). "*The ABC of Communism* was the communist primer at that time," wrote two early activists. Early communists repeatedly cite the book, which focused overwhelmingly on the proletarian revolution, in their memoirs.[28]

Vietnamese Communists at first celebrated foreign communist heroes and events such as the anniversary of the "3Ls" (Rosa Luxemburg, Karl Liebknecht, and Lenin) and the acts of Republican heroes in the Spanish civil war. They entangled themselves in international polemics over Stalin and his followers: "Long live comrade Stalin! Long live comrade Thorez!" one pamphlet proclaimed, defending the Soviet leader and his French acolyte against Trotskyist attacks.[29] They celebrated annually the example of the Paris Commune. As early as 1929, Vietnamese communists commemorated the 1927 Canton commune, in which proletarian communists tried to seize control of the city. (The uprising was a disaster: the Guomindang crushed it and killed thousands in the process.)[30] The choice of many of these commemorative acts must have puzzled new recruits.

An intriguing article that appeared in *Lao động* (Labor), a newspaper published by the General Association of Workers of Tonkin (Tổng Công Hội Bắc Kỳ) in 1929, captures the proletarian spirit of the time. In the article, a Vietnamese "worker" emphasized the importance of developing the consciousness of being a worker:

I was born into a family of workers (*con nhà lao động*), lived in a working milieu, and have yet to see anyone say how important labor and workers are; it is as if workers are all ignorant, only in the darkness of slavery, only for the capitalists to use them to make themselves rich, while they have no idea what their interests are.

Fortunately, now there are newspapers like *Lao động* (Labor), *Mỏ than* (The coal mine), *Tia sáng* (Ray of light), *Lá cờ cộng sản* (Communist flag), and so forth ... all organs serving the interests of the brothers and sisters of the proletarian class. So our brothers and sisters already have people pointing the way.... I dare say that we brothers and sisters, thanks to these newspapers, will be stirred awake and will become enlightened (*giác ngộ*) to bring together the collectivity so that there will be enough strength to struggle with the capitalists.

As for my feelings about the newspapers that have come into existence, it is as if [I were] a patient with a dangerous, life-threatening heart and lung ailment, but a healer (*thầy thuốc*) finds a cure (*phương thuốc*) to get rid of the poison. My happiness is indescribable! May these newspapers live forever![31]

The article's language would have been novel to most Vietnamese.[32] While European in origin, its vocabulary had taken a step toward "localization" through the act of translation. Vietnamese communists appropriated Chinese translations of European terms and gave them Vietnamese pronunciations. The writer celebrates the fact that the worker's existence has been recognized and is considered of value. This existence can now be named, since it has its own conceptual vocabulary. "Workers" can now recast their biographies by saying, as in this passage, that they were born into a "family of workers" (*con nhà lao động*). Vietnamese did not know this term ten years before.

Both the noun "worker" (*công nhân*) and the verb "to labor" (*lao động*) were new to the Vietnamese language at this time. The new term for "worker" is inclusive, subsuming earlier terms that divided workers according to profession or occupation (e.g., *thợ bạc*, silversmith/goldsmith, or *thợ dệt*, weaver).[33] This worker belongs to the "proletarian class" (*vô sản giai cấp*), or literally "[people] of the same rank or level who have no property."

Now that the worker's existence can be named and discussed, other workers can be enlightened. All of a sudden, the author switches to a word familiar in a different context: "*giác ngộ*" usually refers to Buddhist enlightenment. It is quite possible that other readers, when reading the word "*giác ngộ*," conceptualized communist enlightenment as analogous to Buddhist awakening. When the author turns to describe himself as a sick "patient," he uses words such as "medicine giver" (*thầy thuốc*) and "cure" (*phương thuộc*) that have a Vietnamese flavor to them, not a Western one. It is as if the writer, sensing the strangeness of his communist vocabulary, tries to familiarize his thoughts for the reader by injecting Vietnamese Buddhist and medical vocabulary into his discussion.

Clearly, the language of communism was still evolving. For many years, communist texts had to explain new or difficult words. *Búa liềm* (Hammer and sickle), published in 1929 as the central organ of the Indochinese Communist Party, addressed this problem by footnoting articles. In a list titled "The Meaning of Words That Are Hard to Understand," it explained key communist terms. For example, it defined the phrase "imperialist war" as a "war that capitalist gangs carry out to seize colonies and markets." Other phrases glossed included the ones for "going on a march to show off one's strength" (*tuần hành thị uy*), "meeting," "demonstration," "communist international," "civil war," and "dictatorship of the proletariat."[34]

The same source indicates that Vietnamese had not yet settled on a fixed meaning for "worker" (*công nhân*). At this early stage, many communists saw not one class of workers, but workers divided not only along age and gender lines but into the skilled "blue shirts" (*thợ thuyền áo xanh*) and unskilled "brown shirts" (*thợ thuyền áo nâu*).[35] Some thinkers saw even greater gradations of class.[36] Given that some communists initially made such distinctions, these different conceptions of social rank must have hindered the development of notions of a unified and unitary working class.

At this early stage, Vietnamese communists were grappling with a European conceptual vocabulary in which the bourgeoisie, a "city" class that owned the means of production, opposed the proletariat in an urban environment. In the article above, when the worker looked out and celebrated the awakening of a working class, he turned not to fellow peasants but to fellow "laborers" like mine workers or factory workers. But not all Vietnamese interpreted the word in the same way. Part of the communist struggle for the next thirty years would be to try to ensure that communist cadres and their audiences shared the "canonical" interpretation of communist terms. It would be a long struggle.

The day-to-day activities of persons who became revolutionaries present a murkier picture than that presented by the "worker" writing in *Lao động* or by Hoàng Văn Hoan looking back on his life. Many Vietnamese were in a state of "generalized availability" (*disponibilité*), to use Pierre Brocheux's phrase, open to new perspectives. But no clear road lay before them. This state of mind is well captured in Phạm Văn Hảo's memoir, which discusses how one man groped his way to revolution. Hảo faced numerous hurdles in 1931 when he tried to establish contact with the party. Hảo traveled with his "comrade" Hoc Phi to Hưng Yên. Finding no other party members, the two took matters into their own hands and began the clandestine publication of a newspaper named *Tia sáng* (Ray of light). The two militants hoped that this publication would allow other party members to find them while providing them a forum to agitate for revolution. Toward this goal they rented a room in Yên Phu, on the outskirts of Hanoi, with a family of flower growers. "From the outside we appeared to be students, but in reality we often spent all our time in our room writing and printing the paper."[37] The fact that Phạm Văn Hảo and Hoc Phi could come across as students suggests that they did not come from a poor peasant background. They were literate and managed to support themselves without regular jobs. Like some other Vietnamese, these youngsters were searching for revolution but had not yet established contact with fellow travelers.

As Phạm Văn Hảo points out, it was difficult to remain clandestine. The owner of the house, "a good but timid person," left them alone. "We had to print at night or work in a dark room, which was very difficult.... We worked very secretively but could not understand why the police spies took no notice. One day a police inspector named Lanèque and several of his agents came to search my room and examined it very carefully. Luckily, that time I had left no materials in the home."[38] Phạm Văn Hảo and Hoc Phi were lucky, as the French administration found it easier to keep track of suspected "subversives" in the countryside than in the city. New inhabitants stood out, especially if they did not have clearly defined jobs.

One of the greatest difficulties faced by communists was in spreading their message. Since they could not ask printers to publish their illegal tracts, cadres often had to rely on primitive printing technology. Initially, Hảo and Phi resorted to the gelatin method of printing. A slab of gelatin was placed in a tray, and an inked paper was placed on top of it. The gelatin absorbed the ink. The original inked piece of paper was then lifted off and replaced by a blank piece of paper carefully set on the gelatin slab. With this method, several dozen copies of a page could be printed until the ink ran out.[39]

By 1933, Phạm Văn Hảo moved again, becoming a clerk at the Hà Rồng train station in Thanh Hóa province. This time, he was joined by comrade Nguyễn Tạo, who had escaped along with seven other communists from the Phủ Doãn hospital. Tạo brought down to Thanh Hóa a marginally better printing apparatus. The problem with the gelatin method of printing was that one could print an extremely limited number of pages before needing to replace the gelatin and ink. This time around, they used a board on which they placed some potter's clay (đất sét). They mixed the potter's clay with a solvent, making it elastic and level, then dampened it with glycerine water to make the surface "silky smooth." Hảo's younger brother had the best handwriting, so he wrote out the tracts. Once again, the inked paper was laid on the print surface, the glycerine-covered earth absorbed the ink, and then blank pieces of paper were placed on this surface. This method could print more copies than the gelatin method.[40]

As Phạm Văn Hảo has described it so far, printing propaganda was dangerous, and the printing methods were crude and time-consuming. But revolutionaries faced monetary and logistical problems as well:

> From the beginning, our newspaper ran into many difficulties. Whether it was pens, ink, or paper, we lacked everything. We could buy printing paper for several đồng, but for us to get several đồng in the circumstances of the times was never easy, and we had to count upon contributions from comrades and the masses. In addition to the difficulty of having enough money, it was also hard to buy supplies. For the quantity of required newspapers, "gelatin" or "earth" printing was not adequate. We had to print on wax paper (giấy sáp), which was pretty and made many copies. But to buy wax paper, one had to travel far to buy it, since it was only sold in three places: Hanoi, Huế, and Saigon. If you bought this paper, police inspectors would keep an eye on you.... We frequently went to Saigon to buy it, would go to Cholon, enter a Chinese person's shop for help while being spied upon. Printing ink also had to be bought in this manner. [We could find] paper for printing newspaper in the markets or shops in the Phan Rang (Tháp Chàm) region, but we could only buy two or three sheets at a time: if we bought more, they would suspect us immediately.[41]

Despite problems getting paper, the search was worth it: one could print far more copies using wax paper than with clay or gelatin. One wrote with a sharp pen nib onto the wax paper, thereby indenting it. After placing the paper in a frame, the printer inked the wax paper with a roller. The ink would roll off the waxed surface and into the indentations. At this point, one could place a sheet of blank paper on the wax paper and transfer the ink to it. While an improvement on earlier methods, it could still be tricky to roll the ink right and to make the ink flow into the inscribed letters.[42]

As Phạm Văn Hảo's experiences show, colonial law had numerous effects on illegal printing. Most obviously, communists and others had to print their publications themselves, as very few publishers dared to publish tracts that broke the law. These legal restrictions gave rise to aesthetic differences as well. Communist leaflets were hand-lettered, printed using cheap ink. Some leaflets had hand-drawn pictures on the cover. One issue of *Thanh niên* (Youth), a communist publication printed in Canton, displayed a drawing on the cover of Lenin standing atop a globe and pointing at the hammer and sickle.[43] Through such clandestine propaganda here and there and perhaps reading a book such as the *ABC of Communism*, Vietnamese communists pieced together their picture of communism.

Given the novelty of so many Marxist concepts, the ambiguous meanings of terms, and competing idioms of class and political action, Vietnamese communists were unable to reconcile competing tendencies within a young Vietnamese communism. Gareth Porter's contention that the early years of the Vietnamese revolution saw the "successful resolution" of the issues of applying the Leninist theory of a proletarian-based party to an agrarian country strikes me as misguided.[44] Far from resolving such issues, communists encompassed contradictory understandings of them. Phạm Văn Hảo's search for revolution and the varied understanding of peasants in Nghệ Tĩnh defined early Vietnamese communism as well. Diversity, not unity, characterized this early period.

The Nghệ Tĩnh uprisings, a milestone in the formation of Vietnamese communist consciousness, occurred against this backdrop. The proletarian concerns of 1928 and 1929 and the mostly rural ones of 1930–1931 Nghệ Tĩnh differed starkly. Indeed, it is unclear that many peasants had encountered much of the propaganda discussed above. To what extent did peasants think of their plight in terms of a peasant jacquerie revolving around common tax issues and to what extent had they appropriated the revolutionary message? Fording the divide between a revolutionary theory focused on proletarians and the reality of a rural uprising dependent on peasants proved to be a formidably difficult task.

NGHỆ TĨNH: FROM A MESSAGE OF STRUGGLE AND COMMEMORATION TO ITS AUDIENCE

Communists faced three key problems at the end of the 1920s and the beginning of the 1930s. First, they needed to organize themselves effectively. Second, they needed to build on their organizing skills by conveying a clear message to their audience. Finally, they had to ensure that their audience, in reading and hearing the message, understood the message and used it as a basis for organizing. They had to accomplish all these tasks faced with French counterpropaganda and repression of the Nghệ Tĩnh soviets.

The Nghệ Tĩnh rebellion formed part of a larger pattern of social upheaval in Vietnam at the end of the 1920s and into the 1930s: the Vietnam Nationalist Party, after all, launched its Yên Báy rebellion in 1930. Communists claimed credit for a wide array of strikes and peasant demonstrations throughout the country. The north was quiet, with only one strike and one peasant demonstration organized by the communists. In contrast, five strikes and thirty-four peasant demonstrations took place in the south. In the center, seven strikes and twenty peasant demonstrations occurred.[45] While these and other statistics would seem to suggest that the communists were having the most organizing success in the south, the document that provides them states emphatically that the center, and in particular Thanh Chương in Nghệ An, was the key locus of struggle. This was the epicenter of the Nghệ An rebellions. According to a document apparently authored by Hồ Chí Minh, 66 percent of the party members in Annam and Tonkin (1,209 of 1,828), and an astonishing 94 percent of members of peasant organizations (34,078 of 36,230), were found in the provinces of Nghệ An and Hà Tĩnh alone.[46] It was here that French authority was most deeply contested.

The nature of the Nghệ Tĩnh rebellion (1930–1931) is heavily debated. Not surprisingly, the French colonial government blamed outside agitators for fomenting rebellion. Vietnamese and Western scholars have argued over the extent to which the Central Committee of the Indochinese Communist Party was in charge of the uprisings.[47] Scholars have arrived at no consensus on the matter, although it seems clear to me that the Party Central Committee lacked tight control over local Nghệ Tĩnh communists at the outbreak of rebellion.

Agitation in central Vietnam can be traced to 1928 and thus predates the formation of the Indochinese Communist Party. From late 1929 into early 1930, "rural radicals were in a state of ferment," contributing to the burning of temples and village communal houses (*đình*).[48] Widespread rebellions broke out in Nghệ An and Hà Tĩnh provinces in 1930. By late April, the newly united Communist Party had organized a series of demonstrations in support of May Day; the French reacted with force and killed some of the demonstrators. But the weakness of the French presence meant that the French (and their "protectorate," the court of Annam) could not stamp out demonstrations: "Strikes, demonstrations, and the burning of pagodas and *đình* continued throughout the summer."[49] After August, however, when the French bombed a mass demonstration in Vinh and killed an estimated 140 demonstrators, "most of Nghệ An exploded; in some *huyen* [districts], all administration below the county level disappeared."[50] It was in this context that communists began establishing soviets governed by Vietnamese peasants. These soviets soon came under attack by the French, and by the end of 1931 the movement was finished and its leaders were in prison.

The schematic account above does not mention exactly who was responsible for leading the rebellion. Communist historians writing after the event have emphasized the key role of the Indochinese Communist Party. At the same time, there is sufficient evidence that the central committee of the Party was initially caught off guard by the outbreak of violence and the establishment of soviets. As the Annam regional committee itself said in a letter on the topic, "In Thanh-Chuong and Nam-Dan the regional committee has advocated violence (*bao dong*), establishing soviets, dividing land, and so forth. This kind of proposal is not yet appropriate because the level of preparation of the party and the masses is not yet sufficient. There is not yet an armed uprising, and scattered violence in various places would at present be premature putschism."[51] Faced with this fait accompli, the Party's Central Committee both criticized the local committees and exhorted them to use whatever means they could to preserve influence with the masses "so that when defeat comes, the significance of the soviets will penetrate deeply into the minds of the masses."[52]

Debates over the nature of the Nghệ Tĩnh rebellions have often become wrapped up in arguments about the origins of rebelliousness in this region—its "revolutionary tradition"—and in the link between this rebellion and the eventual success of Vietnamese communism. I will put those arguments aside and focus instead on the links among propagandizing, practice, and understanding the communist message. When the Nghệ Tĩnh uprising occurred, communists devoted less and less time to explaining communist theory and more and more time to agitation. How successful were communists, then, in conveying their message? Was the message articulated by communist cadres the same as that understood by the populace?

Propagandizing in Nghệ Tĩnh took place in a symbolic economy different from that of the north or south.[53] The French administration was already warning that, while "the virus of new ideas" on nationalism had not touched the peasantry in 1926, it was spreading to the educated in the smallest villages of northern Annam. The administration grew even more alarmed the next year.[54] Đào Duy Anh in Huế introduced some of the first Vietnamese-language texts on Marxism to Vietnam from 1926 onward, and at least some Vietnamese found their way to radicalism via these books. One example is the female revolutionary Tôn Thị Quế: "gradually," through reading and discussing books produced by Đào Duy Anh's publishing house, "brother explained clearly the revolutionary Party rules to me."[55] But as Trương Tửu argued in 1945, these very books presented new and unfamiliar ideas, and thus people often overlooked them. Đào Duy Anh himself mentioned a concrete sign of limited appeal: his books did not sell briskly.[56] Thus, although some early Marxists such as Đào Duy Anh and Trần Văn Cung came from Annam, and Vietnamese were able to read newspapers and tracts from outside the region, Marxism initially had a muted impact on the region.

Vietnamese in the center were able to gain some access to legal publications from the south and north as well as clandestine Vietnamese communist publications printed in Thailand, China, and France.[57] Nonetheless, they faced great obstacles. The French-controlled court imposed greater restrictions on the Annam press than on that of the south. At the time of the outbreak of the Nghệ Tĩnh uprising, the center had only one major independent newspaper, the Huế newspaper *Tiếng dân* (Voice of the people). The French resident superior controlled the other major newspaper before 1930, *Hà Tĩnh tân văn* (News of Hà Tĩnh). One source has estimated that during the uprisings, the authorities forbade the circulation in Annam of up to twenty-two legally published newspapers from the south and the north.[58] This control of the printed word, combined with the fact that literacy in romanized script was probably lowest in the center, affected the spread of communist ideas.

The court and the French administration realized, however, that they had to combat movements against colonial and royal authority. A 1930 newspaper article that appeared in the government-established news-paper *Thanh Nghệ Tĩnh tân văn* (News of Thanh Hóa, Nghệ An, and Hà Tĩnh provinces) captures well the administration's and the court's fear of communism. The article shifts from one rhetorical strategy to another, in turn belittling communists, claiming that they do not respect proper social relations, and attempting to point out contradictions about com-munists' claims about their ideology. But the article stresses in its intro-duction and its conclusion the foolishness, gullibility, and ignorance of those who follow communism: "Our Vietnam (*Nước Nam ta*) for the last several years has unfortunately encountered a very harmful calamity, the calamity of communism. Most of the people affected by its venom are the inferior ranks who did not succeed in their studies or who had excessively grandiose dreams and so they lose hope; workers, of whom most are lazy; and a number of gullible peasants who have yielded to temptation."[59] Communism "is a wicked way," the article states. Those who spread communist propaganda abandon the three social bonds (*tam cương*) and the five moral obligations (*ngũ thường*).[60] Ignoring the trauma of colonialism, the article poses a rhetorical question: who can imagine abandoning the way of the three social bonds and the five moral obligations, a way that "for several thousand years has made our country glorious?"[61]

Against this type of argument, communists constructed a radically different one. One of the most powerful methods used by communist cadres to convey the revolutionary message was to introduce fellow Vietnamese to new acts of commemoration, like May Day, around which the new revolutionary identity could be structured. Unlike Buddhists, Vietnamese communists at first had no indigenous heroes to commem-orate, nor did they have any sites of commemoration. If Buddhists could go to temples or to pilgrimage sites and Confucians to village shrines, Vietnamese communists lacked these physical locations and temporal occasions that could invest written knowledge with concrete signifi-cation. They had, in other words, no preexisting sites of memory. They had to create them. They had no "communist" poetry, so they created songs like ones about the Guangzhou uprising of 1927 in China and "Remembering Lenin" (Kỷ niệm Lê nin).[62] By early 1930 it appears that they had not yet created poetry that linked communism to local events.

In April 1930, workers at the Bến Thủy match factory (four kilometers from Vinh, the capital of Nghệ An province) in central Vietnam went on strike. Three hundred of the five hundred workers were women.[63] This strike followed other significant strikes: that of the Phú Riềng rubber plantation in the south, in which three thousand rubber workers supposedly participated, and the March 25 strike at the Nam Định textile factory in the north.[64] In its propaganda, the local Communist Party linked this labor struggle to International Labor Day (May 1). Propaganda was filled with stock communist phrases, abstract and perhaps unintelligible to many participants in the strike. Still, the message, by centering on an act (a strike) and a day of commemoration (May Day), provided a context for concretization of the propaganda message.[65]

The stock phrases in propaganda include the way the audience is identified: "Brothers and sisters—workers (thợ thuyền), peasants, soldiers, and youth!" the newspaper Người lao khổ (Toilers) proclaims. An article in the newspaper announces that May 1 is International Workers Day, which is news to many since it had not been celebrated in Vietnam before. The text is filled with terms that are commonly found in Vietnamese communist writings: "sacrifice," "serve the interests of all workers," "French imperialism," "strike," and "repression." Many Vietnamese only imperfectly understood the meaning of many of these terms, meaning that the gap between the message that communists hoped to convey and the ones that readers and listeners created (concretized) was wide indeed. But after much general and abstract prose, the article returns to the strike of the Bến Thủy match factory and links it to French imperialism.[66]

By the time that the Nghệ Tĩnh soviets had developed and French troops had struck back, the propaganda took on a greater urgency and sharper contextualization. The message, nonetheless, is not unified. On the one hand, some objects of commemoration were events in the past that were being actualized in Vietnam (e.g., the Russian soviets) or bloody examples of French repression (e.g., the French bombing of Hưng Nguyên in September 1930). On the other hand, the Communist

Party was trying hard to make communist holidays such as International Workers Day relevant to local Vietnamese. Clearly, the Party hoped that these days would acquire an indigenous meaning through their celebration on Vietnamese soil.

The writers of propaganda still had problems conceptualizing their audience. This is demonstrated by *Gương vô sản* (Proletarian example), published by the district committee of Anh Sơn (Nghệ An), which pushed a strong proletarian line. "Only the proletariat rises to the responsibility of leading the revolution, only the proletariat serves the interests of the toiling masses, only the proletariat is capable of overthrowing capitalist society and building a Communist society."[67] This statement is a clear rebuke to those who imagined that the Nghệ Tĩnh soviets were peasant-led. The peasantry is not identified as an important class in itself. While it is doubtful that there were many (if any) "proletarians" in the small town of Anh Sơn, they were supposed to lead the "toiling masses" (*quần chúng lao khổ*).[68] This particular announcement asserts the key role of the proletariat in Vietnam, but its thick jargon and lack of specificity undermines the clarity of its message of struggle. How could one struggle if one didn't know what was meant by words in revolutionary newspapers such as "struggle," "proletariat," "class," or "imperialism"?

Ironically, propagandists sharpened their message in defeat and invested it with emotional power. Earlier writings spoke of the "ardor" and "heroism" of the working class, but these were cliches with little relationship to actual emotions. But after the French attacks, the propaganda changes. Ngo Vinh Long quotes such a leaflet, handed out in the spring of 1931 to Vietnamese soldiers. The leaflet was raw in its emotion: "We're dying of hunger! We have to demand food! Brother soldiers, you must not kill us! You must support us!"[69] There was also some bitter anti-Catholic propaganda, chastising priests for seducing people with honeyed words to follow teachings of Jesus and stating that, far from forgiving people who had sinned, the French would shoot people who had committed crimes.[70] Another source states: "Today the French brigands (*giặc*) are plotting to drag the workers of Nghệ Tĩnh down the road of death!" The source continues that French troopers have set fire to houses and belongings, shot and killed people, and raped women: "Hundred of families have had their houses set afire, thousands of people have been shot, have been tortured savagely, and countless people are lying in jail awaiting death." The leaflet expresses despair at this suffering.

The conclusion to the leaflet above is a paradox. It calls an incident in which villagers from Nghị Lộc killed some persons, including two members of the secret police, an act "that will accomplish little" but claims that the painful repression will "push the masses down the path of revolution."[71] The Communist Party had lost control of the revolution, and individuals took matters into their own hands. But through remembering and commemorating such suffering and vengeance, a shattered Communist Party would be able to construct a heroic revolutionary Vietnamese identity.

The Nghệ Tĩnh uprising ultimately failed because the French overwhelmed the opposition through force. While communist sources recognized this fact, they also examined ways in which their errors contributed to the failure. They saw that their errors were not simply in the message. They also suffered from poor organization and misguided action.

One newspaper suggested that it was precisely in the midst of disorder and difficulties that cadres needed to use printed materials to raise consciousness. To increase communist influence among the masses, "every cell must set up a section that specializes in the reading of books and newspapers to the masses." That section would convene meetings to read aloud to the masses, and in these meetings take care that people enjoyed themselves while they listened to careful explanations of the text.[72] Other publications stressed the need to expand propagandizing, be more lively in doing so, and reach out to people who had not participated earlier.[73]

The Party faced problems not simply in bringing the message to others, but with its own followers. The newspaper of the Nghệ An provincial committee chastised some people, presumably cadres: "There are people among you who do not look [at publications], there are people who do not read or who read once and throw [publications] into the corner."[74] Furthermore, cadres and communist sympathizers held attitudes that must have undercut the message of revolution, such as prejudices against people of lower social status. A student paper published by the Red Students Association of Nghệ An (Sinh Hội Đỏ Nghệ An) in 1930 proved this point. Replying to the literatus Huỳnh Thúc Kháng, who had stated that "disseminating propaganda leaflets is a child's game," one article pompously replied: "[We] disseminate propaganda leaflets to enlighten the masses, make the masses understand clearly that the country has a Communist Party, which is the party of the masses."[75]

In a self-critical mood, the Party further stressed that it needed to strengthen its system of organization, improve communications, and prepare for a situation where communications were cut off. As part of this overall strategy, the article counseled that cadres "must make proletarian command a reality and centralize the command of the party."[76] Another paper told cadres "to resolutely eliminate the sickness of rightist deviation in the party."[77] The Communist Party, on the defensive, reacted to repression by stressing revolutionary purity and reiterating the ascendancy of the "proletarian" line.[78]

The story told here so far is a familiar one in the study of communism: it is a party-centered account of success and failure. It examines how communist cadres succeeded or failed in framing a message of struggle. Yet the most fascinating part is the reaction of the audience who read newspaper articles and propaganda leaflets or heard oral propagandizing to the new and strange message that cadres brought them. Put in other terms, how can we go beyond the way that communists saw and organized themselves to understand their supposed audience?

Huỳnh Kim Khánh begins to answer this question when he writes that for peasants "communism was appealing not for its Bolshevik revolutionary techniques but because of its millenarian message."[79] But after this enticing sentence, which suggests that the study of communism is doomed to failure if it does not try to understand the way that peasants reconceptualized communist doctrine, Khánh jumps back to a study of organization and ideology. The promise of that one sentence goes unanswered.

Given the lack of sources, a full understanding of peasant consciousness in Nghệ Tĩnh during 1930–1931 is impossible to achieve. There are, nonetheless, highly suggestive traces of peasant and worker consciousness in memoir accounts. This chapter began with a quotation from Chánh Thi, who described his father's unsettled reaction in 1930 or 1931 to a communist propagandist: "Father was increasingly troubled. Could he really be one of us?" Chánh Thi's father sensed that the political and cultural horizons of the propagandist and the peasant differed radically.

Another part of Chánh Thi's memoir contains this discussion: "He [Chánh Thi] told of a naive fellow who asked, 'If we *làm cộng sản* [to act as a communist], could we make three piasters a month?' 'Of course not,' the author replied. '*Làm cộng sản* is for us to get together and cut off the heads of the French, of the landlords, and take their properties and divide them among the poor, like ourselves.'"[80]

A second account underlines the gap between revolutionary theory and its practical understanding. In his memoir of participation in the strike at the Bến Thủy match factory (1930) in Vinh, Nguyễn Phúc mentions how the educated Thuật spoke to him of the conditions at the match factory. "Sitting and listening attentively to my friend explain, I felt something both strange and interesting. It was all words that I had never ever heard before: 'masses,' 'organize,' 'struggle,' and so on.... Although I did not yet understand the full meaning of those words, I understood deeply the ideas that my friend was bringing up."[81] This statement is contradictory and begs the question of the extent to which listeners and readers really understood the communist message. Has the speaker imposed a suspicious logic and clarity on faded memories of the past? That he did is suggested (in a very different context) by a mostly perceptive French report not on the Indochinese Communist Party, but on their rivals in the south, the Trotskyists. The report, speaking of the leaders of one of the most famous papers in Cochinchina, explains:

> The popularity of the "Lutteurs" [named after their paper, *La lutte*, or *Struggle*] is great among the little people of Saigon, Cholon, and Giadinh. For the man on the street, the "gentlemen of *La lutte*" are persons who speak well and loudly, who put their knowledge at the disposition of the humble sort to protest, to write up petitions on the occasion of the thousand and one anarchic little events of Annamite daily life. They are not afraid to talk to the French on equal terms.... It is said that they have high-ranking relations in France, Russia, China, that they are "stronger" than the governor of Saigon and the governor-general in Hanoi.... It is even said, in a loud voice, since people no longer hide saying it, that the "French" are afraid of the "gentlemen of *La lutte*" and that in several years [they] will take power, chase out the oppressors, do away with taxes and divide up the wealth of the rich and of foreigners.[82]

If memories of first encounters with the communist message in the early 1930s are interpreted in light of the French report above, several observations come to mind. Vietnamese workers and peasants grasped communism through preexisting interpretive grids. (This point of view is far more tenable than its opposite: that Vietnamese understood both the original intention of the writer of the message and the Marxist-Leninist ideology on which much propaganda was based.) If they admired communists, they often saw them as potentially powerful champions of the people who could right wrongs. But the specifics of communist ideology often eluded them. Rather than understand communism on its terms, people often understood it on their terms. To most peasants, commemoration of Karl Liebknecht, Rosa Luxemburg, and Lenin—strangely named persons from faraway lands who promoted novel ideas—must have seemed quite peculiar.

In this light, it is clear how little is known about communism and how it was understood at the time of the Nghệ Tĩnh soviets. How did most Vietnamese concretize the message of communism? How, faced with gaps in their understanding of the communist message, did readers and listeners reformulate the message of revolution? Such questions point to the essential plurality of the past. Quite clearly, the gap between the Communist Party's intended message and its actual comprehension by peasants and workers was too wide to bridge in the space of a year.

The Nghệ Tĩnh soviets ultimately failed because rebels lacked organizational and military strength and because the French used overwhelming repression. In Hà Tĩnh province alone, one study claimed that 474 persons were killed and 3,107 thrown in prison during 1930 and 1931 for participation in the uprisings.[83] Nguyen Khac Vien, apparently referring to all of Vietnam, noted that 699 persons were killed in 1930 alone while participating in strikes and demonstrations. By 1932, the French had sent approximately ten thousand Vietnamese political prisoners to jail in Indochina and Guyana.[84] But the "failure" of such uprisings was, as well, the story of a failed attempt to communicate the communist message. The story of much subsequent communist history is a story of the attempt to narrow the gap between intended message and actual concretization, to impose authoritarian readings of communism on audiences, to turn a disparate group of readers and listeners into a more homogeneous audience of the revolutionary word.

VIỆT MINH PROPAGANDIZING AND ITS AUDIENCE, 1941–1945

The Việt Minh's propaganda work of the 1940s took place in a context vastly different from that of the Nghệ Tĩnh soviets ten years before. If not clearly understood by most Vietnamese, communist concepts were certainly better known in 1940 than in 1930. The Indochinese Communist Party had garnered a good deal of publicity, especially in the 1936–1939 period. Before turning to the actual propaganda and the way that it became transformed, I shall pause to sketch out important political and social changes set in motion by the coming of war.

From 1936 to 1939, a Popular Front government led by socialists ruled France. This government relaxed repression in the colonies, and as a consequence, Vietnamese enjoyed more freedom to publish than ever before. A wide variety of Stalinists, Trotskyists, socialists, and independent radicals published their views in the press. Some of these views are surprising: for example, the Marxist Triệu Vân, discussing the proletarian revolution, stated that, "obviously, when classes and all vestiges of classes are wiped out, then government will no longer exist."[85] Utopian views, such as the one above, were mixed with more practical ones focused on the struggle at hand. For example, from 1937, the Indochinese Communist Party began publishing articles on Maoist politics, organizational methods, and guerrilla strategy.[86] "By the eve of the Second World War," Huỳnh Kim Khánh writes, "a confusion of many voices characterized the Vietnamese Communist movement."[87] This confusion attested to the vitality of communism and radicalism in Vietnam. The situation abruptly changed in 1939.

When the French government declared martial law in late August 1939, it arrested many suspected subversives and banned all communist publications. Communists were forced into completely clandestine action. The new Vichy government appointed Admiral Jean Decoux as governor-general of French Indochina in July 1940, and he continued the repression. On 22 November 1940, the southern branch of the Indochinese Communist Party, without confirming its plan with the Central Committee, launched an insurrection. This insurrection was a massive failure. In November and December alone the French apprehended 5,648 suspected communists; eventually as many as 8,000 were arrested.[88] By late February 1942, the governor of Cochinchina could conclude that "the apparatus of the Communist Party [in the south] is almost completely destroyed."[89] Eventually, one hundred communists in the south, including high-ranking cadres like Nguyễn Thị Minh Khai, Nguyễn Văn Cừ, Hà Huy Tập, and Võ Văn Tân, were executed.[90] This uprising shifted the center of the revolution away from the south, to which it had been gravitating, and back to the center and the north. But the repression from 1939 onward did not simply weaken the southern Party: in the center and north, French crackdowns weakened an already debilitated Party as well.[91] This repression set the stage for the united front strategy championed by the Việt Minh.

The Việt Minh (short for Việt Nam Độc Lập Đồng Minh, or Allies for Vietnamese Independence) was created at the Eighth Plenum of the Indochinese Communist Party.[92] This meeting of 10–19 May 1941 in Pác Bó (Cao Bằng province) marked the decisive shift away from a proletarian internationalist line to a united front strategy that emphasized the national liberation revolution. As David Marr has pointed out, the decisions at Pác Bó ignored the Comintern line of the time (that line would change in six weeks).[93] Communist cadres in the Việt Minh now downplayed rhetoric of class struggle in favor of a more inclusive message, one that both addressed the vast majority of Vietnamese and situated them on the Allied side of a global conflict against fascism.

The symbolic economy in which the Việt Minh operated had changed remarkably since 1939. The French administration rounded up suspected subversives and clamped down on freedom of the press, of thought, and of association. In reaction, the Việt Minh formally decided in June 1941 to forgo demonstrations and distribution of tracts and to conduct propagandizing through infiltration and cell building.[94] Propagandizing was aided, ironically, by one aspect of Vichy rule. While the Vichy administration repressed communists harshly, it encouraged Vietnamese to celebrate the "National Revolution." Thus in 1943 Vũ Văn Hiền was free to write that Vietnamese did not need to borrow beliefs or ideologies from afar: one belief "has already been imprinted in our hearts and souls. That is the belief in the Vietnamese nation and race (*chủng tộc*)."[95] Nguyễn Thế Mỹ's 1944 book *Hai bà Trưng khởi nghĩa* (The Trung sisters' uprising) is also a fruit of this growing interest in nationalism. The book uses the uprising of the Trưng sisters against Chinese rule in 40–42 C.E. to reflect on the nature of nationalism and revolution through the ages.[96] In short, the Vichy regime opened up a space to develop a legal, carefully circumscribed but potentially subversive discourse on revolution.

Vietnamese also articulated a range of other options, such as Hòa Hảo millenarianism and pro-Japanese associations. Notably, by the 1940s, intellectuals began to explore the limitations of urbanized and Westernized views of culture. Groping for alternatives, they seriously considered the importance of the countryside and its inhabitants and, more broadly, Vietnamese popular culture. These intellectual shifts form the backdrop to the Việt Minh's reconceptualization of culture and its link to liberation struggle. By stressing the cultural commonalities binding Vietnamese together, the Việt Minh moved from an exclusionary rhetoric of confrontation and division to one that stressed inclusion of all but French, Japanese, and "traitors." It is in this larger semiotic field that one must seek to understand the Việt Minh's clandestine discourse for anti-French and anti-Japanese revolution.

In 1943 the Communist Party defined three fronts: the political, the economic, and the cultural. The Party stated that in its cultural work it would have to acquire the character of the people or nation (*dân tộc hóa*), of the masses (*đại chúng hóa*), and of science (*khoa học hóa*).[97] Following the Party's lead, the Việt Minh set up the Lê Hồng Phong propaganda brigade to develop new and simple propaganda and began publishing a range of newspapers, including its main organ, *Việt Nam độc lập* (Vietnamese independence).[98] In practical terms, the Việt Minh refined its art of propagandizing.

Ironically, as the Việt Minh refined its message, it encountered an unforeseen problem: printing supplies in Vietnam diminished as the war dragged on. Shortages had always bedeviled printers of propaganda, but they now became increasingly acute. The situation worsened as paper imports were cut off and the government rationed paper. Vietnamese started to experiment with the production of paper.[99]

At the beginning of the war, cadres had to travel far to buy paper, while evading police agents on the lookout for anyone who made large purchases of paper. Phạm Văn Hảo, who worked in central Vietnam on the clandestine newspaper *Chiến thắng* (Armed victory), complained that, "whether it was pens, ink, or paper, we lacked everything."[100] *Việt Nam độc lập*, published in the north, printed one hundred to six or seven hundred copies per issue. (This calls into question the claim that the masses "welcomed" and "loved" this newspaper.)[101] The fact that press runs were so low had a deep impact on the nature of Việt Minh propaganda efforts, forcing cadres to rely a great deal on oral methods.

REFINING THE ART OF PROPAGANDIZING:
THE MESSAGE

About ten years ago [i.e., 1928], on hearing the two words *"giai cấp"* (*class*) spoken, we usually pursed our lips and said: what has society done to have classes?!

At that time, we only knew of the nation (*quốc gia*) and compatriots (*đồng bào*). In one country, from the king to the people, all people shared the same bloodline (*huyết thống*), were of the same race, were all brothers and sisters.[102]

Another big shortcoming was not only that of our own people who wrote for the Party newspapers but concerned the political Party line [from 1936–1939]. We called for a democratic people's revolution, but in our newspapers at that time … we only talked of class.… The words "compatriot" (*đồng bào*) [and] "land of our ancestors" (*Tổ quốc*) did not appear in our newspapers, our conversations, or our propaganda leaflets. We had international anniversaries like Labor Day (May 1), Women's Day (March 8), the Day against Imperialist War (August 1), October Revolution Day (November 7), a week to celebrate the anniversaries of the great leaders Lenin, Liebknecht, and Luxemburg (the 3Ls), and the day to celebrate the founding of the Party (January 6) … but as for days to celebrate the nation or people (*dân tộc*), we never acted on them. Reading the newspaper *Tin tức* [The news], many people eulogized the poetry of Dương Lĩnh about the civil war in Spain, but not one poem spoke of our people's exploits against foreign invaders.[103]

In this section I focus on the Việt Minh's 1941–1945 experiences, especially in the mountainous region north of the Red River delta known as Việt Bắc. As the two quotations above illustrate, the Việt Minh moved quickly from the communists' class-centered discourse in the late 1930s to a new message of unity and armed struggle in the 1940s. In 1938 Sơn Trà had accentuated the importance of recognizing divisions in society. Trần Huy Liệu, however, implies that Vietnamese communism succeeded by eliding such divisions and developing a consciousness of acts that brought Vietnamese together, by deepening primordial ties of belonging and place. Liệu also implies that 1930s communists had misread their audience. Both of Liệu's points have merit. But it is no less true that in times of weakness, like 1940 and 1941, communists were forced to renounce ideological purity and reach out to other potential allies. The survival of communism was at stake.[104]

It is safe to say that in the early 1940s most Vietnamese still had murky ideas about the communists. Earlier propagandizing had not effectively conveyed the communist message. After the Việt Minh was formed, many persisted in believing that only communists belonged to the organization. One article summarized popular beliefs about communists in this manner: "Communists fight the French, they requisition lands and property of landlords and capitalists. Communists are thrown in jail."[105]

If examining the Việt Minh message is straightforward, the question of audience turns out to be complex. In reality, the Việt Minh did not aim its publications at only one audience. One can distinguish three: the audience that is assumed by writers and implied by the rhetorical conventions of the text, the actual audience that read the publications, and a third audience that did not read Việt Minh publications but heard about the Việt Minh through oral propagandizing. I will return to the problem of these shifting audiences.

While communists formed the backbone of the Việt Minh, Việt Minh publications played down that fact by underlining that the front comprised a variety of groups.[106] This statement formed part of a larger Việt Minh effort to develop a clear identity for itself. "From the [city] streets to the countryside," one source proclaimed, "from the deep forest to the mines, everyone should know clearly: WHAT IS THE VIỆT MINH? WHAT DOES THE VIỆT MINH DO?"[107]

From the beginning, the Việt Minh tried to counter Vichy propaganda for the "National Revolution." Indochina's Vichy regime, led by Admiral Decoux, launched a massive campaign from 1941 to 1943 that compelled newspapers to print sayings of Maréchal Pétain, changed school curricula, subsidized literary movements, and stressed a "return" to traditional practices and values. The Vichy government subsidized film tours with clips of the Maréchal speaking; it printed thousands of pictures of the French leader and of "traditional" pastoral scenes. It also invented new days of commemoration and embraced old ones. The main targets of Vichy propaganda were French Gaullists and Vietnamese subversives.[108] Around the master themes of "National Revolution" and a celebration of the cult of the Maréchal, the administration invented new holidays and elevated old ones. Joan of Arc returned to favor, and a holiday in her honor was celebrated. Instead of International Workers Day, the Vichy regime celebrated "a Festival of Work and Social Peace."[109]

The Việt Minh struck back by reconceptualizing French holidays. On Bastille Day, one of the key holidays in the French secular calendar, one Việt Minh newspaper argued that Maréchal Pétain had sold out to the German Fascists. He had "transformed the Republic of France into a second Bastille prison."[110] While the Việt Minh used powerful rhetoric, it initially allowed the French administration to determine the parameters of debate. Philippe Devillers has argued that the Việt Minh used a "regime of terror," "a very violent propaganda," and "a certain deception" in its attempts to win over the Vietnamese populace in this period. But for this early period, this notion of a regime of terror may well be exaggerated. Devillers also admits that the population "protected" the Việt Minh and opposed the administration.[111] Only as the French administration lost power to the Japanese and Vietnamese began to suffer from Japanese exactions and then from famine could the Việt Minh make much headway.[112]

The Việt Minh gradually moved from reacting to French administration propaganda to developing a message on its own terms. Cadres developed a sophisticated notion of audience, had great flexibility in propagandizing, and succeeded in writing concrete and interesting tracts. Even in prisons at this time, communists abandoned highly theoretical writings for ones that allotted more space to articles on daily life and literature.[113] While the success of the August General Uprising of 1945 was not attributable to a greater understanding of semiotics, it is nonetheless apparent that Việt Minh writers became more effective at framing the uprising as an act of collective will.

Việt Minh authors addressed their implied audience—the audience implied by the texts themselves and their rhetorical strategies—through a rhetoric of inclusion. They recentered their articles around new key symbols: they addressed compatriots (*đồng bào*), or the people or nation (*dân tộc*), and called for "national salvation" (*cứu quốc*) and "revolution" (*cách mạng*) through a joining together of Vietnamese.

These writings, although more inclusive than earlier communist ones, nonetheless set clear boundaries for the message. They did not welcome the French, the Japanese, "traitorous Vietnamese" (*Việt gian*), and "reactionaries" (*bọn phản động*). The language of class division common to earlier communism disappeared. One publication summarized the new Việt Minh position: "one should not distinguish classes, parties, religion, or people, because the highest interest is of the people (*dân tộc*)."[114]

If the implied audience was very large, encompassing almost all of the Vietnamese people, the actual audience (the people who read Việt Minh publications) was quite small. Because of paper shortages, press runs for Việt Minh publications were low, and these publications became precious commodities. While revolutionary cadres claimed, for example, that *Việt Nam độc lập* targeted a wide audience, this statement must be taken with a grain of salt. Given its small press runs, its greatest function was to bind together different Việt Minh organizations. One Việt Minh book called the newspaper "the soul of salvation organizations in Việt Bắc."[115]

Việt Minh publications pursued several rhetorical strategies to move from the generalized implied audience ("all Vietnamese") to the smaller, actual one ("you, the readers"). They adopted a tone of intimacy, one that sealed a bond between the writer and the reader. Note the friendly, inclusive, and familiar tone of the following 1945 article. It is addressed to readers of *Quân giải phóng* (Liberation Army).

> In response to the wishes of troops (*bộ đội*) and citizens, the newspaper *Liberation Army* is now appearing today for friends.
> *Liberation Army* will be a friend to brigade leaders, political specialists, and fighters....
> *Liberation Army* is a forum for fighters in the Liberation Army and others for military matters. It is hoped that readers all over, and especially comrades in the forces, will send articles and news to journalists so that the new newspaper can reflect the military life in the region and fulfill its responsibility of exchanging their experiences.[116]

Such strategies involved the audience more than many earlier Vietnamese communist texts. They served to establish a sense of group cohesion.

Việt Minh publications presented readers with a range of materials to read. In 1945, for example, *Khởi nghĩa* (Uprising) published articles on the world situation and linked this situation back to that in Indochina. Given the level of detail in these articles (including carefully drawn maps), they must have been based on radio transmissions from Allied forces. Slogans appeared in every issue. Readers and listeners could memorize these slogans easily. Linking the end of hunger to national liberation, one July 1944 poster listed the evocative lines "rice, freedom, independence." The 15 April 1945 issue of *Khởi nghĩa*, appearing six days after the Japanese seized power from the Vichy French government, had the following slogans: "Do not cooperate with the Japanese!" "Expel the Japanese!" "Eradicate Vietnamese, Chinese, and French traitors!" "Independent Vietnam!"[117] The Việt Minh targeted both readers and the larger pool of listeners with such sayings.

Though the Việt Minh commanded a small actual reading audience, it tried to mold this audience to read its texts in a strictly prescribed way. It developed a highly authoritarian model of reading to ensure that the message it sent and the message understood by readers were more or less the same. (The contrast with Nghệ Tĩnh is noteworthy.) It then used these readers to spread the Việt Minh message through oral propaganda to larger and larger circles of people. Writers explained to readers how they should understand newspapers and how they should discuss them in groups. Ideally, one noted, recruits should learn revolutionary ideology through training classes. But when the Việt Minh could not organize such classes, "discussions over books and newspapers are even more necessary."[118]

One article suggested a manner of reading and discussion that, at first glance, strikes one as involving all participants actively. After group members had read articles in the newspaper, this article suggested the following: "At the next meeting, the convener (*chủ tịch*) requests every person to repeat a paragraph or the entire article that he/she had agreed to read. The listeners should ask questions about the meaning of the entire article, the meaning of each paragraph, each word, and the person who agreed to read must explain [to them] clearly. Before turning to the next lesson, the convener sums up the meaning of the entire article and rereads the article one more time."[119] Of course, such a method of reading is highly authoritarian: the convener is the final interpreter. Although listeners are supposed to ask question of the reader, the intent

of such questions is not to underline the open and polysemic nature
of the text but to prevent "erroneous" interpretations from gaining
credence.

The Việt Minh leadership encouraged cadres to learn from the good
and bad experiences of other cadres. One booklet stated that the
main newspaper of the Việt Minh, *Việt Nam độc lập*, "taught cadres
about many work experiences ... gave rise to a spirit of unity in the
mass-organization, [and] criticized the common shortcomings of local-
ities."[120] In short, reading was not a dispassionate act. Through reading
and discussion of it, cadres and others could draw on the experiences of
others to develop correct thinking and "a spirit of unity."

Between the giant implied audience of millions of Vietnamese and the
actual audience of readers lay, as I have mentioned, a third audience:
those Vietnamese who lived in areas where Việt Minh propaganda
groups operated. Front publications repeatedly discussed this audience
and how to reach it. Writers expressed ambivalence about the level of
understanding of this audience, an ambivalence that calls into question
many views of Việt Minh success.

Since Việt Minh cadres were reaching out to a wide audience, the
front encouraged its members to know the horizons of their audience's
world. For example, when speaking with soldiers serving the French, "if
one wanted to spread the revolutionary message, one would have to
speak about how hard the life of a soldier was." But spreading a message
was not enough: one also had to understand this life through experienc-
ing it oneself.[121]

The Việt Minh strived to make its message more relevant and interesting to its audience. Comrades who propagandized had to take the
initiative and look at matters in new ways, or their work would seem
tiresome. "We need to find the initiative to work in small things of daily
life that occur around us," one writer counseled. He suggested that the
American bombing in Indochina, the forced roundup of coolies, and rice
and tax collection could be used to spark discussions and decide on
propaganda techniques. Furthermore, cadres should use different types
of propagandizing, such as singing, and "mix in" ideas about the salvation of the country.[122]

Ultimately, however, the Việt Minh stressed that cadres had to spread
a message that was simple and easy to remember and that listeners could
understand easily: "Whatever methods you use to propagandize, the

contents of propaganda should be limited to these slogans: 'all the people unite,' 'prepare for armed uprising,' 'attack the French and the Japanese,' 'independent Vietnam.' And always position [yourself] in terms of the inner experiences of the masses, using methods that are easy to understand in order to enlighten and gain the trust of the masses."[123]

This message was hammered away. Articles emphasized that cadres were to combine the use of leaflets and banners with oral propagandizing. Cadres were to use any opportunity to reinforce the propaganda message and to be alert for misunderstandings among the target audience. They could do this in numerous ways. They would talk with groups of people to further explain the meanings of slogans and of leaflets. For those who did not understand or who understood incorrectly, they would have to explain it clearly. "One has to be on the lookout for expressions of opinion by all categories of people, every person, in order to thoroughly understand if they are paying attention or are indifferent, if they are happy or resentful."[124] In short, there was a realization that without understanding the audience, the revolution was doomed.

Việt Minh leaders realized that they had to go beyond their own "horizon of expectations" to try to understand those of people unlike themselves. But there are signs that the audience sometimes refused to understand the message on the revolutionaries' terms. These traces of misunderstanding suggest that bridging the gap between the revolutionary and the peasant world was difficult, as the preconceptions that each side brought to the message were so different.

By stressing that its oral propaganda be limited to several slogans, the Việt Minh hoped that, through repetition, such slogans would be imprinted in everyone's minds. But it also realized that, if listeners only heard their message in such abbreviated form, they would frequently understand it incorrectly.[125] Indeed, the extreme brevity and simplicity of these slogans encouraged the listener to fill in the interpretive gaps to make their understanding more concrete. Many of these slogans were abstract, and listeners needed to translate them by appealing to their own experience. What did "all the people unite" mean? Did it mean that Vietnamese should join together under the village elders? Should they form parties? The possibilities were endless.

Việt Minh publications themselves mention that Vietnamese interpreted propaganda in unexpected ways. One author, for example,

claimed that almost all Vietnamese "thirsted for revolution" but lamented that not all Vietnamese understood its meaning. Catholics were
suspicious of the Việt Minh. Others did not believe that the revolution
would succeed or rejected the organization's stated logic for success.
And some Vietnamese simply did not accept that the Việt Minh victory
was due to the unfolding of a Marxist-Leninist logic of history: for
example, some understood the outbreak of war in 1940, the coming of
peace in 1945, and Hồ Chí Minh's entry into Hanoi at the head of troops
as the realization of a sixteenth-century prophecy by Nguyễn Bỉnh
Khiêm![126] As one Việt Minh cadre complained: "Many spread the rumor
that propaganda leaflets are dropped from airplanes, cars, or by people
who can make themselves invisible, like characters in legends or 'knight
errant' (*kiếm hiệp*) stories. Don't these people know that revolutionary
fighters are also people of flesh and blood?"[127]

David Marr has noted that, in August of 1945, "many local groups
calling themselves Viet Minh had almost no idea what the organization
stood for."[128] In short, one cannot simply assume that the Việt Minh
message was transparent and open only to one possible interpretation.
When some Vietnamese believed that invisible beings instigated revolution, it is clear that not everyone had heard the revolutionary message
that the Vietnamese should take charge of their own destiny.

CONCLUSION

Vietnamese communist historiography is structured by interpretive
grids that the Vietnamese Communist Party established after 1945. Since
the histories of these events written in the 1950s by Trần Huy Liệu and
his colleagues,[129] historians have increasingly distanced themselves from
the writings and experiences that should be the basis for these interpretations. Only from the 1990s onward has a scattering of serious research begun to undermine these Communist self-representations and
rethink the nature of Vietnamese radicalism, communism, and power
in the 1920–1945 period.[130] To a certain extent, this process has been
pushed forward by studies that reevaluate the Communist Party and its
leaders by drawing on previously untapped sources. But perhaps more
important, fresh approaches—like focusing on the theme of prisons,
examining the process of the construction of a hero, or integrating the
concept of space into a discussion—have placed communists and their

historiography in a new light. This chapter attempts such a focused inquiry into actual propagandizing, the spread of and appropriation of the Communist message, and the nature of shifts in communist language itself.

The author of the official French account of the Nghệ Tĩnh uprising falls back on a racial explanation for communist success: "pseudo-intellectuals" and "failures" spread communist propaganda, which "had the effect ... of catalyzing the instincts of cruelty characteristic of the yellow race."[131] In this view, the communist message did not contain any possible intellectual truth but fueled the basest instincts of the Vietnamese. In the standard Vietnamese discussions of Nghệ Tĩnh, on the contrary, the communist message "enlightened" the masses. Communists traced some of the failures of the uprising to peasants and workers not heeding the enlightened line of the Communist Party. The argument between French and Vietnamese views, then, is an argument over the ideological truth of communism and its impact on human nature.

The role of the audience is lost in this disagreement. A gap separated the revolutionary language of communist cadres from the practice and understanding of its audience. This language did not "reflect" reality; it played a part in imagining and constructing one. To most readers and listeners, this new language was confusing; the reality that it constructed was not at all clear. Communists introduced new notions of causality, hierarchy, and identity. But they had no monopoly on the way that Vietnamese would understand such notions.

The audience of the communists in Nghệ Tĩnh differed from that of the Việt Minh. On reflection, the symbolic economies of 1930–1931 and of 1941–1945 were starkly different. In 1945, many Vietnamese were familiar with ideological concepts and forms of organization that had been bewilderingly new in 1930. In 1930, for example, many Vietnamese did not know what constituted a political party or the meaning of the word "movement." Such was not the case in 1945. During the Nghệ Tĩnh period, the gap between the intended message and the actual understanding of that message seems to have been exceedingly wide. In 1941–1945, this gap had narrowed, but it never disappeared completely.

The truth that, to succeed in propagandizing, one had to draw on language and beliefs familiar to one's audience was stressed once again by Trường Chinh in 1950. In his article on "popularization" (*dân tộc hóa*), he stated that writers should avoid using foreign words whenever

possible. They should not estrange themselves from the "precious traditions of the people" or hold popular writing in contempt.[132] A following
section on "acquiring a mass character" (*đại chúng hóa*) stated that
writers "should not write a sentence that the average reader cannot
understand" and that writers should not write for the upper class or for
intellectuals.[133]

Trường Chinh's comments are unwittingly ironic. From the point of
view of 1943 or 1950, Trường Chinh's statements make sense. But when
communists first started writing in Vietnamese, they referred to a European reality, with its conceptions of class and human agency, that resonated little with the experiences of most Vietnamese. They used foreign
concepts understood by few and belittled the "precious traditions" of
the people. Communists had radically changed their practices between
1929 and 1945, but they also benefited from the fact that their conceptual vocabulary now circulated widely and no longer sounded "foreign."
Communist signifying practice was on the road to becoming common
signifying practice. Or, as Merleau-Ponty might say, fertile language was
being institutionalized: it no longer needed to be explained.

The change, however, was not simply that the message of communism had spread. Communists learned to pay attention to their audience
to both understand and manipulate it. If communists did not understand
the horizons of their audience's world, they would not be able to tailor
a message to resonate with the life experiences of Vietnamese. A 1950
propaganda guide stated this truth pithily: "A proverb says: 'play music in
a carabao's ears' (*gẩy đờn tai trâu*), ridiculing listeners for not understanding. But if people who propagandize and write and speak are hard
to understand, then *they* are the 'carabaos.'"[134] It was precisely the problem for much of the 1925–1945 period that cadres saw their audience,
and not themselves, as "carabaos."

The propaganda guide insinuates that the relationship between
propagandizer and audience has a dialogical nature to it. After all, prop-
agandizers have to "understand" their audience. This apparent dialogic
edge only slightly masked a different truth: from the 1920s to the 1950s,
the Communist Party moved to more authoritarian models of reading
and understanding than before. There was a tension between this move
to authoritarian models of reading and the fact that readers brought
different life experiences to reading texts, which are open to multiple
interpretations. Ultimately, with the institutionalization of practices of

self-criticism (*tự phê bình*) and ideological indoctrination and rectification (*chỉnh huấn*) under Maoist influence in the 1950s, the limited space of interpretive freedom that cadres had previously enjoyed was narrowed yet further. That development constitutes a different chapter in Vietnamese communism.

Reflecting on the 1929–1945 period, I discern commonalities with the fate of the Javanese *pergerakan* ("movement") that lasted from 1912 to 1926. Like the *pergerakan*, the period from the 1920s through the Nghệ Tĩnh uprising saw Vietnamese introduce new forms of thinking, organization, and protest (such as the "party" and the "meeting") to fellow Vietnamese. As in Java, this period "provided a whole series of new forms and languages in which people could 'say' what they had been unable to 'say.'"[135] In the period after the Nghệ Tĩnh uprising, as in the period after the Javanese *pergerakan*, people began to take this new language for granted.

But what does it mean to say that Vietnamese, like Javanese, had found new language? As this chapter has shown, it is not enough to point to the use of new language and new forms in which people could finally express themselves. Such words have to resonate with the expectations of the audience, or they fall on deaf ears. A few comparative examples may drive this point home. In the Philippines, Ileto has argued, orators in the early period of American rule seized the attention of crowds by making oblique and overt references in their speeches to a preexisting radical discourse that gave meaning to the lives of many Filipinos. They used commemorative events (such as Rizal Day) "not just to remember and pay homage to the past, but to relive its intensity as well."[136] By reaching out, fitfully, to establish a common sentiment of purpose and meaning, speaker and audience bonded to one another. A similar process was at work when so-called communists attempted to seize power in Banten (on Java) in 1926. This call for revolt resonated with the populace precisely because leaders, in their speeches and organizing, emphasized local and Muslim concerns: "even Lenin and the Bolsheviks were portrayed as defenders of Islam."[137] In short, whether one is speaking of the Philippines, the Dutch East Indies, or French Indochina, novel political views only made sense when they could be domesticated and rendered somewhat familiar.

Early Vietnamese communists, faced with the choice of indigenizing communism (as in Banten) or maintaining its ideological purity, usually chose the latter. At first, this severely limited its appeal. Vietnamese often fell back on preexisting frameworks of interpretation, thus subverting the communist message. But as communists slowly succeeded in institutionalizing their language, the range of meanings a word, a sentence, or a text could have narrowed substantially. The story of 1929–1945, then, is a tale of an attempt to construct an audience that would use new language in commonly accepted ways. It was an attempt that had only partially succeeded by 1945: it may not have been until the 1950s that a large percentage of Vietnamese came to understand the communist interpretive matrix.

From Popular Visions of Paradise to the Buddhist Revival

On 1 February 1930, Nguyễn Kim Muôn quit his job in Saigon at the Bank of Indochina. The next year, he moved to the island of Phủ Quốc in the Gulf of Thailand to establish the "Đạo Phật Thích Ca," or the Way of Sakyamuni Buddha. Accompanied by thirty followers of both sexes, he bought ten hectares on the island to grow coconuts. Muôn himself built two temples on Suối Đá Mountain dedicated to the Buddha, the Paradise Temple and the Heavenly Way Temple. In addition he and his followers built four smaller shrines and thirty houses to shelter the faithful.

For seven years, Muôn claimed, he had toiled alone while other religious communities ignored him. Writing to a Vietnamese man in Phnom Penh in 1933, he underlined that "all by myself I built these temples, purified the religion and the Buddhist faith for the greatest good of the community; these are great works. I received no subvention and had to toil without cease to achieve these results: I see this as a true proof of celestial protection that allowed me to spread the religion."[1] But now, Muôn stated, he planned to come down from the mountain to build another temple with the help of others, all in order to spread the message of the Buddha. In the same year, he claimed that two bodhisattvas had descended from heaven and blessed his work.

And how would he spread this message? Muôn's story shows the potential importance of print in spreading the teachings. In 1929, he implored recipients to distribute his Buddhist "catechism." This "would be a great service for our country, worth more than building seventy-two temples." Four years later, he was planning to have his new temple serve as a center for printing prayers and other Buddhist tracts. "Economize on tobacco and betel nut; buy prayers and distribute them free throughout Cochinchina," he stated. After this point, the French seem to lose

interest in Muôn: his actions probably struck them as quirky and ultimately harmless. Muôn drops out of the archival record. But is he so
unimportant? Muôn published over thirty tracts and prayer books, some
of which were reprinted. His story, while far from the usual tales of
political and social change that characterize the writings on his period,
suggests that the printed word was making inroads into a heavily oral
society.

Muôn's story is suggestive in another way. While it is common for
scholars to assert that Confucianism defined the Vietnamese past, Buddhism may have shaped Vietnamese society more profoundly. In the
1930s, the northern scholar Trần Văn Giáp addressed this issue of popular culture. Noting that a village of five hundred people will have both a
temple and a Confucian shrine, he continued: "Nowadays, if you ask
what the Confucian shrine venerates, we can be certain that of those 500
people, only about 50 will know exactly that the Confucian shrine is for
the veneration of Confucius and the sages. But if one goes to the temple,
all 500 persons will know that it is to worship the Buddha. We must recognize that in terms of doing good and avoiding evil, we Vietnamese are
more influenced by Buddhism than Confucianism."[2] Given this statement by a well-known Vietnamese historian, it is surprising that serious
scholarship on the history of Buddhism in Vietnam is so meager.[3] This
chapter takes a small step toward rectifying that neglect. It explores an
important topic: how Vietnamese Buddhism began a major transformation between 1920 and 1945, forming an autonomous realm of discourse
in which printed matter played a key role. I focus on the Mekong delta,
looking at two distinct topics: the Buddhist Revival (*chấn hưng Phật giáo*)
and popular Buddhism.

Few scholars have tackled the topic of the Buddhist Revival.[4] The
followers of this movement, which took place from the 1920s onward,
were dismayed at Vietnamese religious practice. Drawing inspiration
from the Chinese Buddhist revival, they argued forcefully that Vietnamese had to improve their knowledge of key Mahayana Buddhist texts.
Initially, the Buddhist Revival made inroads only among educated Buddhists. The Huế monk and scholar Thích Mật Thể, a partisan of this
movement, doubted its effectiveness: "The great majority of monks in
the temple (*sơn môn*)," he stated, "are still daydreaming or sleeping, and
have not yet done anything to show that they have been aroused from
their slumbers. Although there has been a revival, in reality it has been a

revival in name only."[5] While the Buddhist Revival was ultimately of great significance to Vietnam, its impact from 1920 to 1945 was admittedly limited.

The same cannot be said for popular Buddhism. In the period under study, a popular Buddhism centered on salvation and rebirth in paradise affected more Vietnamese than the so-called Buddhist Revival. It focused on simple acts (such as prayer) to help one escape the wheel of death and rebirth. While focused on practice, popular Buddhism increasingly relied on texts as well, especially in the Mekong delta. These texts included simple catechisms, poetry on Buddhist themes, and fragments of the basic texts of Vietnamese Buddhism (such as the *Amitabha sutra*). Such printed matter, used in combination with oral transmission, multiplied the accessibility of religious texts. In other words, a popular version of religion followed by literate and illiterate believers benefited greatly from printed materials.

The view that Buddhism prospered from 1920 to 1945 goes against the grain of most commentary. French administrators, Marxist critics, and Buddhist intellectuals, who agreed on little, nonetheless concurred that twentieth-century Buddhism had degenerated from a golden age. Reflecting a common belief, Thích Mật Thể dated the Buddhist decline from the late eighteenth century: "Because of ... the war with the Tây Sơn, temples were destroyed [and] the monkhood fell into disorder.... From this point on in history, we find nothing more on which to base a glorious era in Buddhist history."[6]

As a general rule, the French administration saw most monks as poorly educated do-nothings with little influence. It believed that, while Buddhism itself posed no threat to the state, unscrupulous monks and others abused the religion to advance political goals.[7] The iconoclastic Nguyễn An Ninh, who flirted with Marxism, shared the belief that Buddhism had degenerated. Perplexed over why so many Vietnamese were passionately religious, he had a typically elitist response: the people were "extremely ignorant and bewitched."[8] Educated monks and lay followers shared some of these concerns: looking at the condition of monasteries and the people's knowledge of doctrine and ritual, they argued that Vietnamese had sunk into superstition. They believed that most Buddhists had a poor grasp of the Buddha's teachings and practiced a deformed version of the religion.

Despite this rhetoric of decline, one fact stands out: in the years from

1920 to 1945, Vietnamese circulated more Buddhist texts than at any time previously in history. Buddhists used print technology to spread the dharma to wider and wider audiences. They printed five hundred to a thousand different Buddhist texts during this period, many of which were second editions or partial editions. Why? Did they distribute these texts simply to improve their karma, or did they do so because there was a hunger for reading? To what extent did the Buddhist Revival lead to this propagation of texts, and to what extent was it simply an indication of the generalized spread of print culture to Vietnam? Finally, does this propagation of texts indicate that Buddhists formed a separate sphere of discourse insulated from both the concerns of the French colonial state and those of the increasingly Westernizing nationalist elite?

SITUATING VIETNAMESE BUDDHISM

Within the Mahayana branch of Buddhism, two streams of Buddhist thought exerted the greatest influence on Vietnam: the Pure Land (Viet.: Tịnh Độ) and Zen (Ch.: Ch'an; Viet.: Thiền) traditions. Discussing the place of these schools in East Asia, Chappell has commented:

> Pure Land and Ch'an [Zen] are often described as the two major poles of Buddhist practice in East Asia. Pure Land devotees emphasize the inadequacies of their own capacities and the futility of their times; salvation can only be achieved at another time (in the next rebirth), in another place (the Western Pure Land), and through another power (Amitabha Buddha). By contrast, Ch'an affirms the completeness of the present moment and human capacities ... arguing for the non-duality of oneself and the Buddha, as well as the identity of this realm with the Pure Land. Whereas Pure Land devotionalism calls upon an external power, Ch'an affirms self-reliance and rejects dependence on external religious objects.[9]

Vietnamese, like Chinese, selected freely from Pure Land and Zen Buddhism, and showed little interest in defining adherence to a particular sect or school.[10] In terms of popular devotional practice, most Vietnamese Buddhists followed a simple version of Pure Land doctrine. Indicating that Zen exerted greater influence over learned than popular Buddhism, the scholar and Buddhist monk Thiều Chửu noted:

If one asked Buddhists in our country what school they belonged to, 99 percent would reply that they belonged to the Pure Land school. If one asked what one had to do to be a Pure Land believer, then most would reply: The Saha world [i.e., this world of suffering] is very miserable. One must pray to be reborn out of it to enjoy the pleasures of paradise. If one asks what one must do to be reborn in paradise, the majority will say that you need only pray to the Buddha, pray to be quickly released from this world to go over to that shore [i.e., to the Pure Land].[11]

Pure Land Buddhism focuses on prayer and faith, not on rigorous textual study, mastery of Tantric techniques, or meditation practice. The rewards of faith are not achieved in this world. And yet, given the Buddhist belief that we are born into endless cycles of death and rebirth, and can only escape this cycle through rebirth into a higher existence (e.g., as a bodhisattva), what is one mere lifetime?

In Vietnam, scholars have slighted the study of Pure Land beliefs and practices. They have often presented the Lý and Trần dynasties (1009–1400) as the high point of Buddhist influence, when the dominant "schools" of Vietnamese Zen (Vinitaruci, Vô Ngôn Thông, and Thảo Đường) were founded. From this "golden age," they argue, Vietnamese Buddhism entered a slow, uneven decline. But did it? The record is far more ambiguous. Nguyễn Lang argues that "the number of temples and monks in the period we call one of decline continued to increase," and Phan Đại Doãn suggests that while Buddhism declined in political power, its influence among the populace may have increased. An influx of Chinese monks from Guangdong appears to have revived the sangha in the seventeenth and eighteenth centuries.[12] Indeed, from Hội An to Gia Định (what was to become Saigon) and into the Mekong delta, Chinese temples dotted the landscape. Buddhist influence was most marked in the center and the south, where the Nguyễn lords presided at the head of a militarized Buddhist state for much of the seventeenth and eighteenth centuries.

Nguyen Tu Cuong has argued for a more fluid understanding of Buddhism and its impact on Vietnam. He attacks the common view that the dominant Zen schools were founded in the Lý and Trần periods. Furthermore, he suggests that a focus on carefully delimited "schools" misrepresents "many hidden cross-currents and intermingling" that characterized premodern Vietnamese Buddhism.[13] For example, "some of the most beloved eminent monks in Vietnamese Buddhist history ... are the wonder-workers, healers, and magicians. These monks were believed to possess magical powers such as prophetic abilities, the ability to cure disease, and the ability to bring rain."[14] Indeed, numerous currents of beliefs and practices were interspersed with ones based on the Buddhist classics. Buddhists often believed in divination, astrology, and the existence of powers to confer invulnerability. Among other things, Vietnamese incorporated fertility cults; cults to tigers, dogs, whales, and rocks; worship of Indian gods and Cham lingas; and beliefs in magic and Khmer healing arts into their beliefs.[15]

Vietnamese incorporated a range of local deities, some of them not Vietnamese in origin, into their Buddhist pantheon. The Cham world of central and southern Vietnam, for example, was not completely obliterated: it was often refashioned into a Vietnamese idiom. In Nha Trang, Vietnamese worshipers have given the name "Tháp Bà" (Stupa of the Lady) to the religious complex of the Cham female deity Po Nagar. They have appropriated it, linga and all, into a Buddhist pantheon.[16]

Finally, the Vietnamese constructed temples, which (through their names) linked the Vietnamese landscape to East Asian and Indian Buddhism. For example, the name of the Xá Lợi temple in Saigon literally refers to a reliquary (Skt. *sarira*) of the Buddha—and recalls King Asoka's attempt to define the realm of Buddhism by establishing stupa reliquaries all over the Indian subcontinent. The name of the Linh Sơn temple (literally, "Magic Mountain") refers to Mount Grudhakuta near the city of Rajagriha, where the Buddha preached the dharma.[17] Vietnamese, in other words, remapped the landscape to fit into pre-existing symbolic structures.

In this process of remapping the environment, texts played a key role. Works such as the *Sutra of the Master of Healing* (*Dược sư*) and the *Universal Gate Chapter* (*Phổ môn*) of the Lotus Sutra circulated widely in their Chinese versions.[18] But along with sacred texts, Vietnamese developed other tastes. Several popular Nôm texts, such as the *Tale of Kiều* (*Truyện Kiều*), discussed Buddhist themes. Others, such as the *Story of Guanyin–Thị Kính* (*Quan Âm Thị Kính*) and *Guanyin of the Southern Seas* (*Nam Hải Quan Âm*), centered explicitly on Buddhist themes and in particular on women becoming bodhisattvas.[19] Indeed, tales about the female Buddha Quan Âm (Ch.: Guanyin; Skt.: Avalokitesvara) were highly popular in Vietnam, where a cult to her dates back at least to the eleventh century.²⁰ They continued to be popular in the twentieth century.

Vietnamese combined textual transmission of the dharma with oral practice and ritual. Commenting on the importance of oral transmission, one text quotes the Diamond Sutra: while giving alms is very precious, no action is as meritorious as reciting and explaining four lines of the sutra so that people may hear.²¹ Devotees also practiced *kể hạnh*, in which they told stories about the lineage founder. In this temple practice, "the voices of older persons were interpolated with those of young women. The women would learn by heart the words that they would narrate. If they forgot anything or made mistakes, the masters, using copies of the *Khóa Hư* and the *Tam Tổ Thực Lục*, would correct or fill in the missing parts."²² Vietnamese also sung *hát kệ*, or songs about the founders of the lineage. "Listeners could not understand completely the deep meaning of the Buddhist litanies, but they could enjoy the melodies."²³

The above examples show that marking a divide between literate and popular cultures is impossible. Reading and recitation, as well as orality and literacy, were intertwined, thus extending the reach of texts over a mostly illiterate populace. Several writers noted that many monks themselves had heard others explain the dharma but did not themselves understand Chinese texts and have a clear sense of their meaning.²⁴ This opened the way for believers to fashion a Buddhism in line with their own practical and interpretive concerns.

Thus, Nguyen Tu Cuong's comment that "hidden cross-currents and intermingling" characterized premodern Vietnamese Buddhism remained true in the twentieth century. Complaints that writers made about religious practice also bear this out. The northern monk Thiều Chửu stated, for example, that most Vietnamese saw Buddhism as "magical" (*thần dị*) and "bizarre" (*kỳ quái*); they valued monks for telling fortunes, reading physiognomy, predicting the past and future, and similar abilities, and not for moral character or knowledge of doctrine.²⁵ Nguyễn An Ninh criticized monks "who sold prayers, amulets, and magical incantations [*chú*, or *dharani*] in order to make themselves rich."²⁶ Mộng Vân chastised believers who worshiped sincerely and knew the correct rites but did not understand the meaning of sutras or prayers. He compared such persons to lazy and ignorant pupils who could not bear to listen or study but then kowtowed before their teacher, beseeching him to pass them in the examination so that they could gain fame.[27] Nguyễn Khắc Hiếu zeroed in on women's failings in particular: he opined that women were excessively fond of divination and giving offerings, and stated that this was a "great harm" for the country.[28]

Such comments are laments by the highly literate over the failings of those who do not share their reverence for texts. They assume that texts should not bewitch or seduce, that accuracy in reading is important, and that there is such a thing as an authoritative interpretation of a text. But historically, in Vietnam and elsewhere, documents have served multiple cultic, ritual, and interpretive needs. These complaints suggest, ironically, that in its broad outlines, Vietnamese Buddhist practice had always been inclusive. It was impregnated with popular beliefs and practices that devotees of the text might frown upon, but this has been true of Buddhism everywhere.

Given the above observations, the common notion that Vietnamese Buddhism declined from a position of Zen authenticity should be questioned. Despite the repeated statements by Buddhists that their Way was in decline, Buddhism in the 1920s probably differed little in its broad outlines from a century earlier. Popular texts, while discussing the decline of Buddhism in general spiritual terms, rarely discussed "sociological" issues like the health of the sangha. They focused on conceptions of Paradise, the Pure Land, and Nirvana.[29] In contrast, partisans of the Buddhist Revival did initiate discussions of the monastic order and its malaise; Buddhism's decline was not in question for such writers. Whatever the truth of such assertions of decay, it does seem that educated Vietnamese had a greater awareness than before about the gap between practice and precept.

MEKONG DELTA BUDDHISM AND PRINT

As a general rule, writers have observed that the culture and customs of the inhabitants of the Mekong delta differed from those in the north. The eighteenth-century writer Trịnh Hoài Đức wrote that southerners venerated the Way of the Buddha, believed in spirit mediums, and ascribed great importance to female divinities.[30] More recently, Sơn Nam, citing an unidentified scholar, has asserted that in more recent times "the people of Saigon and the delta, fundamentally, adhere to a particular form of popular religious belief: those of women and the poor."[31] Because of their lack of money or time, on the one hand, they do not go to the temple often, and they sometimes forget rituals; on the other hand, they go on pilgrimages, eat vegetarian food, and engage in other such practices.

Both statements have merit. Today, for example, cults to women saints are still popular: witness the attraction of the cult to the Black Maiden at Black Maiden Mountain near Tây Ninh and the attraction of Quan Âm, or Guanyin, the female Buddha. Sơn Nam has further noted that, in Saigon, the "popular classes" liked to go to Hindu temples to worship the female deity Mariamman ("Rain Mother," originally a south Indian form of the Great Goddess, or Mahadevi). Today that goddess is variously referred to by Vietnamese as the Black Lady, the Indian Lady, the Lady of Tây Ninh, the Lady of the Realm, and Lady Buddha.[32] These cults illustrate the power of cults to mothers and female deities in Vietnamese popular religion. Clearly, canonical texts do not define the full range of Vietnamese religious practice. Even the extremes of Mekong delta religion seem more notable: it is here, for example, that millenarian and apocalyptic movements were most likely to be found in Vietnam.[33]

From the late nineteenth century onward, Buddhist print and manuscript culture began to change slowly. Vietnam saw a slow reorientation from small centers of knowledge (e.g., Buddhist temples, villages with prominent literary lineages) scattered around the countryside to two major centers of power and production of knowledge: Hanoi and Saigon. These changes were partly attributable to the French, who established their political and cultural mark on these two cities. Yet the French were never able to transform the production and circulation of printed material completely. Countless pilgrimage sites, temples, and other sites attractive to the faithful remained scattered across the landscape, served as centers of religious prosletyzing, and linked Vietnamese both to local cults and practices and to the larger world of East Asian Buddhism. They remained as a counter to the new, more secular city culture that arose in the twentieth century.

One reason for the Mekong delta's peculiarities is simple: historically, this had been a thinly populated zone under nominal Khmer control. While Vietnamese settled in Saigon as early as the seventeenth century, large parts of the western Mekong delta remained wild or thinly inhabited. The main exceptions were Hà Tiên (on the Gulf of Thailand), Vietnamese military outposts in places like Châu Đốc, and the scattered Khmer settlements near rivers and the sea. The wildness of this frontier region is attested to by Vietnamese reports of tigers, which still roamed parts of the western Mekong delta up through the nineteenth century.[34]

Up to the twentieth century, one of the wildest places in the south was probably the far western part of the Mekong delta. Political refugees, vagabonds, mystics, and monks favored this sparsely inhabited zone on the border between Vietnam and Cambodia. Pilgrims from all over the delta gathered here: Vietnamese worshipers incorporated a former Khmer site of power in Châu Đốc, the Seven Mountains on the current Vietnamese-Cambodian border, into a Buddhist worldview.[35] Hue Tam Ho Tai notes: "It was an article of faith among the Strange Scent of Precious Mountain (Bửu Sơn Kỳ Hương) sectaries that Maitreya Buddha would be reborn in the Seven Mountains of Châu Đốc province, hence the idea that these were precious mountains (bửu sơn)."[36]

In addition to attracting lay pilgrims, this area also attracted religious practitioners who established temples. At least two prominent Buddhists from the nineteenth and twentieth centuries lived in this area. They included the nineteenth-century Buddha Master of the Western Peace and Huỳnh Phú Sổ (founder of the Hòa Hảo sect in 1939), who both claimed to be reincarnations of the Buddha. The inhabitants of the region "are very religious," an outside observer wrote in 1935, and "practice evil magic (tà thuật) that we cannot fully understand."[37] Indeed, a Vietnamese monk claimed in 1929 that, in the Phi Lai temple of Châu Đốc, many "concealed heroes" lived, including warriors who had sprouted out of peas when a monk with supernatural powers uttered an incantation.[38]

Not surprisingly, some Vietnamese worshipers associated this part of the Mekong delta with Mahayana notions of the Western Paradise. This religious significance has endured: as two Vietnamese observers put it in 1955, "Anyone except an atheist or a sceptic recognizes that the Seven Mountains region harbors very strange and mysterious things." They underlined: "But what is most noteworthy is the mysterious and magical power of [its] deep forests and high mountains. Invisible beings on mountain peaks are always ready to show friends the mountains' miraculous powers."[39] In short, the Seven Mountains region, with its sites of sacred power and with religious leaders who amassed followers, attracted a great number of pilgrims and in so doing helped to define popular religious beliefs and practices of the Mekong delta as a whole.

It was in this context that Buddhist texts circulated in the Mekong delta. Before the advent of large print runs, Buddhist manuscripts and printed materials were but one constituent of the Vietnamese symbolic world. The symbolic transformation of the Mekong delta was thus an attempt to establish a human mark on a frontier wilderness, to "Vietnamize" an area that already had scattered Khmer and Chinese settlements, and to link the area to preexisting religious conceptions. Common landmarks in East Asian Buddhism were linked to local deities, Buddhist temples, and the practice of pilgrimage to the Seven Mountains region.

The print culture of the Mekong delta reflected the eclectic religiosity of the region. While books on Buddhist history and philosophy did circulate, far more common were fragments of sutras important to Zen and Pure Land practice, commentaries on the sutras, instructional manuals on prayer, or prayers themselves. Tracts with titles like *Niệm Phật qui tắc* (Method for praying to the Buddha) abounded. Short and relatively simple, these latter publications were printed by Saigon and delta publishers. In these prayer tracts and in the introductions to sutras, the correct ways to recite and pray are favorite topics.

A few Buddhist groups printed monthly magazines and polemical religious texts. The monks Lê Khánh Hòa and Thiện Chiếu published the first Buddhist reviews in Vietnamese history, *Pháp âm* (The sound of the law) (1929) and *Phật hóa tân thanh niên* (New Buddhist youth).[40] The first issue of *Pháp âm* had a press run of ten thousand copies, a very high number for a religious magazine.[41] Other Buddhists in Saigon, Trà Vinh, Huế, Hanoi, Bà Rịa, and Sóc Trang also put out Buddhist magazines.[42] The Tam Bảo temple in Rạch Giá even published a newspaper, as did an association of Pure Land disciples in Cholon.[43] But these periodicals reached a limited audience: publishers rarely printed more than five hundred to three thousand copies of an issue. With their difficult and abstruse philosophical debates, they catered to highly educated Buddhists. In contrast, the simpler Pure Land tracts found a broader audience.

The question of audience has always been a key concern for Buddhists. They have understood that different individuals have different capabilities, and not everyone can appreciate the Buddha's wisdom in an equally profound way. In Vietnam (as in many other Buddhist countries), the fact that many of the sacred texts were in Chinese added a barrier to comprehension. Ironically, this did not lead to the quick eradication of Chinese in religious ceremonies: the Chinese language had greater staying power in the religious sphere than in other realms of discourse. Monks, for example, were supposed to learn to read the sutras in the "original" Chinese characters. And although the vast majority of believers could not read Chinese, they appear to have accorded it some reverence.

Despite the staying power of Chinese, Vietnamese began to be used increasingly in Buddhist practice. More and more catechismic texts and fragments of Buddhist sutras appeared in romanized script from the 1920s on. To supplement completely romanized works, Buddhists sometimes printed ones that transliterated the Chinese writing or that presented Chinese characters side by side with the romanized equivalents. Readers could choose from a variety of textual forms.

For the average reader, early translations from Chinese were probably difficult to understand: for one, they contained a very high percentage of erudite Sino-Vietnamese words. Later translations had a more colloquial (and "Vietnamese") flavor. In the past, readers had relied on authoritative Chinese versions, such as those of Kumarajiva; now, the heterogeneity of translations gave rise to a plethora of interpretations.

Scattered evidence supports the claim that Buddhist literature appealed to a wide audience. First of all, it was gender-inclusive. Buddhist articles and catechismic texts often use the phrase "male and female believers" (*thiện nam tín nữ*), a kind of locution absent from other Vietnamese printed works. This inclusionary phrase underlines the importance of women in Vietnamese Buddhism and contrasts sharply with the male-centered discourse of Vietnamese Confucianism. Beyond such textual clues, it is known that Buddhism held great appeal to women. Many Buddhist tracts list the names of persons who gave money to defray printing costs, and one can identify a high proportion of women among them.[44]

Second, Buddhist texts influenced oral culture. Unlike many other texts, Buddhist ones were often meant to be read out loud. Catechisms, for example, combined instructions for praying with the prayers themselves. Monks read sutras out loud, thus ensuring that the texts could reach the literate and the illiterate, rich and poor, and men as well as women. Temples, wandering monks, and book hawkers distributed Buddhist tracts in the countryside. Finally, some devout Buddhists sold tracts for a low price or gave them away: the poor and well-off alike could have access to them.[45]

Third, popular imagery, often sold during the Tết holidays, complemented these Buddhist texts. Durand estimated that before World War II Hanoi artisans manufactured about 1,800,000 pictures each year; "at Tết, popular imagery was sold in Hanoi and in all the villages of the delta."[46] The same held true of the south. These images often showed religious figures or illustrated scenes from religious poems (such as *The Story of Quan Âm and Thị Kính*).

Given the low literacy rate of Vietnamese, most Vietnamese directly encountered the Buddhist message through oral transmission and popular imagery. Cultural brokers, such as literate monks, spread the textual message far and wide as well. But the slowly increasing popularity of Buddhist texts, demonstrated in the printing of works designed to help in the practice of rituals at home, suggests that rural society, in which oral means of communication predominated, was slowly changing.

Vietnamese read, heard, used, and transformed Buddhist works in multiple ways. Buddhist monks and nuns often attached great importance to the correct technique, comportment, and sincerity in prayer.[47] Monks and followers usually read prayers out loud, often accompanied by the ringing of a bell and the beating of a wooden fish.[48] A nun argued that one must recite the sutras before knowing their meaning in order to discipline one's nature; only then can one release one's heart from its bonds. "A person's heart is like a gibbon in the forest, like an untamed horse": if one frees it, it will wander all over. But if one keeps one's eyes on the book and expands one's understanding, then daily recital of the sutras and disciplining one's heart to be pure will help the reciter to become a Buddha of the Western Paradise.[49] As for prayers, it did not matter whether or not one prayed "quickly or slowly, silently or aloud." It was, however, important to have "a completely respectful heart."[50] Such, at least, was the model that Buddhists should strive to emulate.

In practice, even monks often conducted themselves poorly and read badly. Trần Quang Thuận lamented that many of them recited the sutras incorrectly: they recited words in the wrong order and yelled without the faintest idea what they were saying. One reason: many could not read Chinese characters. As for the populace at large, this same writer counseled those praying that when they were standing "before an altar to the heavens, the Buddha, spirits, or sages, one should not laugh or joke, say anything ill-mannered, chew betel or smoke, wear dirty clothes, or be in rags that expose the body to the outside."[51] One gathers from the above list that such practices may have been common.

Many Vietnamese valued Buddhism for its magical side and expressed little interest in the particularities of textual interpretation. Many of them believed in the efficacy of *chú*, or *dharani*, that could supposedly help protect the reader from harm or misfortune; these texts, in Sino-Vietnamese transliterations of Sanskrit, made no sense to the reader or listener but were held to have magical power.[52] Others believed that amulets, with Chinese writing on them, could confer magical power on them. But this magical power was often channeled into social uses, as when sectaries who took part in the 1916 Phan Xích Long rebellion in the south thought that their amulets made them invulnerable to police bullets.

In the twentieth century, Buddhist texts continued to be created, printed, circulated, read, and heard in ways quite different from other texts. Buddhism and secular discourse occupied social, ritual, and symbolic spaces that overlapped but were never identical. Geographically, political materials (including Marxist writings) tended to circulate in and around cities. In contrast, Buddhist materials circulated more in the countryside. Women formed the largest audience of Buddhist preaching, which contrasted with the public sphere of print in general, where men made up the primary audience. Buddhist materials were produced the most in the south: for whatever it is worth, the southerner writer and monk Thiện Chiếu suggested that northerners tended to put all their energy into making a living, not into religion.[53]

For all the attention I have given to the local developments that shaped Vietnamese and Mekong delta Buddhism, it is important to remember that a broader Buddhist world shaped the circulation of discourses. Historically, Vietnamese Pure Land and Zen teachings drew on Chinese schools. In the modern era, conversations taking place throughout the Buddhist world—from China to Siam and Cambodia and on to Vietnam—shaped Vietnamese encounters with the Way of the Buddha. Chinese immigrants to Vietnam may have influenced Vietnamese Buddhist practice as well. Such was the transnational context in which the Buddhist Revival was launched.

THE BUDDHIST REVIVAL AND THE PUSH FOR
TEXTUAL ORTHODOXY

By the 1920s, the religious world of southern Vietnam was changing. On the one hand, French colonialism influenced daily life in the south more profoundly than in the north: from the penetration of the capitalist economy to the French state's nominal supervision of Buddhist affairs, southern Vietnamese perceived change in the wind. Some of them became distraught over questions of moral and spiritual decay. "All countries are the same," the writer Viên Hoành stated in 1923. "Rituals and customary practices are the foundation of society." But, Viên Hoành observed, while some Vietnamese championed progress and civilization, they appeared to "want to destroy [old] rituals and customary practices."[54] Some writers argued that such persons held nonsensical and dangerous views. In particular, they asserted that everyone needed a *đạo*, or religious and ethical Way: "a person without a Way is no different from a country without people [or] a tree without roots."[55] Nonetheless, given the common perception that Buddhism was in decay, it was not at all clear which path Vietnamese should take.

The Buddhist Revival was one response to this moral anomie. Thích Thanh Từ implies that this movement began as early as 1911, but the first major actions of its proponents date from 1920. In that year, two senior monks from Tuyên Linh temple, Từ Phong and Lê Khánh Hòa, established the Hội Lục Hòa "in order to unite the monks on the founders' death anniversaries at the temples and to launch a movement to revive Buddhism in the six provinces [i.e., southern Vietnam]." With this action, monks gave organizational form (linking far-flung temples) to their desire for revival. In the decade that followed, Từ Phong, Lê Khánh Hòa, and monks at other large temples in the south opened classes to teach about the sutras and monastic discipline.[56] Southern newspapers like *Đông Pháp thời báo* published articles that discussed Buddhism and called for its renovation.

Faced with the perceived decline of Buddhism, some southerners turned to the Cao Đài. This religion, founded in the south in 1926 by Ngô Văn Chiêu, drew on Confucianism, Buddhism, and Christianity. It was structured on the model of the Catholic church, with a clear ecclesiastical hierarchy. Followers worshiped a pantheon of selected Vietnamese and foreign heroes. The Cao Đài extended its reach with the extensive use of published materials, including posters, to gain converts. The rise of this religion siphoned away Buddhist believers. In some cases, the Cao Đài took over Buddhist temples. In 1927, Nguyễn Mục Tiêu expressed his bewilderment at Cao Đài growth:

> I don't know if I should be happy or afraid: happy because in my situation today, I scorn base material things and turn toward the spiritual path; or afraid, because in [this] era the hearts and minds of our country's people are in turmoil (*rối loạn*), are no longer able to distinguish orthodoxy from heresy, no longer want to accept the order and discipline of the religions of the world, but want to create a topsyturvy religion (*đạo lộn xộn*) that's like a Western "Salade russe"—such is the Cao Đài's new religion.[57]

Tiêu ended up attacking the Cao Đài sect and arguing that Vietnamese needed to revive Buddhism.[58]

If the perceived decline of Buddhism vexed believers, the rise of the Cao Đài from 1926 on marked a turning point in discussion about the Buddhist Revival. Up to that point, lay Buddhists and monks had discussed the need to rescue Buddhism from its decrepitude but had accomplished little. The Cao Đài directly threatened Buddhists and pushed believers to fight back. In this sense, those who championed the Buddhist Revival were reacting to events within Vietnam.

In key ways, however, the Buddhist Revival reached beyond Vietnam to draw inspiration from other Asian countries. Thiện Chiếu argued that "the problem the Buddhist Revival needed to resolve was to provide our citizens with a base of correct beliefs."[59] But where would such beliefs come from? Vietnamese Buddhists noted with approval the renovation of Theravada Buddhism in Thailand.[60] They reserved their greatest interest, however, for the Chinese Buddhist revival. Monks read Chinese Buddhist reviews from China and translated a few works by Chinese reformers into Vietnamese. They heeded Tai Xu, one of the most important Chinese monks of the twentieth century, who called in the 1920s for a religious revival: "Aroused by the destruction of temples ... I launched a movement to defend the religion, propagate the faith, reform the order, and promote education."[61] Showing the influence from the north, Thiện Chiếu translated *Phật học tổng yếu* (Fundamentals of Buddhism) from Chinese into Vietnamese to introduce compatriots to new currents of thought from China.

By 1929, the Buddhist Revival was gaining adherents and developing an institutional base. In that year, a prominent monk wrote: "Now, many virtuous persons (*vị đạo đức*) in the south want to propagate Buddhism so that everyone can know which religious beliefs are useful, not to venerate Buddhism in a superstitious manner, not to curry favor with the Buddha, make offerings, bow, and pray, [all] for one's personal good fortune. That completely misses the goals of Buddhism."[62] In the same year, this movement for renewal of Buddhism could apparently count on the support of fifteen temples. They, with the support of some well-off lay benefactors, ordered 1,500 books from Shanghai publishers as well as French books on Buddhism. These works were housed in the movement's library at the Linh Sơn temple in Saigon.[63]

By the early 1930s, the movement, centered on the Linh Sơn temple, linked Buddhist monks, nuns, and lay believers throughout the Mekong delta. Buddhist study associations emerged, led by monks, nuns, and lay followers. The 1934 statutes of the Buddhist Studies and Mutual Help Association of Sóc Trăng (in the Mekong delta) give a typical view of why Buddhism had declined and what the aims of these new Buddhist associations were:

> Buddhism in southern Vietnam has declined because no schools exist and monks lack sutras and books to study. There are no collections of books translated from Chinese into romanized script for the faithful to use to verse themselves in doctrine.
>
> Consequently, the Thiên Phước temple (Kế An market), Sóc Trăng, has founded a Buddhist studies and mutual aid association ... to spread the Buddhadharma (*Phật pháp*) and to enlighten.[64]

The monk Lê Khánh Hòa, a major force in the Buddhist Revival, also urged Buddhists to cooperate with one another, build libraries, carry out research on the sacred texts of Buddhism (especially the Tripitaka, or three-part "canon" of Buddhism), translate the Tripitaka from Chinese into romanized Vietnamese, and popularize it so that everyone could read, understand, and follow the Buddhist way.[65] Vietnamese also translated works of the Chinese Buddhist revival into Vietnamese. To realize such ambitious goals, adherents called for better instruction for monks.

By the 1930s, proponents of revival could see cause for celebration. At least some of them looked at Buddhism's struggle against the Cao Đài with less alarm. Thanks to the Southern Buddhist Study Association's actions against the Cao Đài and other "enemies" of Buddhism, one pamphlet proclaimed, Buddhists of the lay believers' Pure Land sect in the countryside "are now able to recite the sutras . . . in peace . . . without anyone daring to stop them."[66] At the same time, proponents realized that the Buddhist Revival had a long way to go. A 1932 *Từ Bi âm* (Sound of compassion) editorial despaired: "The majority of monks today chant prayers and look at Chinese books in darkness, in ignorance, not understanding their meaning. It is all the more comprehensible that believers don't understand the doctrine (*đạo lý*). Not understanding, how can they avoid heresy and follow orthodoxy?"[67] This comment reflects a common refrain in twentieth-century discussions of Vietnamese Buddhism: that Chinese religious texts have become indecipherable. Revivalists also worried that the inability to read Chinese would lead to poor ritual practice. One writer, comparing the monks' reading of the sutras at the temple to the muttering of "secret incantations," concluded: "How can it be that Buddhism is not in decline?"[68]

The repeated claims of Buddhist decay and decline, and the need for a renaissance of sorts, suggest that the writings of the Buddhist Revival are characterized by rhetorical excess. They assert that the revival stands for a renunciation of heretical and superstitious thought, for rescuing Buddhism from perdition, and for creating a new, orthodox Buddhism. The revivalists targeted the Buddhist practice of the Mekong delta and the rest of Vietnam in their attacks. Although proponents of the Buddhist Revival stressed that their movement opposed the degeneracy of doctrine, one can see their arguments through a different prism: as a movement by literate, text-oriented monks to develop a print culture that would eradicate the practices of an oral culture.

To Revivalists, one of the key problems facing Vietnamese Buddhism was a lack of Buddhist scriptures circulating in the country. Most monks and followers knew fragments of sutras (if at all), but they were incapable of placing these fragments in the larger framework of schools of Mahayana Buddhism. Many Vietnamese monks were unaware of the long history of disputes between Pure Land and Zen schools in China. Furthermore, Vietnamese knowledge of texts on monastic discipline seems to have been poor. In short, Revivalist monks saw Vietnamese Buddhists becoming too much a part of the Vietnamese landscape and acquiring the particular vices of Vietnamese as a whole. They strongly advocated, then, a turn to the text to move from the particularities of

Vietnam to link up again with the universal message of East Asian Mahayana Buddhism. They assumed that the propagation of texts in itself would be a prime motivator in the change to more orthodox and text-oriented practices.

This reassertion of Buddhist teachings brought the wider Buddhist world to the Mekong delta. As a result of the turn to China and the translation of key Chinese texts, new currents of thought penetrated Vietnamese consciousness. Vietnamese Buddhists, never very print-oriented, began to read debates over the nature of Buddhism, the relationship of Buddhism to science, whether there was a soul or not, and the latest writings of the Chinese monk Tai Xu translated into Vietnamese. By the 1930s, Vietnamese were even reading arguments from China that Buddhism and science should fuse together instead of opposing one another.

The tensions and contradictions of the Vietnamese Buddhist Revival were manifested in the writings of Thiện Chiếu, one of the most prominent monks to introduce new currents of thought from China. Thiện Chiếu seemed to want both to return to orthodoxy and to transcend it. Like many of his fellow Revivalist monks, he was dispirited at the state of Vietnamese Buddhist practice. In 1927, he wrote that the majority of monks "did not know their duties and responsibilities"; they were "superstitious [and] only knew how to light the incense and pray to the Buddha and protecting spirits." Furthermore, they treated the temple as a kind of "insurance company."[69] In 1929, Thiện Chiếu took his criticisms further by taking a swipe at rich patrons of Buddhism: "The rich, with their slave natures, don't realize that ... happiness and misfortune are caused by one's own actions, but imagine that rewards and punishments are handed down by a divine power; not only can they never understand deeply the Buddhadharma (*Phật lý*), but furthermore, they are a kind of poison that will destroy Buddhism."[70]

Thiện Chiếu believed that Buddhism was atheistic. He belonged to the group of Revivalists who engaged modernity and science. Others, however, promoted the revival in order to encourage "correct" or "orthodox" thought. Their quest was fraught with difficulties. How can one define orthodoxy in the Mahayana context? One can try to argue that one is faithful to the teachings of a particular school like the Pure Land. But unlike Theravada Buddhists, who arguably have a Pali textual core and an orthodox, unchanging, tradition, Mahayana Buddhists have a difficult time delimiting a canon and an orthodox practice. Further-more, Vietnamese Buddhists tend to locate orthodoxy not in the original Pali and Sanskrit texts, but in Mahayana ones written in Chinese. Some of these texts were composed in China long after the Buddha's death.[71]

I will sidestep the vexed question of whether or not there is such a thing as Mahayana orthodoxy by accepting for the moment that some writers invoked notions of orthodoxy to promote their particular understanding of revival. This revival can be seen as a dialogue among educated monks and lay followers, a conversation in which readers and writers came up with a wide variety of interpretations of the meanings of *suy đồi* (decline, decadence) and *chấn hưng* (improve, make prosper, revive). The constant call for revival continued into the next few de-cades, although Vietnamese never shared a common understanding of the concept. The notion of *chấn hưng*, or revival, was plastic enough to incorporate all sorts of possible changes. In 1940, for example, a north-erner from Hải Dương province suggested, in an essay on the revival, that it would help if different ranks of Buddhists distinguished them-selves by wearing differently colored lotus seals (*hạng dấ hoa sen*)![72]

While partisans of the Buddhist Revival often reiterated longstanding concerns, social changes often shifted the framework of this debate and thus gave it different meanings. For example, proponents of revival drew a distinction, implicitly, between themselves (a group of textual exegetes who could read Chinese) and the great number of ignorant, superstitious monks who peopled the sangha. But as the explosion of cheap or free religious tracts in the 1930s indicates, Vietnamese who did not know Chinese could increasingly gain access to the Buddhist message. Clearly, the rise of vernacular religious texts took some control of religious orthodoxy out of the hands of such highly trained exegetes and allowed more and more Vietnamese to interpret these texts on their own.

The advocates of revival pitted themselves against two classes of enemy: those within the religion and those without. Outside the religion, the opponents were most modern, Westernizing intellectuals, who were beginning to assert themselves from the 1920s, as well as the Cao Đài sect and Catholic proselytizers.[73] Inside Buddhism, reformers opposed "traditionalist" groups within the sangha. But more important, they opposed a general indifference among the populace to strict notions of orthodoxy and heresy.

Advocates of the Buddhist Revival, while not always in agreement with each other, often stressed the need to propagate Buddhist texts and magazines more widely and to fight superstition. Almost all educated Buddhists thought that Buddhism was in decline, but they disagreed over the reasons for this decline and its solution. Their philosophy differed. In contrast to the credulous who stressed the wonders of the Western Paradise, some monks stressed that enlightenment came from one's own actions and was located in one's person: "Buddha is in the heart."

What conclusions then, can be drawn about the Buddhist Revival? Bửu Tín, a monk from Rạch Giá in the Mekong delta, stressed in 1936 that it was a great success:

> For the last seven or eight years, the movement to revive Buddhism in our country has developed vigorously and enthusiastically throughout the three regions of the south, center, and north; everywhere [people] have established Buddhist associations. Whether it is with weekly newspapers or monthly reviews, monks and lay believers cooperate with one another, publish on and study the canonical classics, translate into Vietnamese and publish collections of Buddhist books, speak out on the aims of the Buddha, and proselytize among humanity.
>
> Thus, today, of the citizens of our country, many are deeply knowledgeable about Buddhist dogma ... know to venerate the Buddhadharma (*Phật pháp*), [and] are resolved to abandon heresy and return to orthodoxy.[74]

Many did not agree with this assessment. Some Buddhists who favored the Buddhist Revival did not believe that human action could save Buddhism from its decline. Invoking the three stages concept of the sixth-century Chinese Buddhist Xinxing, Thích Mật Thể stated: "Some people say that Buddhism today has entered decline because of the proselytizing vigor of Catholicism. But in my opinion, this is not true; it's simply that [we find ourselves] in an era of destruction of the dharma."[75] Instead of using a Social Darwinist or Marxist narrative of progress, such Buddhists perceived the current situation of the Vietnamese in terms of a cyclical process of the establishment and decay of the dharma. And while the theory of the three stages made it clear that it would be harder, in the Age of the Destruction of the Dharma, to reach enlightenment, it did not foreclose the possibility.

In the end, the significance of the Buddhist Revival before 1945 was limited. This text-oriented movement did not represent all of Vietnamese Buddhism in the interwar period. It could not encompass the breadth of Vietnamese appropriations of the Buddha's message. Advocates of revival remained a distinct minority among those who spread the dharma. Among themselves, revivalists showed a lack of unity. Nonetheless, the organizational and intellectual changes suggested by reformers in this period would later come to shape the slow transformation of Vietnamese Buddhism after 1945.

POPULAR BUDDHIST DEVOTIONALISM

Proponents of the Buddhist Revival like Thiện Chiếu flirted with the idea that Buddhism was atheistic and that the Pure Land "was in the heart." In contrast, popular Buddhist texts spread a devotional message that stressed that the Pure Land where Amitabha Buddha resided was outside, a place that one could enter, a locus of devotion where other followers could congregate in an afterlife to live with the Buddha for innumerable eons.

From the 1920s on, texts that discussed the related themes of paradise, the Pure Land, and Nirvana played an important role in the construction of a symbolic universe for many Vietnamese. Heavily devotional, these texts often stressed that through faith and prayer followers could ensure their rebirth in the Western Paradise.

Not only did many inhabitants of the Mekong delta believe in such visions of paradise, but some linked them to the magical power of the Seven Mountains in the western Mekong delta. This rootedness contrasts sharply with the rise of more philosophical and abstract texts of the Buddhist Revival that took as their context the larger world of East Asian Buddhism.

Sutras favored by the Pure Land school and tracts that discuss liberation from suffering in the Pure Land circulated frequently from the 1920s. I refer not only to texts that are considered, canonically, to be important to Pure Land belief or to poems and commentaries written by monks, but to all texts that discuss themes important to the Pure Land school in Vietnam. I focus on Pure Land texts because temples and lay followers printed them much more often than Zen ones. Zen focuses on practice; in contrast, Pure Land emphasizes devotion and, to a limited extent, the use, through reading and listening, of a few key Buddhist sutras.

Even as it drew on core Pure Land beliefs, this popular Buddhist culture remained highly eclectic. It was composed of numerous currents of thought and belief. Scholars and practitioners have tended to isolate this popular Buddhism from the story of an "orthodox" version defined by schools, lineages, and prominent temples. Popular Buddhism is often seen as a heterodox (and inferior) version of the standard teaching. This view skews the reality of Buddhist practice in southern Vietnam, however, where such popular groupings predominated in a bewildering variety of local "sects." Far from being "self-conscious dissenters from the mainstream,"[76] to borrow David Ownby's words, these popular groupings simply expressed variants of fundamental Buddhist beliefs on enlightenment, salvation, and the decay of the dharma.

The rapid growth and dissolution of new religious sects was a perennial feature of southern Vietnam. The Cao Đài, founded in 1926, persists to this day. Most cults or "ways," however, attracted far fewer believers than the Cao Đài. In 1928, for example, French police noted that a new sect called the Banana and Coconut Way (Đạo Dừa Chuối) had gained followers in the Mỹ Tho area. A Chinese fruit merchant had convinced Vietnamese to follow this religion, which encouraged believers to venerate Chinese heroes from the *Tale of the Three Kingdoms*. In the same year, the police reported on the activities of the Amitabha sect in Trà Vinh led by a rich landowner, as well as sects by the same name in Bạc Liêu and Rạch Giá. The main aim of the groups seemed to be fasting and the recitation of prayers. Some adepts also practiced boxing and ingested potions to confer invulnerability. While these groups proselytized, some did not: the French reported as well on a reclusive "sect" of Giảng Đạo Sĩ, or ascetic Preachers of the Way, who lived in the mountains around Châu Đốc and Hà Tiên and professed to have supernatural powers.[77] These few examples show how revivalist concerns with textual orthodoxy had a limited impact. Buddhism's lack of a central guiding body meant that when these kinds of associations proliferated, little stopped them from incorporating features not found in self-professed "orthodox" Buddhism.

While French colonial administrators remained wary of Buddhist heterodoxies, most monks caused no problems to the state. (As one French source put it, only women paid attention to such religious practitioners.) The French seemed particularly concerned about a small number of "mountain monks" (*thầy núi*) from Châu Đốc: according to their sources, these included trouble-making vagabonds who gathered suspicious characters (such as thugs) as followers and distributed "alarmist tracts" during their wanderings.[78] The state constantly feared that individuals would use the cover of religion to hide political agitation against the French.[79] There is a grain of truth in such fears, but the French focus on political issues obscured a deeper understanding of this heterogeneous religious culture that resisted the state's attempts to domesticate it.

What, then, characterized the message spread by such popular associations and their followers? Given an interest in correct devotion and the belief that there had been a deterioration in Buddhism in general, it is not too surprising that, beginning in the 1920s, Buddhists of the Mekong delta printed up prayer books as well as tracts. Correct prayer, after all, was a gateway into the Pure Land, and thus a means of escaping from this "ocean of suffering" (*bể khổ*). Buddhists also printed up parts of sutras. While Buddhists drew on multiple influences, Pure Land influences seem stronger than Zen ones.

Popular texts came in various genres, but the most popular were probably poetic ones. In a culture that was still overwhelmingly oral, this fact is not surprising. To cite one example, Phong Vân, a prolific writer of the 1930s, published a variety of songs in Saigon on the Buddha as well as on his female incarnation, Quan Âm (Guanyin). From the late 1920s into the 1930s, various presses from Mỹ Tho, Cần Thơ, Long Xuyên, and Bến Tre in the Mekong delta printed *Quan Âm giác thế ca* (Song on Quan Âm awakening the world) in versions that ranged from two to eight pages. The popularity of such material is attested by the fact that tracts with this exact title were printed ten times between 1928 and 1940.

Generally speaking, the life and actions of Quan Âm were a favorite theme of such songs.[80] The cult to Quan Âm had been prominent in Vietnam since at least the eleventh century.[81] Showing how closely linked Quan Âm and the Pure Land were in many minds, the Quan tế Phật Đường temple of Long Xuyên set up a "Pure Land–Quan Âm Buddhist Association" in 1940.[82] Such popular concerns manifested themselves in the Buddhist print culture of the Mekong delta.

Given the proliferation of stories about paradise, the Buddha, and Quan Âm, the average believer had a rich conception of the possibilities of life after death. As time passed, however, fewer and fewer Vietnamese had access to the authoritative Chinese text that described this realm. Presumably, through listening to learned commentary and hearing popular poetry on Buddhist themes, listeners acquired a Vietnamese gloss on religious texts. One catechismic text describes this land of bliss:

> *Tịnh* means silence (*im lặng*). *Độ* means land (*quấc độ*), the location of *Tịnh Độ* is the location of silence, purity. Sakyamuni Buddha's Pure Land ... is described in the *Amitabha sutra* as follows: "From here to the West is very far, there is a world known as Paradise, where the Buddha Amitabha preaches the dharma; everyone in that world is utterly happy, at leisure. If they want something they can have it. There is no suffering, no cruelty. It is a place of beauty and solemnity. . . .
>
> The Buddha sees sentient beings undergoing suffering, whether it is [because of] birth, old age, sickness, or death, and expresses compassion and mercy, teaches the dharma-gate (*pháp môn*): if one "enters the religious path" in one life, one can become a Buddha.[83]

The quintessence of the Pure Land message is captured in the counsel of a catechismic book: "The dharma-gate to the Pure Land taught here is no different than chanting the six words "Nam Mộ A Di Đà Phật" over and over again.[84] Or in one nun's statement: "One thousand sutras are nothing more than the words 'Amitabha.'"[85] Pure Land texts counsel believers that if they are sincere, keep the faith, and chant these words, they will be reborn into the Western Paradise. Whether functionaries, tillers of the soil, merchants, or skilled workers, all can enter the religious path to the Pure Land, a path that will end the cycle of death and rebirth, bring peace to the country and to the family, and harmony to husband and wife.[86] Poor, learned, ignorant, male, female, all have a chance at salvation. All have a chance to escape the world of suffering and cross over into a paradise so wonderful that it is virtually impossible to describe.

Many of the concerns that I have discussed are brought to the fore by the following tract. It is not a canonical Pure Land text. It is a 1935 song in the *vọng cổ* style, a genre popular in the south. Indeed, while the Pure Land is not even mentioned in the text, a similar "destination," Nirvana, is. The song discusses the attractions of Nirvana in a very modern context, the battle between idealists and materialists. But it is also a printed song and as such illustrates the intersection between oral culture, print, and Buddhism. I present the end of this song, titled "A *Vọng Cổ* Song on the Buddha Entering Nirvana," by Huỳnh Kim Long.

People born into this world, although [belonging to] many
　　factions, are divided into two main factions,
The idealists and the materialists
The materialists, whether speaking of life or death, say that
　　human fate (*kiếp*) is simply to be a corpse
That's why we are born with selfish characters, argue,
Kill one another . . . whether speaking of misdeeds or good fortune
　　in life,
[The materialists] do not believe that there are rewards and
　　punishments, do not believe that there are *kalpas* (*kiếp*) of the
　　transmigration of souls
Thus, [they believe that] submerged in the ocean of suffering, in
　　human destiny (*kiếp*) the passions are joined with the bitterness
　　of the transmigration of souls
The idealists, relying on spiritual power, know that there is
　　misfortune and happiness but do not know from where
　　misfortune and happiness arise
[They] know that passions are deep [and] engulf one in suffering
But about these things, [they] do not know from where these
　　things arise
Oh, believers! After we enter into the land of Nirvana
　　then we will tell people to devote themselves
　　to spreading the Way
To help the people later to cast off their passions, escape from
　　sinking into suffering
Thus at peace is the teacher [?]
For the teacher takes pity on humanity that is suffering in this
　　world
The Great Being of Compassion takes pity on his foolish children
　　but in his heart has difficulty in liberating them completely [?].
If we want [our] teacher to help [us] escape from the sea of
　　suffering, escape the circle [of death and rebirth], cast off the
　　Three Passions, escape *samsara* (*luân hồi*), then the people must
　　make great efforts.

Follow the profound and magical Way, transform wickedness into
   goodness, rectify one's nature.
Practice *dhyana* devotion, lead a religious life
Today is the day we arrive in Nirvana, believers
   should not lament, should not sink into melancholy
Believers should know that in this world, it is possible to
   escape from separation (*biệt ly*)
[When] life has gone, death comes again.[87]

This song illustrates the powerful attraction of Nirvana to Buddhist
believers. It also illustrates that a new Buddhist print culture in romanized script was developing to spread the Buddhist message. This print
culture cannot be easily pigeonholed as traditional, modern, oral, or
literate. The printed song crossed oral-print boundaries and mixed
doctrinal Buddhist beliefs with modern concerns.

The text in question clearly is modern: that is to say, it touches on
materialism's arrival into Vietnamese consciousness. Or more accurately,
it gives a Buddhist representation of materialist thought. Key features of
materialism are ignored, such as its view of human progress, its understanding of human agency, and its focus (in its Marxist version) on class
struggle. Rather than understand materialism on materialist terms, the
author judges it according to Buddhist ones and finds it lacking.

This text and many others like it present a starkly different worldview
than that usually discussed in modern Vietnamese literature and history.
The voice that is speaking was heard far and wide in the first half of the
twentieth century, but most histories suppress or ignore it. The text resonated with the life experiences of many Vietnamese, for it diagnosed
their current condition, their existence in a "sea of suffering," but provided them with hope for a future in Nirvana.

In this song and in related ones, Vietnamese loosely used the concept
of Nirvana to mean paradise. Indeed, Vietnamese authors often used
Nirvana (Niết bàn), the Pure Land (Tịnh Độ), and the Western Paradise
(Cực lạc Tây phương) interchangeably. Nirvana here does not refer to
the experience of *moksa* (extinction) or *samadhi* (enlightenment), but to
the travel to a land of bliss. In this sense, this song is fully within the
framework of Pure Land texts that stressed how, through devotion, the
believer could escape from the sea of suffering and reach the Pure Land

of Amitabha Buddha. And if this text refers to a recent development in Vietnam, the arrival of materialist thought, it nonetheless stands outside the flow of history. The Buddhist message that comes across in this text is not historically contingent: it is inscribed in the cycles of prosperity and decay of Buddhism itself.

CONCLUSION: BUDDHISM, PRINT CULTURE, AND THE CREATION OF A RELIGIOUS PUBLIC SPHERE

Print played a key role in the Buddhist Revival and in popular Buddhism. In the twentieth century, Buddhism slowly became more text-oriented, heralding a long-term process of change in Buddhist practices and beliefs that took decades to realize. Most Vietnamese expressed far more interest in gaining access to "traditional" Buddhist writings than in becoming acquainted with modern reformers like Tai Xu or Thiện Chiếu. Popular religiosity was devoted to the intensive use of a few texts and to the intensive elaboration of a few key symbols like the Pure Land. Revivalism, in contrast, aimed to be more learned; it claimed to be based on the reading of a wider range of Mahayana works. But how well did it succeed?

Revivalist claims to have succeeded in promoting orthodoxy were always suspicious. Ironically, even some partisans of the revival have agreed. In 1940, the Huế monk Thích Mật Thể complained that the nearly one hundred temples in and around Huế "have certainly not become a collectivity (*đoàn thể*) with any systematic organization" and showed shortcomings in culture, spirit, and education.[88] His views encapsulated the views of some partisans of the Buddhist Revival in the center and in the Mekong delta. When Thích Mật Thể complained four years later that, "although there has been a revival, in reality it has been a revival in name only,"[89] he generalized his earlier criticisms to Vietnamese Buddhism as a whole. Given the power of popular Vietnamese Buddhism and the deficiencies of the Buddhist Revival, was the latter a failure?

Framing the question in terms of the success or failure of the Buddhist Revival misses some fundamental changes that were occurring in Vietnamese Buddhism. One change was conceptual. The Buddhist Revival was important in deploying a new language among small groups of believers with which they could talk about the situation of Vietnamese

Buddhism. But, as Thích Mật Thể so acutely observed, this conceptual leap forward was not accompanied by institutional revolutions. Vietnamese Buddhism remained as organizationally anarchic as before.

A focus on the Buddhist Revival and its success or failure masks as well another important change that took place in this period: the spread of Buddhist printed material aimed at a popular audience. I began this chapter by mentioning a striking paradox: why, given the laments over the poor condition of Buddhism, did Vietnamese Buddhists print such a large number of texts between 1920 and 1945? The question, as earlier formulated, is slightly naive. Buddhists have long emphasized that individuals can gain merit by propagating Buddhist teachings. With the recent spread of modern print technology (which was far easier to use than woodblocks), Buddhists found it easier than ever to do so.

Previous writings on modern Vietnamese Buddhism have assumed that because there was a Buddhist Revival, Vietnamese published an abundance of tracts and sutras. This logic is exactly backward: the publication of the writings of the Buddhist Revival formed part of a larger urge to publish and spread the dharma. Whether believers in the revival or not, many Buddhists understood the karmic rewards of printing the Buddha's message. They reproduced Buddhist texts and at the same time provided others with an opportunity to read or hear the Buddhist message of human liberation. Print technology simply made this process easier to realize. The impetus behind the explosion of cheap (and even free) Buddhist texts was not print capitalism. To the contrary, print in romanized script was simply a technology that allowed Buddhists to propagate the truth of the Buddha's message.

In this sense, one can also step outside the Buddhist discourse and see the revival not so much in terms of "orthodoxy" but as a movement that advocated that Vietnamese move from an oral understanding of texts to critical approaches based on written and printed texts. Buddhist articles and tracts of the 1920s through 1940s often stated that the religion had declined for want of books (especially sutras), implying that oral transmission gave rise to heterodoxy and that print culture could restore purity to Buddhist thought and practice.

What can be concluded about the place of these currents of Buddhist thought within the Vietnam of the interwar period? In the north, Buddhists continued to have a muted influence in rural areas. In the south, however, Buddhists fared quite well in the symbolic struggles between religious forces and the secular avant-garde that took place through the late 1930s. Their message of human liberation was probably more widely heard in southern Vietnam in the 1930s than its Marxist counterpart. While Trần Văn Giàu has argued that the followers of dialectical materialism engaged in dialogue with Buddhists at this time,[90] it was far more common to find antagonism between these two groups. In general, Buddhists and communists operated in different realms, and communists attacked Buddhists for their superstitions.

David Marr has argued that, in the period from 1920 to 1945, Vietnamese put "tradition" on trial. He is absolutely correct: these years saw young Westernized intellectuals savagely attack the "old" and promote the "new." But not everyone paid equal attention to this trial. As the study of Buddhism indicates, at least one facet of this "tradition" was actually quite lively. The verdict on "tradition" was not, in other words, foreordained.

Conclusion

How does one understand Vietnam during the colonial period: as a country defined by a hegemonic colonial state or as one that finds its identity through a search for a revolutionary nationalist path to independence? This book has rejected both approaches to the past. While the preceding chapters have outlined the character of colonial repression with regard to printed matter and have discussed revolutionary opposition to colonial rule, their main focus has been elsewhere: on the complex public sphere. In some realms political contestation was crucial: the chapter on communism underlines this point. But the chapters on Buddhism and Confucianism show that Vietnamese thought about far more than politics.

Much writing on twentieth-century Vietnam has centered on the political themes of state, nationalism, and revolution. Many Vietnamese and foreign scholars have framed the twentieth-century history of the country as a transition from Confucianism to communism. More recently, as the Vietnamese Communist Party's Marxism-Leninism has lost its ideological coherence, writers have resurrected the colonial era contrast between Confucianism and a vague modernity to structure their arguments; some are even attempting to construct a new ideology that synthesizes Confucian past and modernizing present.[1] There are obvious reasons for such choices. First, key political activists from the 1920s onward articulated their views through such binary contrasts: they rejected the "old," like Confucianism, and embraced the "new," like Westernization or communism. Their modes of analysis have shaped representations of the past. Second, the post-1945 struggles for independence and reunification have refashioned the country's identity, and scholars have searched for the origins of such conflicts in the colonial period.

The philosopher Trần Đức Thảo has suggested two other reasons for the character of writing on Vietnam's twentieth-century history. The difficulty of understanding the colonial past, he argues, lies both at the level of language and at the level of the horizons within which we have framed the problem of colonialism. Questioning the nature of the colonial encounter in 1946 (as war was about to break out), Thảo noted that any answer faced a basic stumbling block: "Words do not seem to convey the same meaning to Annamites and French and discussions usually end with accusations of bad faith."[2] With the deceptively mundane point that different individuals could interpret the same words in radically different ways, Thảo introduced a powerful phenomenological and nationalist argument about colonialism.

Implicitly drawing on Husserl, Thảo argued that interpretations of commonly known facts depend on the horizon within which one perceives the real. The Frenchman views the "Annamite" from "within the horizon of the imperial community," in which the states of French Indochina formed but a peripheral part. From the vantage point of this community, "Annamites" occupy a lower rung of the racial and cultural hierarchy defined by the ultimate authority of France. In contrast, "Annamites" view reality from within the horizon of Vietnam itself: far from being on the margins, they define the center. Theirs is a Vietnam that finds its ultimate identity outside of colonialism:

> Vietnam as it would have been without colonialism is not for him a "mere hypothesis," but a project actually lived, the project even of his existence, that which defines even his existence as an Annamite. This world of possibilities forms the *background* (*fond*) on which appear perceived realities and which provide them with their meaning. Erupting into this world, colonialism's contribution reveals its negativity immediately.[3]

Trần Đức Thảo argued that Vietnamese needed to transcend colonialism's negativity. To Thảo, the task of Vietnamese intellectuals was to seize back the symbolic terrain from colonialists and show that colonialism did not define their very being. They needed to excavate a "hidden" or "negated" history—a nationalist history—that had been submerged by the French imperial state and to make it visible. Indeed, many postcolonial intellectuals shared the view that the colonial legacy needed to be rejected or transcended. These writers articulated a view of

Vietnam in which differences within the borders of the country were recognized but ultimately subsumed into nationalist and revolutionary views of the Vietnamese past that stressed similarities.

Ironically, such views could take hold precisely because young Westernized Vietnamese often had a poor grasp of Vietnam's history. As Đào Duy Anh complained: "Among our country's intelligentsia today, there is something appalling, the modern scholars ... believe that our teachings from the past are corrupt and so they do not wish to give them any attention. They know everything about Plato and Aristotle, they know Thomas Aquinas by heart, they're enamored of Pascal and Descartes. But as for Sakyamuni [Buddha], Laozi, and especially Confucius, they don't need to know anything."[4]

Trần Đức Thảo formed part of this emergent young Westernized generation. Members of this group, faced with the absence of a deep scholarship on pre-twentieth-century Confucianism and Buddhism, accentuated the importance of revolution and nationalism. They placed the construction of meaning at the center of their reevaluation of the past and its legacy to the present. In the sense that they rejected the notion that a French colonialist perspective could encompass the significance of this past, their search for meaning was a welcome event. One of the supreme ironies of all these approaches, however, is that their partisans placed themselves on one side of an intellectual divide (for progress and modernity) that was alien to many Vietnamese. This enlightenment discourse failed to capture the richness of Vietnamese life in the interwar era.

Trần Đức Thảo's arguments represent the triumph of such an "enlightenment" view. This view, with all its strengths and limitations, has dominated the post-1945 representations of the Vietnamese past. It serves as a useful foil against which to understand this book. Speaking of a fellow "Annamite," Thảo insists that "all that he sees is immediately located within a certain horizon, a horizon that defines his existence as such."[5] All facts, in other words, are conditioned by the frame through which one perceives the real and acts out one's life. It follows that Vietnamese and French, situated within different horizons, cannot help but come to divergent understandings of the same facts.

This book, in focusing on the printed word and how Vietnamese understood it, accepts that different horizons within which one exists shape the perception of reality. Yet Trần Đức Thảo's pioneering attempt to link phenomenology to nationalism is not exempt from criticism. Thảo did not push his phenomenological approach to its logical conclusion: Vietnamese themselves did not agree on shared meanings for the simple reason that they did not inhabit identical perceptual universes. By asserting that the relevant horizon of subjectivity was the national one, Thảo ignored the ways that Vietnamese drew on oral and printed discourse to construct multiple horizons through which they perceived the real. In retrospectively "uncovering" a hidden history of nationalism, he ironically ignored the remarkable diversity in Vietnamese thought exemplified by its print culture. One of the implications of this book's examination of Confucian, communist, and Buddhist fields of discourse is that these fields provided different horizons through which to perceive the real.

In his simultaneous "discovery" of the past and its elision, Thảo was joined by a wide range of postcolonial scholars. In the years after the August General Uprising of 1945, these scholars increasingly began to see themselves in radically different terms than before and framed their plight in terms of nationalism. Given the outbreak of war in 1946, this shift is quite understandable. Activists such as Hoài Thanh, Nguyễn Đình Thi, Nguyễn Hữu Đang, Trương Tửu, and Đào Duy Anh called for a "new culture" that was not hostage to the French. Xuân Diệu had shaken up the world of poetry in the 1930s with his romantic verse that drew inspiration from French symbolist poets. After the war, he turned into a poet of the revolution. Hoài Thanh, who in the early 1940s stated that "the West today has penetrated into the deepest part of our soul,"[6] rejected his earlier romantic individualism to champion socialist realist literature rooted in the people and their traditions. Some of the Marxists and nationalists active in the 1920s and 1930s, men such as Đào Duy Anh, Trần Huy Liệu, Trần Văn Giàu, and Khuất Duy Tiến (Minh Tranh), have shaped the writing of Vietnamese history in the post-1945 era.

After 1945, the Democratic Republic of Vietnam slowly began to try to institutionalize a modernist view of history and identity in which nationalism and revolution were prominent themes. In the 1950s, the state sponsored the practices of rectification and self-criticism in order to push intellectuals to transform themselves and rid themselves of vestiges of "feudal" and "backward" culture. But if in the north saw the eclipse of many traditional cultural practices by the late 1950s, the experiences of the north cannot stand for all of Vietnam. The official northern-oriented perspective on the past that has come to dominate general historical narratives of twentieth-century Vietnam has marginalized southern voices and voices of tradition, ones that came back into prominence in the 1990s.

Not all Vietnamese, of course, accepted the views of Trần Đức Thảo and his modernist colleagues. In 1946, the same year that Trần Đức Thảo published his seminal article on phenomenology and nationalism, the Buddhist monk Tố Liên penned an article that implicitly, and modestly, suggested the limits of such approaches. Writing at a time of great enthusiasm in the north for "national salvation," he remarked that monks should support such work. But he added that "the salvation of the country can take many different paths, and we need to recognize whatever path is truly compatible with the principles and tendencies of our religion (*giới nhà tu*)."[7] Such comments show that Vietnamese history from 1920 to 1945 cannot be reduced to the rise of modernity or the triumph of communism. Buddhist and Confucian discourses, as well as Western ones, circulated in the public and clandestine arenas. They all shaped Vietnamese encounters with the modern age.

ALTERNATIVES: PRINT CULTURE, REALMS OF DISCOURSE, AND AUDIENCES

In the first chapter of this book, I quoted the words of the communist Võ Nguyên Giáp at the Independence Day ceremonies in Hanoi on 2 September 1945. In a speech that was modern in tone but with some traditional inflections, Giáp orated: "The center, the south, and the north share one heart. Literati, farmers, artisans, merchants, and soldiers share one will. Even Buddhist and Christian priests, even King Bảo Đại have warmly responded [to the call]."[8] It was as if the message proclaimed by the Việt Minh was the same as that received by the populace. Each group, hierarchically ordered in the public realm, nonetheless shared a common understanding and a common identity. Giáp implied that this identity could be articulated by the leadership elite.

But intellectual and revolutionary claims to speak for others must be taken with a grain of salt. The intentions of the writer may be irrelevant to the audience of the printed word. Audiences refashion and reinterpret texts in line with their own predilections. Vietnamese did not always interpret communist texts in the way that cadres would have liked them to: thus, some of them insisted that invisible beings had deposited propaganda around villages. Some Buddhists, rejecting calls to orthodoxy, framed the Buddhist message in terms of a Western Pure Land with a physical base in the western Mekong delta. Others, rejecting a Western progressive and linear logic to events, insisted that the end of the Second World War proved that the prophecies of the sixteenth-century sage Nguyễn Bỉnh Khiêm had been realized. The audience of the printed word, in other words, did not always act in the ways that political and cultural elites demanded.

This book has focused on the print culture of 1920–1945 and the way that it constituted Confucian, communist, and Buddhist spheres of discourse. A legal and secular public sphere dominated intellectual and cultural life, but a clandestine sphere and a religious sphere also existed in which different groups pursued their interests and agendas. The existence of these different realms of discourse illustrates two important cleavages in the print culture of Vietnam: that between the secular and the religious, and that between the legal and illegal. The significance of these cleavages was momentous. After all, the argument that modern Vietnam has been defined by nationalism presupposes that people have access to a common realm of discourse in which beliefs about the nation can form and be shared. But in the Vietnamese case, it is not at all clear that this is true.

If the colonial state tried to put its imprimatur on Vietnam, an examination of Vietnamese materials shows that it had an ambiguous impact on the Vietnamese public sphere. It was hardly hegemonic. Some Vietnamese were deeply marked by French culture; others seem to have been little influenced. Urban educated youth often embraced Western trends, while their rural compatriots did not. In areas like politics, censorship and Westernization shaped the public sphere the most strongly; it was in these realms that Vietnamese partisans most persistently insisted that nationalist and revolutionary discourse was "new." Despite such repression, Vietnamese managed to speak on all sorts of topics and published a wealth of material on a wide range of topics in the interwar period. While the colonial state crushed all rebellions against its rule up to 1945, it was far less successful at shaping what Vietnamese thought.

In the process of reconstructing the past and reevaluating the present, print played an important role. Printers in Saigon and Hanoi dominated the printing of Vietnamese-language materials. Confucians, communists, and Buddhists all drew on the technology of print to disseminate their views, but the modernist communists were no more sophisticated in its use than the others. Forced into the clandestine realm, communists frequently relied on the most primitive methods. Without printing presses, they had to improvise: much communist propaganda was hand-lettered and printed using a gelatin slab that held the ink. Confucians and Buddhists both relied on linotype. In fact, the supposedly "traditional" Buddhists enthusiastically embraced the use of such presses, as many Buddhists saw the karmic merit of propagating the message of the Buddha. Being "modern," in other words, did not make one more technologically savvy.

The increasing importance of print technology meant that printed materials increasingly defined Vietnamese consciousness, slowly making inroads into Vietnamese oral culture. But print hardly replaced orality: it would be more accurate to say that it energized the oral circulation of knowledge in new ways. Old patterns in the circulation of knowledge remained; when Buddhists invoked Amitabha Buddha with the aid of new printed tracts, they did so in the context of a preexisting symbolic economy.

While revolutionary nationalism did not supplant the Way of the Buddha or the Way of Confucius in Vietnam, it is nonetheless true that Confucianism's hold over Vietnamese weakened. At the level of high culture—the Confucianism of the literati and the court—Vietnam saw a sharp change after 1920. With the exception of the Huế court, state patronage of the Way ceased to exist. As a consequence, fewer intellectuals had the competence to carry out scholarship on the topic. The existing Confucian scholars wrote for one another and evinced little interest in reaching out to the populace as a whole: they were more interested in writing about the highly educated "superior man" than about the peasant. Their male-centered discourse appealed to few women. Nonetheless, the proliferation of morality tracts and moral advice, often drawing on Confucian beliefs, indicates that Confucianism was not dead. For example, women in the 1930s were still debating the significance of the "three submissions," whereby a woman was supposed to submit to her father when young, her husband when married, and her son if widowed. This example suggests that, if Confucianism as a coherent system of beliefs on statecraft and behavior had weakened perceptibly, fragments of the Confucian conceptual scheme continued to circulate widely. This was particularly true in the north and center of the country.

Communism's impact on Vietnam before 1945 is surprisingly ambiguous: if organizationally the communists showed great skill, they had difficulty transmitting their revolutionary message to the populace as a whole. Communism entered Vietnam with none of the advantages of Confucianism. No preexisting class of literati naturally advanced this ideology, and the French colonial state attempted to eradicate it. A few Western-educated Vietnamese like Hồ Chí Minh and Đào Duy Anh stumbled upon it and embraced it. Most Vietnamese, however, had a poor grasp of this teaching. Communism's success, then, has to be found less in the specifics of Marxism-Leninism than in its broad opposition to French rule and the organizational acumen of its leaders.

One reason for communism's initial lack of success was the continuing significance of Buddhism in the lives of many Vietnamese. Buddhism remained influential in rural Vietnam in the interwar period, though its strength was most marked in Cochinchina. While some scholars have suggested that the Buddhist Revival that took place in those years invigorated the religion as a whole, this claim is suspect. The reasons for Buddhist vitality lie instead in a popular Vietnamese Buddhism, with a powerful message of liberation and salvation, which continued to appeal to many Vietnamese, particularly those in rural areas. In particular, a Pure Land vision of the future circulated at the same time that revolutionary nationalist visions stirred the minds of Vietnamese in the 1920s, 1930s, and 1940s. And in contrast to Confucianism and communism, both of which appealed mostly to men, Buddhism found its greatest adherence among women.

The three fields of discourse examined in this book were linked to distinctly different intellectual and physical pilgrimages as well as different notions of audience. Anderson, in explaining the rise of colonial nationalism, has argued that "the geography of all colonial pilgrimages" is isomorphic with the boundaries of the nation.[9] But colonial pilgrimages were more complex than Anderson's formulation would allow. If one thinks of the nation-space as the area where printed discourses and people circulate, one can distinguish different pilgrimages and different imaginings of community. Consider the case of the communist pilgrimage. Most lower-level communist cadres probably stayed within their province or region. Key higher-level cadres, in contrast, circulated outside the boundaries of Tonkin, Annam, and Cochinchina, and even outside the boundaries of areas controlled by France.[10] Vietnamese communist experiences in Siam, China, and Russia had a formative impact on the Communist Party. When imprisoned, communist cadres often were in areas on the margins of the nation-state, not in the deltas (e.g., Lao Bảo or Kontum prisons, or Poulo Condore, an island off the coast of Cochinchina). For high-level cadres, then, one can make a strong argument that their experiences on the margins of the colonial state and outside of it, seen together, collectively define the internationalism so essential to communist theorizing. Their publishing abroad played an important role in the early years of the party as well.

The Buddhist experience was markedly different. Few Buddhists who spearheaded the Buddhist Revival of the 1920s through 1940s left the confines of Annam, Cochinchina, or Tonkin. But intellectually, these Buddhists occupied a very different place. Some turned not to the metropolis but back to China, appropriating the Chinese monk Tai Xu's message of revival and the example of the Chinese Buddhist sangha. Most other Vietnamese Buddhists in the Mekong delta, relatively untouched by the "Buddhist Revival," imagined themselves going on yet different pilgrimages. Some imagined themselves going to the Western Pure Land after they died. Some traveled to the frontier between Cambodia and Cochinchina, from which came the Buddha Master of the Western Peace. The west of Cochinchina and the Western Pure Land were their actual and imagined centers of the universe.

The Vietnamese intellectuals who reconceptualized Confucianism and popular culture show yet another intertwining of intellectual trajectories. On the one hand, their eventual turn inward to Vietnam and to peasant culture shows the unmistakable combination of French notions of "popular culture" with Vietnamese interest in native place. Their perceived need to come face to face with Confucianism shows the lingering power of a legacy centered on China. But, whether they were quoting Kang Youwei, Liang Qichao, Hu Shi, or other Chinese critics of Confucianism, the intellectual power of that discourse was not eradicated. This discourse far transcended the boundaries of the nation-state-to-be of Vietnam.

In short, Vietnamese took different intellectual and physical pilgrimages. They were not isomorphic with the confines of the three regions of the south, the center, and the north. The multiplicity of pilgrimages suggests as well that there were different audiences of the printed word. Confucian scholars aimed their discourses at others who were interested in the life of the "superior man" of virtue. The difficult language of their scholarly tracts shut out the vast majority of readers, whose knowledge of Confucianism centered on popular discussions of topics like a women's duty to her husband. Communists initially struggled to define, shape, and reach their audience. But they encountered repeated frustration in translating this new Western ideology for a mass audience. Buddhist writers reached out, more than most, to both men and women: "Virtuous men and devout women," their tracts often began, implying that both genders were the intended audience of the word. These writers had different styles of imagining their audiences. They articulated different views on the ways to read printed texts. And their audiences, not surprisingly, reacted to the printed word in different ways.

Far from subscribing to a bounded notion of identity defined by the territorial limits of today's Vietnam, Vietnamese participated in public and clandestine realms of discourse that transcended such frontiers. Indeed, it was precisely the experiences in Siam, Cambodia, Laos, China, France, and Russia, and the different discourses that they encountered, that enabled Vietnamese to turn to themselves and focus more and more on their commonalities rather than their differences. In this process of redefinition, print played a key role.

As we enter a new century, a religious revival has brought a wide variety of religious groups, and especially Buddhists, back into the public eye. State intellectuals, once fervent critics of Confucianism, now invoke some of its teachings as compatible with a new modernity. Realizing the obvious benefits of tourist dollars, local governments promote pilgrimages to temples and shrines. From village to village, Vietnamese continue to worship their tutelary divinities. Last but not least, elements of the print culture of the interwar years are back as well: from the reprinting of texts from the 1930s on Confucianism and Buddhism to the reappearance of novels of the dissolute life (such as those of Vũ Trọng Phụng), Vietnamese are becoming reacquainted with their past. As Vietnam hurtles into the future, the past refuses to go away.

INTRODUCTION

1. Arlette Farge, *Le gout de l'archive*, 11–12.
2. Ibid., 14; italics in original.
3. For an excellent example of such scholarship, showing how one biography was constructed in part through fabrications and the suppression of acts, see Christoph Giebel, *Imagined Ancestries*.

CHAPTER 1: TRANSFORMING PRINT CULTURE AND THE PUBLIC SPHERE

1. See "Sấm giảng khuyên người đời tu niệm" (Prophecy advising people on the religious life, 1939), in Đức Huỳnh Giáo Chủ [Huỳnh Phú Sổ], *Sấm giảng thi văn toàn bộ* (Prophecies, poetry and prose: collected works), esp. 25; Hue Tam Ho Tai, *Millenarianism and Peasant Politics in Vietnam*.
2. On the importance of print to the Hòa Hảo in these early years, see Hue Tam Ho Tai, *Millenarianism*, 118–119, 145–146.
3. Đức Huỳnh Giáo chủ [Huỳnh Phú Sổ], *Sấm giảng thi văn toàn bộ*, 6.
4. For representative examples of this view, see Trinh Van Thao, *Vietnam du confucianisme au communisme*, and Huynh Kim Khanh, *Vietnamese Communism, 1925–1945*. Numerous Vietnamese-language texts fit this mold: see, for example, Trần Bá Dệ, Nguyễn Ngọc Cơ, Nguyễn Đình Lê, *Lịch sử Việt Nam 1930–45*. (History of Vietnam, 1930–1945). Alexander Woodside's *Community and Revolution in Modern Vietnam* is a partial exception: while he focuses on such themes, he does give some attention to topics that others neglect, like Buddhism.
5. Vũ Ngọc Phan, *Nhà văn hiện đại* (Modern writers), 1167.
6. Hoài Thanh and Hoài Chân, *Thi nhân Việt Nam (1932–1941)* (Vietnamese poets, 1932–1941), 11.
7. John Fitzgerald, *Awakening China*, 6.
8. This search for organized communities is the theme around which Alexander Woodside structures *Community and Revolution in Modern Vietnam*.
9. Hoàng Đạo, *Mười điều tâm niệm* (Ten things to ponder), 15; Hoài Thanh, Lê Tràng Kiều, and Lưu Trọng Lư, *Văn chương và hành động* (Literature and action), reprinted in Nguyễn Ngọc Thiện, Nguyễn Thị Kiều Anh, Phạm Hồng Toàn, eds., *Tuyển tập phê bình, nghiên cứu văn học Việt Nam (1900–1945)* (Selected works of literary criticism and research), vol. 3, 178.

10. Lương Đức Thiệp, *Xã hội Việt Nam tiến hóa sử* (History of the evolution of Vietnamese society), 458–459.

11. Nguyễn Tế Mỹ, *Hai bà Trưng khởi nghĩa* (The Trưng sisters' revolt), 186–187.

12. Nguễn [*sic*] Mục Tiêu, "Nên chấn hưng Phật giáo ở nước nhà" (We need to revive Buddhism in our country), 2.

13. There is a voluminous scholarship on literacy. See Walter Ong, *Orality and Literacy*, and Jack Goody, *The Domestication of the Savage Mind*, both of which argue that the acquisition of literacy leads to a major cognitive shift away from oral practices of recording, storing, and using information. More recent scholarship, however, has called the sharp distinction between orality and literacy into question, and tends to stress the importance of situating the technology of print in a social and historical context. Michael Clanchy, *From Memory to Written Record: England, 1066–1307*, to cite one example, shows how complicated the interplay of oral and written modes of conveying information could be. The great majority of recent historical work continues the trend of underscoring the complexity of the appropriation of the written and printed word. In Asian studies, discussion of literacy has been scattered about: see, for example, Evelyn Sakakida Rawski, *Education and Popular Literacy in Ch'ing China*, which argues that a restricted literacy was surprisingly widespread in China.

    The study of print culture is quite obviously linked to that of literacy. Elizabeth Eisenstein sees printing as a key technology of transformation in *The Printing Press as an Agent of Change*. For newer approaches to the history of print culture, see, for example, Roger Chartier, *Les usages de l'imprimé*, and Adrian Johns, *The Nature of the Book*. In Asian studies, print history seems to have been studied little. A welcome exception was a special issue of *Late Imperial China*, 17:1 (June 1996), on the theme of "Publishing and the Print Culture in Late Imperial China." See, for example, Kai Wing Chow, "Writing for Success," 120–157. See also David Johnson, ed., *Popular Culture in Late Imperial China*, which contains a variety of illuminating studies addressing literacy and popular culture. One of the most thoughtful reflections on literacy and print culture is the extended introduction in Susan Rogers, ed., *Telling Lives, Telling History*. For Vietnam, see Christiane Pasquel-Rageau, "L'imprimerie au Vietnam de l'impression xylographique traditionelle à la revolution du quôc ngu (XIIIe–XIXe siècles)."

14. Jürgen Habermas, *The Structural Transformation of the Public Sphere*, 27.

15. For a critique of Habermas that emphasizes how the public sphere was gendered, see Joan Landes, *Women and the Public Sphere*; for other critiques see, for example, Craig Calhoun, ed., *Habermas and the Public Sphere*.

16. Robert Darnton, "A Police Inspector Sorts His Files," in Robert Darnton, *The Great Cat Massacre and Other Episodes in French Cultural History.*

17. David Strand, *Rickshaw Beijing,* 167–168.

18. Mary Elizabeth Berry, "Public Life in Authoritarian Japan," 133.

19. Ibid., 139.

20. See Benjamin Elman, *From Philosophy to Philology.*

21. Katsuhisa Moriya, "Urban Networks and Information Networks," in Chie Nakane and Sinzaburo Oishi, *Tokugawa Japan,* 122.

22. Phan Huy Chú, *Lịch triều hiến chượng loại chí* (Classified survey of the institutions of successive courts), vol. 3 (fascicle 42), 63.

23. Hoa Bằng (Hoàng Thúc Trâm), "Lịch trình nghề ấn loát Việt Nam—Từ lối in mộc bản xưa đến thuật in hoạt bản bây giờ" (From woodblock printing in the past to modern printing techniques), *Tri tân* 49 (3–9 June 1942), 2. In a 1970 article, Hoa Bằng states (without providing proof) that woodblock printing in Vietnam dates from the tenth century. But the only proof of Trần period (1225–1400) printing is in Trần Anh Tông's reign, when the court ordered the printing of the *Ksitigarbha bodhisattva sutra* (*Địa Tạng*). See Hoa Bằng, "Kỹ thuật ấn loát của ta thời xưa," 52.

24. Nguyễn Thị Dương, "Hải Học Đường và việc in sách đầu thế kỷ XIX" (The Sea of Learning Hall and the printing of books at the beginning of the nineteenth century), 63.

25. Trần Văn Giàu, *Sự phát triển của tư tưởng ở Việt Nam từ thời kỳ XIX đến Cách Mạng Tháng Tám* (The development of thought from the nineteenth century to the August Revolution), vol. 1, 99.

26. Alexander Woodside, *Vietnam and the Chinese Model,* 187.

27. Hoa Bằng, "Lịch trình nghề ấn loát," 1–2; Trần Hồng Liên, "Vài nét về Phật giáo thời Nguyễn (1802–1862)" (Several features of Buddhism under the Nguyễn), 188; Woodside, *Vietnam and the Chinese Model,* 123–124.

28. Trần Văn Giáp et al., *Lược truyện các tác giả Việt Nam* (Biographical sketches of Vietnamese authors), vol. 1, 442.

29. Trần Nghĩa, "Bước đầu tìm hiểu các kho sách Hán Nôm và lịch sử thư mục học Hán Nôm" (Toward a preliminary understanding of the Han-Nôm repositories and the history of Han-Nôm catalogs), 3–4; Hoàng Lê, "Vài nét về công việc sưu tầm thư tịch Hán Nôm trong lịch sử" (Aspects of the collection of Chinese and Nôm books in history), 30.

30. Jean Louis de Lanessan, *L'Indochine française,* 230; Yoshiharu Tsuboi, "Politique et confucianisme dans le Vietnam du XIXe siècle," 134.

31. An intriguing 1938 study of literacy shows that in one village (Phu Quang, Thanh Hóa province), 20 percent of the men sixty-one and over could read Chinese, but that 0 percent of the women could. This pattern

was repeated in two other villages studied: male rates of literacy for the age cohort sixty-one and older fluctuated, but women always had a o percent literacy rate. Most of these persons would have learned to read in the late nineteenth century. See Dr. P. Chesneaux, "Enquête sur l'analphabétisme en milieu rural dans une province du Nord-Annam," 267.

32. Nguyễn Lộc, *Văn học Việt Nam nửa cuối thế kỷ XVIII nửa đầu thế kỷ XIX* (Vietnamese literature from the second half of the eighteenth century to the beginning of the nineteenth century), vol. 2, 308.

33. Thanh Lãng, *Văn chương chữ Nôm trong Bộ khởi thảo văn học sử Việt Nam* (Nôm literature in the history of Vietnamese literature), 79.

34. This is tentatively confirmed for parts of Annam by Chesneaux, "Enquête," 267.

35. Well into the colonial period, French administrators complained about hawkers selling "seditious" books in the provinces. See, for example, National Archives Center–I (hereafter TTLTQG-I) (Hanoi), M. Le ... Tong Doc de Bac Ninh à M. le Résident de France à Nam Dinh, "A.[u] s.[ujet] des pamphlets séditieux," Bac Ninh, 8 January 1908, Résidence de Nam Dinh (hereafter RND), d. 2029.

36. If one is to believe A. Bouinais and A. Paulus, *L'Indochine française contemporaine*, 213. Many works say that the first Vietnamese-run newspaper was *Phan Yên báo*, published in 1868. Bằng Giang, *Văn học quốc ngữ ở Nam Kỳ 1865–1930* (Southern literature in romanized script, 1865–1930), convincingly argues that this date is wrong (pp. 130–133). Bằng Giang suggests that the first newspaper was *Thông loại khóa trình*, published from 1888 to 1889.

37. "Tiểu tự (Note[?]), *Nam kỳ* (The south) (Saigon), 63 (January 5, 1899), 1000.

38. Bình Nguyên Lộc, "Thời vàng son của nghề xuất bản tại Sài Gòn" (The golden age of publishing in Saigon), 15. French publishers were the first to sell these works. Thanks to Đỗ Văn An for providing me with this article.

39. Phan Châu Trinh, *Bài diễn thuyết đạo đức, luân lý Đông Tây* (Address on Eastern and Western philosophy and morality), 23. Note that scholars disagree over whether one should refer to this man as Phan Chu Trinh or Phan Châu Trinh. Although the Chinese character for his middle name should be pronounced "Chu," I have decided to use the name that appears on the cover of his 1926 book and the one that he appears to have used in conversation. Thanks to Li Tana and Keith Taylor for clarification on this issue.

40. Centre des Archives d'Outre-Mer, Aix-en-Provence (hereafter CAOM), Gouvernement Général (hereafter GG), 7F d. 22 (2): "Notes de Sûreté concernant la situation politique indigène au 25 mai 1923."

41. Đặng Thai Mai, *Hồi ký thời kỳ thanh thiếu niên* (Memoirs of my youth), 64–65. This memoir, filled with detailed descriptions of the environment in which the author grew up, is one of the best to come out of Vietnam.

42. TTLTQG-I (Hanoi), 1907 or 1908 statement [untitled, transcribed into romanized script] in RND, d. 2629.

43. Đặng Thai Mai and others have stressed how the Tonkin Free School played a crucial role in propagating new currents of thought around Hanoi in 1907 and in encouraging other free schools in the provinces of Nam Định, Nghệ An, Hà Tĩnh, Quảng Nam, and Bình Thuận. Đặng Thai Mai, *Văn thơ cách mạng đầu thế kỷ XX (1900–1925)* (Revolutionary prose and poetry from the beginning of the twentieth century [1900–1925]), 74. Cf. Nguyễn Văn Xuân, who argues that the Tonkin Free School formed part of a larger modernization movement that mostly originated in the center and spread north. See Nguyễn Văn Xuân, *Phong trào Duy Tân biên khảo* (Study of the modernization movement), esp. 205–223, and Nguyễn Q. Thắng, *Huỳnh Thúc Kháng tác phẩm* (Huỳnh Thúc Kháng: collected works), esp. 36–39.

44. Trần Huy Liệu et al., *Tài liệu tham khảo lịch sử Cách mạng cận đại Việt Nam* (Materials for research on the modern Vietnamese revolution), vol. 3, 38; TTLTQG-I (Hanoi), M. Le … Tông Doc de Bac Ninh à M. le Résident de France à Nam Dinh, "A.[u] s.[ujet] des pamphlets séditieux," Bac Ninh, 8 January 1908, RND, d. 2029.

45. See "Bài hát khuyên học chữ quốc ngữ" (Song to encourage the study of romanized script) and "Bài hát khuyên người xem nhật báo" (Song to encourage people to read daily newspapers), in Vũ Văn Sạch, Vũ Thị Minh Hương, and Phillipe Papin, comps., *Văn thơ Đông Kinh Nghĩa Thục / Prose et poésies du Đông Kinh Nghĩa Thục* (Prose and Poetry of the Tonkin Free School), 110–111, 132–133.

46. Gouverneur Général Paul Beau, *Situation de l'Indochine de 1902 à 1907*, vol. 1, 80.

47. Đào Duy Anh, *Nhớ nghĩ chiều hôm* (Evening meditations), 73–74.

48. CAOM, GG, 2517, "Liste des Imprimeurs Chinois et Annamites," Hanoi, 21 May 1909.

49. See TTLTQG-I (Hanoi), Résidence Supérieure au Tonkin (hereafter RST), d. 79.515, "Objet: demande d'autorisation de créer un journal par M. Tran Van Co," Hanoi, 18 August 1918.

50. CAOM, Département des Archives et des Bibliothèques, d. 1628 (untitled, 1941 or 1942 text). Note that this includes reimpressions and second editions. I would guess that around ten thousand different tracts and books were printed in this period.

51. Ngô Hà, "Lược sử báo chí thành phố" (Brief history of the city's newspapers), 342–343, 359–362.

52. Statistics based on CAOM, Indochine, Nouveau Fonds (INF), c. 369, d. 2950, "Liste des journaux publiés en Indochine au 30 juin 1937"; National Archives Center–II, Ho Chi Minh City (hereafter TTLTQG-II), IIA45 302 (2), "Réponse au questionnaire" [1941]. In 1937, Vietnamese-language weeklies sold approximately 54,000 copies in the north and 18,000 in the south. (Southern circulation of dailies had risen to at least 35,300 by 1941, showing the increasing popularity of the newspaper.) There was a smaller French-language press aimed at Vietnamese as well. Given that each newspaper was often read (or heard) by several others, the reach of newspapers was undoubtedly greater than it may seem at first.

    Furthermore, Nguyễn Thành has compiled a list of 256 "revolutionary" newspapers published between 1925 and 1945. The great majority of them were illegal and thus never showed up in the collections of the *"dépôt légal,"* or legal repository, of the French state. See Nguyễn Thành, *Báo chí cách mạng Việt Nam 1925–1945* (Vietnamese revolutionary newspapers, 1925–1945), 324–345.

53. On the diversity of titles see, for example, TTLTQG-II, II.45 195 (4), "Liste par ordre alphabétique des collaborateurs de la presse française," 1940; Ngô Hà, "Lược sử báo chí thành phố", 338–339.

54. Thanh Châu, "Hồi ký văn học: Mười năm với tuần báo *Tiểu thuyết thứ bảy*" (Literary memoir: ten years with the weekly newspaper *Saturday Novel*), 79.

55. CAOM, GG, 7F d. 22 (2), "Notes de Sûreté concernant la situation politique indigène au 25 mai 1923."

56. In 1925, for example, 1,095,000 textbooks for elementary-level instruction were printed; by 1930 this number had climbed to 4,884,000. Direction Général de l'Instruction Publique, *Les manuels scolaires et les publications de la Direction Générale de l'Instruction Publique.*

57. Ngọc Giao, "Hồi ký văn học: Chủ nhà in, nhà xuất bản Tân Dân Ông Vũ Đình Long" (Literary memoir: Vũ Đình Long, head of Tân Dân print shop and publishing house), 58. The *Journal officiel de l'Indochine française* gives a list of all the printers in French Indochina and their output that confirms this (1942:1337–1339). Of the seventy-one printers and publishers in Tonkin, Annam, and Cochinchina, the vast majority were in Hanoi and Saigon. Only thirteen of them published ten or more books, with the Imprimerie d'Extrême-Orient (which printed many publications for the government) far in the lead with 140. Most of these publishers probably made their money from publishing newspapers, theater tickets, calling cards, and assorted other publications.

58. This was at least true for Vietnamese printers in Cambodia: see Lê Hương, *Việt kiều ở Kampuchea* (Vietnamese in Cambodia), 25–27.

59. Nguyễn Quang, "Nghề ấn loát ở Việt Nam" (Printing in Vietnam), 888. Thanks to Đỗ Văn An for bringing this article to my attention.

60. The Asia Publishers (Nhà Xuất Bản Á Châu), for example, offered a 25 percent commission for every book sold after the fifth one and offered sole distribution rights in a town or city other than Hanoi and Saigon. For trusted agents, it would send books cash on delivery, and unsold books could be returned and exchanged for new ones. See Nhà Xuất Bản Á Châu, *Thể lệ bán sách và mục lục những sách đã in* (Guidelines on selling books and list of published books), [4]–[5].

61. TTLTQG-II, IIA45 303 (2), Trần Văn Quới, "Réponse aux questions relatives à l'enquête sur le lecteur annamite et les ouvrages lus par lui" [Cholon, 1941?].

62. Lê Thanh, "Quyền tác giả" (The rights of authors), *Tri tân* 55 (15–21 July 1942), 2.

63. CAOM, GG, 7F, L'Administrateur Chef du Service de la Sûreté à M. le Gouverneur de la Cochinchine, "Objet: Sûreté politique," Saigon, 2 April 1921.

64. Cao Văn Chánh, quoted in Phillipe Peycam, "Intellectuals and Political Commitment in Vietnam," 182.

65. CAOM, GG, 7F d. 30 (5), [Rapport à M. le Gouverneur Général de l'Indochine], Hanoi, 21 November 1930.

66. CAOM, GG, 7F d. 22, Chef du Service de la Sûreté à M. le Gouverneur de la Cochinchine, "Objet: Sûreté Politique," Saigon, 2 April 1921.

67. CAOM, GG, 7F d. 22 (2), "Notes de Sûreté concernant la situation politique indigène au 25 mai 1923."

68. Ibid.

69. CAOM, GG, 7F d. 22 (4), Service de la Sûreté de la Cochinchine, "Rapport annuel 1924–1926."

70. For the comments on Cochinchina, see TTLTQG-II, IIA45 243 (11), "La presse en Cochinchine" [1938]; and TTLTQG-II, IIA45 303 (2), Trần Văn Quới, "Réponse aux questions relatives à l'enquête sur le lecteur annamite et les ouvrages lus par lui" [1941?]; for those on Tonkin, see CAOM, Indochine, GG, 7F d. 30 (5), Le Résident Supérieur [Yves Chatel] au Tonkin à Monsieur le Gouverneur Général de l'Indochine, Hanoi, 26 June 1937.

71. CAOM, GG, 7F d. 18 (1), "Rapport Annuel 1926–1927."

72. CAOM, GG, 7F d. 18 (2), "Rapport Annuel 1927–28."

73. Revolutionary Museum (Hanoi), propaganda leaflet from Nghệ Tĩnh (Nghi Lộc?): "Hỡi anh em chị em thợ thuyền, dân cầy, binh lính. Hỡi anh em chị em bị áp bức bóc lột!" [February? 1931]. Note: propaganda leaflets usually did not have titles. I have cited the first words of the text.

74. CAOM, SLOTFOM, série III, c. 54, "Note périodique no. 44 de la Direction Générale de la Sûreté Générale Indochinoise (mois de septembre 1936)."

75. CAOM, GG, 7F d. 30 (5), "Rapport sur la situation politique au Tonkin au cours du mois de novembre 1938."

76. CAOM, GG, 7F d. 18 (1), "Rapport Annuel 1926–1927." On *La lutte*, see Daniel Héméry, *Révolutionnaires vietnamiens et pouvoir colonial en Indochine.*

77. Đặng Thai Mai, *Hồi ký*, 309.

78. Circulaire No. 199/N/IP, 7 March 1941, in *Bulletin administratif de la Cochinchine*, 1er semestre, 1386–1387.

79. Nguyễn Trân, "Nam kỳ văn học năm vừa qua" (Southern literature in the past year), 33.

80. TTLTQG-I (Hanoi), Archives de la Mairie—Hanoi (hereafter AMH), d. 3456, Le Gouverneur Général de l'Indochine [Decoux] à Monsieur le Résident Supérieur au Tonkin, "Objet: état de l'opinion chez les français d'Indochine," Saigon, 6 February 1942, and le Président du Comité local de Contrôle des Informations et de la Propagande à Monsieur l'Administrateur-Maire de la ville de Hanoi, Hanoi, 22 October 1941; CAOM, INF, c. 133, d. 1198, Secrétariat d'État aux Colonies, Service des Contrôles Techniques des Colonies, "Information des Commissions Coloniales du Contrôle Postale et interceptions reçues pendant le mois de novembre 1941, Indochine."

81. J. Habermas, *Structural Transformation of the Public Sphere*, 27.

82. Hoa Bằng, "Các vùng ngoại ô và thôn quê cần có những 'duyệt thư, báo xã'" (The city outskirts and the countryside need "reading societies"), *Tri tân* 37 (4 March 1942), 2.

83. CAOM, Fonds Moutet, c. 5, d. 131, "Le problème de l'enseignment" [1936?].

84. David Marr suggests that, in the mid-1920s, perhaps 5 percent of the population could read, and this figure may have risen to 10 percent in 1939. See David Marr, *Vietnamese Tradition on Trial, 1920–1945*, 34. Contrast these low estimates with confusing statistics from the DRV government's Popular Education campaign, carried out from 1945 onward. Early statistics, which I do not trust, suggest that literacy in the twenty-four provinces of the north (Bắc Bộ) was already at 34 percent in 1945 before the beginning of the literacy campaigns, with one province (Hải Dương) listed as having had a 50 percent literacy rate! These figures seem highly implausible and go against the great majority of (admittedly speculative) estimates of literacy rates. See CAOM, Indochine, Gouvernement de Fait (hereafter GF), c. 24, "Bảng kê tình hình các lối học đến ngày 1-7-46," July[?] 1946.

This is not the place to go into a detailed discussion of the methodology of calculating literacy rates: there is an extensive literature on the topic. With the exception of the Chesneaux study, noted below, Vietnamese and French accounts that I have seen for this period do not explain the criteria for measuring literacy. For Vietnam in this period, it is impossible (given the data) to calculate one general rate for literacy. One would have to calculate rates for French, Vietnamese in romanized script, Vietnamese in Nôm, and Chinese.

85. Calculated from information taken from Chesneaux, "Enquête," 267–278. This is the best study I have encountered on literacy in French Indochina. Some of the comments that follow are based on the findings of this study.

86. Hoài Thanh and Hoài Chân, *Thi nhân Việt Nam*, 57.

87. Ibid., 120.

88. Từ Lâm [Nguyễn Xuân Nghị], *Lược khảo về mỹ thuật Việt Nam* (Short study of Vietnamese fine arts), 166–167.

89. Thanh Lãng, *Bảng lược đồ văn học Việt Nam* (Outline of Vietnamese literature), vol. 1, 550–551.

90. "Để làm 'sang giá' và 'sang gia' tác phẩm văn học (phỏng vấn nhà nghiên cứu phê bình văn học Hoàng Ngọc Hiến)" (Making literary works "limpid" and "illustrious": an interview with the literary scholar Hoàng Ngọc Hiến), 64.

91. Only a scattering of sources break down reading habits. See, for example, TTLTQG-II, IIA45 303 (2), "Réponse au questionnaire" [1941]; TTLTQG-I, Département des Archives et Bibliothèques de l'Indochine (hereafter DABI), d. 451, "Note concernant la Librairie en Annam [ca. 1930]."

92. TTLTQG-II, IIA45 303 (2), Le Chef du Bureau de Traductions [Sûreté], "Influence de la Presse, du livre, et de la littérature sur la population indigène," Saigon, 10 June 1941.

93. TTLTQG-I, AMH, d. 2687, Lương Ngọc Hiển à M. l'Administrateur de la ville de Hanoi, 15 January 1940.

94. TTLTQG-II, IIA45 303 (2), "Réponse au questionnaire" [1941].

95. Phạm Mạnh Phan, "Muốn chữa thanh niên truy lạc, hãy đốt hết những sách khiêu dâm" (If we want to cure our debauched youth, we should burn all lewd books), *Tri tân* 9 (1 August 1941), 7.

96. Thái Phỉ, *Một nền giáo dục Việt Nam mới* (A new Vietnamese education), 55. This book has a litany of complaints against the younger generation, ranging from male youths indulging in dancing and talking coarsely to women neglecting the home.

97. CAOM, GG, 7F d. 22 (2), "Notes de Sûreté concernant la situation politique indigène au 25 Mai 1923."

98. Mme. Lê Trung Ngọc, *Nữ lưu phân sự* (Female duties), 29, 30.

99. [Editorial], "Ảnh hưởng tiểu [sic] thuyết trong nữ giới" (The influence of novels on women), *Phụ nữ tân văn*, 30 August 1934, 1.

100. T. V., "Câu chuyện đọc sách," *Phụ nữ tân văn*, 21 December 1933, 5.

101. Thiếu Sơn, "Sự học và đàn bà" (Women and studies), *Phụ nữ tân văn*, 7 September 1933, 8.

102. Trần Hữu Độ, *Triết học của vô sản* (The philosophy of the proletariat), ii–iii.

103. I have benefited from reading Lydia H. Liu, *Translingual Practice: Literature, National Culture, and Translated Modernity—China, 1900–1937.* On p. 26, Liu defines "translingual practice" as "the process by which new words, meanings, discourses, and modes of representation arise, circulate, and acquire legitimacy within the host language due to, or in spite of, the latter's contact/collision with the guest language."

104. [Anonymous], "Tiểu tự điển" (Little dictionary), *Đại Việt tạp chí* (Đại Việt magazine) (Saigon), 1 (January 1918), 102.

105. I have drawn some inspiration in this paragraph from Catherine Bell's discussion of how one text defined, sometimes in contradictory ways, multiple forms of communities to which they were addressed: what I call "implied audiences." See Catherine Bell, "'A Precious Raft to Save the World.'"

106. Trần Huy Liệu, *Một bầu tâm sự* (A heartfelt concern) (1927), reprinted in *Hồi ký Trần Huy Liệu*, ed. Phạm Như Thơm, 383. Trần Huy Liệu (at this point an admirer of Liang Qichao) also stated that, although Vietnam had been Confucian, many Vietnamese were Confucians not out of conviction but out of fear of deviating from public opinion.

107. Phan Châu Trinh, *Bài diễn thuyết đạo đức luận lý Đông Tây*, 22.

108. Joan Judge, *Print and Politics*, 68.

109. Such comments come from the instruction manual for literacy instructors of the Hanoi Association to Propagate the Study of Romanized Script, which also noted that the laboring poor could be "confused" and "disobedient" in literacy classes. See Hội Truyền Bá Học Quốc Ngữ, *Mấy điều cần thiết các giáo viên của Hội nên biết* (Some necessary things that the association's instructors should know), 8.

110. Nghiêm Xuân Yêm, "Thanh niên tri thức với dân quê" (Intellectual youth and the peasantry), *Thanh nghị* 47 (16 October 1943), 2, 24.

111. Tân Phong, "Học thuật và hành động" (Study and action), *Thanh nghị*, 29 July 1944, 3.

112. Đỗ Đức Dục, "Dư luận chấn chính" (Correct public opinion), *Thanh nghị* 41 (16 July 1943), 2–3, 29.

113. Lưu Văn Ngôn, *Những phương pháp giáo hóa dân quê* (Methods of educating rural people), 1, 13. The implied audience of his suggestion that Vietnamese take up exercise would seem to be the elite: after all, why would

anyone need to counsel peasants to exercise? This example drives home the need to consider the implied audience of much printed matter in the colonial period.

114. Phan Bội Châu, "Vấn đề báo chí" (On newspapers), *Ánh sáng* (Ray of light), 9 April 1935, quoted in *Phan Bội Châu*, 335.

115. Speech of Võ Nguyên Giáp in *Trang sử mới: Tuyên ngôn độc lập* (A new page in history: the declaration of independence), 24.

116. Ibid., 23.

117. François Guillemot has suggested that, from 1945 to 1947, from five thousand to fifty thousand Vietnamese were killed. The Việt Minh was not, it should be underlined, responsible for all of the deaths, as other nationalist and religious groups contributed to the carnage. I would argue that at least ten thousand were killed in intra-Vietnamese violence in these years and that the death toll is probably much higher. See François Guillemot, "Viet-nam 1945–1946."

118. The classic work that articulates the view that Confucianism had a deep impact on Vietnam in the nineteenth century is Alexander Woodside's erudite *Vietnam and the Chinese Model*. In the 1988 preface to a reprinted version of this book, Woodside argues that, while Vietnam was more a part of an East Asian "Confucian commonwealth" by the eighteenth and nineteenth centuries than he had earlier believed, "it was also more dominated by its own medieval past, and by the many pockets of that past that survived." Alexander Woodside, "Preface to the Paperback Edition," 4.

CHAPTER 2: THE COLONIAL STATE AND REPRESSION OF THE PRINTED WORD

1. Nguyễn Bách Khoa, "Những hình thức, sinh hoạt mới: Xã hội và con người đang biến hóa, IV, Thảo luận," (New appearances, new living conditions: society and individuals in transformation, IV, debate) *Văn mới* (New literature), 7 (30 October 1945), 2.

2. James C. Scott, *Seeing like a State*, 4. For more on the homogenizing proclivities of states, see Ernest Gellner, *Nations and Nationalism*; Benedict Anderson, *Imagined Communities*; and Thongchai Winichakul, *Siam Mapped*, esp. 16–18.

3. Scott, *Seeing like a State*, 97.

4. Crawford Young, *The African Colonial State in Comparative Perspective*, 223.

5. Ibid., 253.

6. The general budget rose from 50 million piasters (1920) to 104 million (1930), dipped to a low of 55 million in 1935 (as a result of the depression), then rose back up to 129 million in 1940. See Gouvernement

Général de l'Indochine, Direction des Affaires Économiques, Service de la Statistique Générale, *Annuaire statistique de l'Indochine*, 310.

7. Hương Giang, "Une mesure draconnienne à supprimer," *Écho annamite*, 10 August 1926; "La séance des voeux," *Écho annamite*, 8 December 1926; *Đông Pháp thời báo*, 7 February 1930.

8. Pierre Brocheux and Daniel Hémery, *Indochine: la colonisation ambiguë*, 186.

9. The examples in this paragraph are from Andrée Viollis [Andrée Françoise Caroline d'Ardenne de Tizac], *Indochine S.O.S.*, 57, 101; TTLTQG-I, AMH, d. 2679, Police Municipal de Hanoi, Procès-verbal, Déclaration de To Dinh Hoe, Hanoi, 5 February 1937; TTLTQG-II, IIA45 261 (9), Nguyen Xuan An, le Juge de la Paix de Chaudoc à Monsieur le Procureur Général, Chau Doc, 19 December 1936.

10. Phan Văn Hùm, *Ngồi tù Khám lớn* (In Khấm Lớn prison), 45–46; "Hai chuyện giống nhau mà dư luận lại khác" (Two similar stories, but public opinion differs), *Thần chung* (Morning bell), 10 January 1929, 1.

11. Robert Cribb argues that, while the Netherlands East Indies colonial state had undergone a "political-administrative revolution," it retained a "puzzling weakness" when Japan attacked in 1942 precisely because this transformation had not been finished. Robert Cribb, "Introduction: The Late Colonial State in Indonesia," 5–6.

12. Both James Scott and Hy Van Luong obliquely suggest this view for Vietnam. They have argued that, while the colonial state incorporated Vietnam into the capitalist world system, this state was often ineffective at refashioning the sociocultural logic through which Vietnamese perceived and acted on their world. See James Scott, *The Moral Economy of the Peasantry*; Hy Van Luong, *Revolution in the Village*. Luong sees the persistence of such a sociocultural logic, while Scott focuses more on its breakdown.

13. Hue Tam Ho Tai, *Radicalism and the Origins of the Vietnamese Revolution*, 32.

14. Jürgen Osterhammel, *Colonialism*, 51.

15. Peter Zinoman, "The History of the Modern Prison and the Case of Indochina," 156.

16. Gouvernement Général de l'Indochine, *Les administrations et les services publics indochinois*, 770.

17. Patrice Morlat, *La répression coloniale en Indochine (1908–1940)*, 46.

18. On the liaison of Southeast Asian colonial powers, see Ann Foster, "Secret Police Cooperation and the Roots of Anti-Communism in Interwar East Asia."

19. On such violations, see Zinoman, "History of the Modern Prison," 162–163.

20. Cf. Woodside, who dismisses the importance of law in *Community and Revolution in Modern Vietnam*, 22–27. His comments make sense for large

areas of civil law except that on the press. I might add that, at the microlevel, there are no studies on the interaction of law and practice (e.g., studies of conflicts that arose in court cases).

21. Before the arrival of the French, Vietnamese law was based on the Nguyễn legal code (borrowed from the Qing dynasty, with a few modifications) and customary practice (so-called customary law). Although the Lê dynasty had promulgated the Hồng Đức code, it is not clear to me whether the Nguyễn code completely superseded the earlier code.

   French law in Vietnam sometimes drew on completely different legal traditions (e.g., laws on marriage and the family) and sometimes was based almost exclusively on French precedents (e.g., law on the press). Taking the system as a whole, one can agree with Roberts and Mann (discussing the African cases) that, from a legal pluralism, colonial law developed into "a single, interactive colonial legal system" that differed from both its indigenous and foreign bases. See Richard Roberts and Kristin Mann, "Law in Colonial Africa," 9.

22. Nhượng Tống, *Nguyễn Thái Học (1902–1930)*, 16–17.

23. The 1881 law still required that newspapers have a French manager who had not been stripped of his or her civil rights. Further, the state could crack down on publications that fomented sedition, "directly provok[ed] ... crimes against the internal security of the state," or advocated non-compliance with the law. See Henri Litolff, comp., *Recueil des textes concernant le régime de la presse en Indochine*, 8, 15–16, 36–41.

24. On the evolution of French censorship, see James Smith Allen, *In the Public Eye*, 84–103; L. Gabriel-Robinet, *La censure*; and Léon Sabatié, *La censure*, 140. In France, censorship of drama continued until 1905, while film censorship continued past World War II. Laws on the control of pornography had no teeth, and juries refrained from ordering such material seized.

25. For laws on the press, see Litolff, *Le régime de la presse*; J. Chabas, "Le régime de la presse en Indochine," pt. 1 and pt. 2; J. Chabas, "Le contrôle de l'opinion publique en Indochine depuis 1940"; Emile Tavernier, *Le régime de la presse au Tonkin*; Daniel Hémery, "Journalisme révolutionnaire et système de la presse au Vietnam dans les années 1930"; Nguyễn Thành, *Báo chí cách mạng Việt Nam*; Huỳnh Văn Tòng, *Báo chí Việt Nam từ khởi đầu đến 1930* (Vietnamese newspapers from their origins to 1930).

26. Decree of 30 December 1898, article 2, in Litolff, *Le régime de la presse*, 96; the full text of the law is on pp. 94–97.

27. "Décret rélatif au régime de la presse en Indochine, exception faite de la Cochinchine, promulgué le 10 décembre 1927," in Gouvernement Général de l'Indochine, *Recueil général de la législation et de la réglementation de l'Indochine: supplément de 1926–1927*, 685.

28. CAOM, GG, 7F d. 22, L'Administrateur Chef du Service de la Sûreté à M. le Gouverneur de la Cochinchine, "Objet: Sûreté Politique," Saigon, 2 April 1921.

29. CAOM, GG, 7F d. 22 (3), quotation from 9 August 1924 edition of *l'Essor indochinois* excerpted in "Notice d'Information Politique portant sur la periode comprise entre le 1er Juillet 1923 et le 31 Décembre 1924."

30. CAOM, GG, 7F d. 28, Vinay, "Rapport à M. le Résident supérieur au Tonkin sur le fonctionnement de la commission de Contrôle postal et de la Censure de la Presse indigène dans le courant de l'année 1921," Hanoi, 6 January 1921 [1922?].

31. See for example, CAOM, GG, 7F d. 18 (2), "Rapport annuel 1927–28."

32. CAOM, GG, d. 44.516, "Note sur la propagande bochévique [*sic*] en Indochine," 6 January 1925.

33. CAOM, SLOTFOM, série 5, c. "Revue de la presse annamite de langue française du 1er au 15 Juillet 1927." The passages censored indicate no such thing.

34. "La liberté de penser en Indochine française," *Tribune indigène*, 16 February 1924, excerpted in CAOM, GG, 7F d. 22 (3), [Sûreté de Cochinchine], "Notice d'information politique portant sur la période comprise entre le 1er Juillet 1923 et le 31 Décembre 1924."

35. "Loyalisme et censure," *Écho annamite*, 22 February 1924, 1.

36. "Le temps est encore loin," *La cloche fêlée*, 14 July 1924, 1; Việt Tha and Lê Văn Thử, *Hội kín Nguyễn An Ninh* (The Nguyễn An Ninh secret society), 20; Hue-Tam Ho Tai, *Radicalism and the Origins of the Vietnamese Revolution*, 131.

37. "Le Phap-Viet Nhut-Gia suspendu," *Tribune indochinoise*, 21 May 1927, in CAOM, SLOTFOM, série 5, c. 39, Gouvernement de la Cochinchine, Cabinet du Gouverneur, "Revue de la presse annamite de langue française du 16 au 31 mai 1927."

38. CAOM, INF, c. 31, d. 964, Letter from Paul Monin to Marius Moutet, Saigon, 26 July 1925.

39. CAOM, GG, 7F d. 22 (5), Gouvernement de la Cochinchine, Service de la Sûreté, "Rapport annuel 1er juillet 1926 au 1er juillet 1927, Tôme 2."

40. In 1928, a *dụ* (royal order) from the court declared that any songs, pictures, or printed matter banned by the Résident Supérieur in Tonkin would also be banned in Annam. But the royal court went even further, saying that anything "contrary to public order, whether [against] decency (*bonnes moeurs*) or [against] the respect owed to the representatives of Public Authority, would be punished" with fines or imprisonment. TTLTQG-II (Ho Chi Minh City), Résidence Supérieure en Annam (hereafter RSA), d. 2047, [Lettre sur une ordonnance royale], Huế[?], 24 July 1928.

41. TTLTQG-II (Ho Chi Minh City), Thống Đốc Nam Kỳ (hereafter

TDNK), IIA45 185 (1), J. Krautheimer, Gouverneur de la Cochinchine à Monsieur le Gouverneur Général de l'Indochine, "A.s. propagande subversive par la livre et autres écrits non-périodiques," Saigon [?], 22 October 1929.

42. TTLTQG-II, TDNK, IIA45 185 (1), Le Directeur des Affaires Politiques et de la Sûreté Générale [Lacombe], "Note pour Monsieur le Chef du Service du Contentieux au Gouvernement Général," Hanoi, 21 January 1929.

43. TTLTQG-II, TDNK, IIA45 185 (1), Cochinchine, Service de la Sûreté, "Brochure *Anh hung yeu nuoc*," Saigon, 8 February 1929. Trần Huy Liệu translated this brochure written by the Chinese Lam Van Ly.

44. Prefatory note in Triệu Vân, *Chính phủ là gì?* (What is government?), [2].

45. CAOM, RST, d. 577, stay of 17 December 1938. The Huế court adopted, as a matter of course, the bans promulgated in Tonkin.

46. TTLTQG-II, TDNK, IIA 191 (6), [Stay (Arrêté) of the Governor of Cochinchina Pagès], Saigon, 7 April 1937.

47. CAOM, GG, 7F d. 28, Vinay, "Rapport à M. le Résident supérieur au Tonkin sur le fonctionnement de la Commission de Contrôle Postal et de la Censure de la Presse indigène," Hanoi, 6 January 1921 [1922?].

48. CAOM, GG, 7F d. 22 (5), Service de la Sûreté, "Rapport annuel 1er Juillet 1926 au 1er Juillet 1927, Tome 2." Archival dossiers occasionally contain original intercepted letters—for example, correspondence between Phan Bội Châu and friends can be found in dossiers of the Service de Protection du Corps Expeditionnaire (hereafter SPCE) in the French archives at Aix-en-Provence.

49. CAOM, GG, 7F d. 22 (5), Service de la Sûreté, "Rapport annuel 1er Juillet 1926 au 1er Juillet 1927, Tome 2."

50. In 1928, for example, the post office seized twenty-three copies of a tract by Phan Bội Châu, *Lời hỏi* (Questions), printed in the south but banned in the north. They post office also recorded the addresses of all the people who had ordered the tract. CAOM, SPCE, c. 351, Service de la Sûreté du Tonkin, "Note confidentielle No. 1802."

51. TTLTQG-II, TDNK, IIA45 285 (1), [Réquisition du Gouverneur Général de l'Indochine Pagès], Saigon, 28 December 1935.

52. CAOM, GG, 7F d. 7, "Les associations anti-françaises et la propagande communiste en Indochine (les faits du 3ème trimestre 1933)."

53. J. Chabas, "Le régime de la presse en Indochine," 679. Following the principle that a colonial decree "cannot contradict [French] law" (ibid., 678), the courts declared that the 1898 decree was null and void. In the 1898 decree, the authors had tried to "make an exception [to the 1881 law] ... for newspapers and periodical writings written in the Annamite, Chinese, or any other language, which would have to receive pre-publication approval" (Litolff, *Régime de la presse*, 7). The courts rejected this

subterfuge in 1937, and the 30 August 1938 decree formally recognized this fact by striking them from the 1898 law. See the decree of 30 August 1938 in Litolff, *Régime de la presse*, 238.

54. CAOM, Affaires Politiques, d. 1387.

55. CAOM, GG, 7F d. 30 (5), "Rapport sur la situation politique au Tonkin au cours du mois de décembre 1935." CAOM, SLOTFOM, série III, c. 54, "Note périodique de la Direction de la Sûreté générale indochinoise (3ème trimestre 1935)," discusses a pharmacy that gave away tracts on anti-French heroes.

56. CAOM, SLOTFOM, série III, c. 54, "Note périodique no. 44 de la Direction Générale de la Sûreté Générale Indochinoise (mois de septembre 1936)."

57. CAOM, Affaires Politiques, d. 1387, Governor General of Indochina to the Minister of Colonies, "Lettre-Avion 588, Rapport Politique, septembre 1938," Saigon, 22 October 1938.

58. TTLTQG-II, Tòa Đại Biểu Nam Việt, d. 132, "Regime de la presse au Sud-Viet-Nam"; William Duiker, *The Rise of Nationalism in Vietnam, 1900–1941*, 258–259.

59. CAOM, SPCE, c. 381, "Période du 3 au 5 Octobre 1939"; TTLTQG-II, IIA45 234 (4), untitled, to Chef des Services administratifs de la region de Saigon-Cholon, 12 October 1939; CAOM, GG, 7F d. 26, "Notice sur l'activité des intrigues politiques de tendances subversives dans les milieux indigènes de l'Indochine pendant le mois d'octobre 1939."

60. CAOM, SPCE, c. 381, "Notice de renseignements concernant Nguyen An Ninh," February 1940. Nguyễn An Ninh later died in prison.

61. Duiker, *Rise of Nationalism*, 268–270.

62. See the *Journal officiel de l'Indochine*, 1939 to 1942. This total is certainly too low: it only lists printed matter banned by the Governor-General of Indochina, but the governors of Tonkin, Annam, and Cochinchina also had the power to ban publications.

63. TTLTQG-II, IIA45 303 (2), Police, Le chef du Bureau de Traductions, "Influence de la presse, du livre, et de la littérature sur la population indigène," Saigon, 10 June 1941.

64. CAOM, RST, d. 576, "Subvention de 120$ accordé à M. Michel," 22 March 1940.

65. TTLTQG-I, DABI, d. 2135, Service de l'Information de la Propagande et de la Presse, "Objet: discrimination à faire dans la Presse," Hanoi, 5 December 1941.

66. TTLTQG-I, DABI, d. 2135, Service de l'Information, de la Propagande et de la Presse, "Instruction sur la censure de la Presse," Hanoi, 25 August 1942.

67. Domei (the Japanese news agency) could distribute news releases to newspapers without precensorship. Only when the newspaper presented

its pages to the censor could this information be deleted. Domei was the sole source for news on Japan and in the territories occupied by Japan. See TTLTQG-I, DABI, d. 2135, "Instruction sur la censure de la presse," Hanoi, 25 August 1942.

68. TTLTQG-II, TDNK, II.45, d. 243 (12), "Censure de la presse française du 1er janvier 1942 au 31 mars 1942."

69. TTLTQG-I, DABI, d. 2135, [Governor-General] Decoux à Monsieur le Directeur des Archives et Bibliothèques, "Objet: épuration des bibliothèques," Hanoi, 6 August 1942.

70. CAOM, Gouvernement Général, Direction des Services Économiques (hereafter DSE), d. 91, Le Directeur des Affaires Politiques ... à Messieurs les Présidents des Comités Locaux de Contrôle des Informations et de la Propagande, 17 September 1941.

71. "Đời sống Đông dương: mấy dạo dự về tự do" (Life in Indochina: some edicts on freedom), *Thanh nghị*, 21 July 1945, 23. But these freedoms were actually quite restricted. See Trần Huy Liệu and Nguyễn Khắc Đạm, *Xã hội Việt Nam thời Pháp Nhật* (Vietnamese society in the Franco-Japanese period), 61–62.

72. "Thông cáo thứ nhất của Ủy Ban Giải Phóng" (First communique of the Liberation Committee [of the Provisional Government]), August 1945, in Trần Huy Liệu and Văn Tạo, comps., *Tổng khởi nghĩa tháng tám* (The August General Uprising), 34.

PART 2: THREE REALMS OF PRINT

1. I develop some of these points in greater detail in Shawn McHale, "Mapping a 'Confucian' Vietnamese Past and Its Transition to Modernity," and "Texts and Bodies." For a glimpse of the parameters of the debate, look at Keith Weller Taylor, "Surface Orientations in Vietnam" and contrast his views with, for example, Alexander Woodside, "Territorial Order and Collective-Identity Tensions in Confucian Asia," or Philippe Papin, *Viet-Nam: parcours d'une nation*.

2. On Trần Cao, see Đào Duy Anh, *Lịch sử Việt Nam* (History of Vietnam), vol. 2, 251; also see Keith W. Taylor, "Surface Orientations in Vietnam," 957; on Phan Bá Vành, see Masaya Shiraishi, "State, Villagers, and Vagabonds."

CHAPTER 3: CONFUCIANISM AND VIETNAMESE CULTURE

1. This chapter recasts sections of my "Mapping a Vietnamese Confucian Vietnamese Past." I would like to thank Ed McCord of George Washington University and Keith Taylor, Alexander Woodside, and the other

participants at the 1997 and 1999 UCLA conferences on Confucianism for their helpful criticisms.

2. On this multiethnic region and its culture, see Li Tana, *Nguyen Cochinchina*, 18–36, 99–138.

3. Nguyen Khac Vien, "Confucianism and Marxism in Vietnam," 17.

4. I base my comments on Korean historiography partly on John B. Duncan, "Uses of Confucianism in Modern Korea."

5. In the colonial period, as I shall show, Trần Trọng Kim complained about poor understanding of Confucian texts. This view was taken up by a range of postcolonial scholars: see, for example, Trần Văn Giàu, *Sự phát triển của tư tưởng ở Việt Nam từ thế kỷ XIX đến cách mạng tháng tám* (The development of thought in Vietnam from the nineteenth century to the August Revolution).

6. Phan Đại Doãn, ed., *Một số vấn đề về Nho giáo Việt Nam* (Some topics in Vietnamese Confucianism), 289.

7. Woodside, *Vietnam and the Chinese Model*, 7.

8. Ibid., 25.

9. Ibid., 61.

10. Oliver Wolters, "What Else May Ngo Si Lien Mean?" 106.

11. Woodside, *Vietnam and the Chinese Model*, 2d edition, 4.

12. Alexander Woodside, "Territorial Order and Collective-Identity Tensions in Confucian Asia," 204–209, 211.

13. *Vietnamese Traditional Medicine*, 11–12.

14. *Đại Việt sử ký toàn thư* (Complete Historical Annals of Great Viet), 7: 15a–b.

15. Ibid., 5:9b–10b. For further discussion of these problems and of the post-Trần Confucianization of the Trần dynasty, see McHale, "Texts and Bodies."

16. The Nguyễn dynasty fell to the French in 1883, but the French allowed the court to exercise extremely limited powers of rule in Annam. In 1945, Emperor Bảo Đại abdicated the throne under pressure from Việt Minh revolutionaries, thus ending the Nguyễn dynasty.

17. Li Tana, *Nguyen Cochinchina*, 37–46, 101–112.

18. Cao Tự Thanh, *Nho giáo ở Gia Định* (Confucianism in Gia Định), 28; M. de la Bissachère, *État actuel du Tunkin, de la Cochinchine, et des royaumes de Cambodge, Laos, et Lac Tho*, vol. 2, chap. 5, p. 24. Cao Tự Thanh's book is one of the few that goes beyond the intellectual history of Confucianism in Vietnam to explore social history.

19. *Đại Việt sử ký tục biên* (Complete Historical Annals of Đại Việt, continuation, 1676–1789), 21:4b.

20. Trần Huy Liệu, "Những ngày cửa Khổng sân Trình" (Days of Confucian learning), in *Hồi ký Trần Huy Liệu* (Memoirs of Trần Huy Liệu), 12. The

Song dynasty scholar Wang Bohou supposedly wrote this work, the *Sanzi jing*, for his students, and Wang Jinsheng later annotated it. See the "Préface du Commentateur" (i.e., Wang Jinsheng), in *Tam Tu Kinh ou le livre des phrases de trois caractères*, ii–iii. The translator Abel des Michels wrote in 1879: "The *Tam tự kinh* is, in China as in the colony [of Cochinchina], one of the basic works that is most widespread, to the extent that it constitutes the starting point for instruction in the country's schools." Ibid., viii.

21. For Wang Bohou's views, see *Tam Tự Kinh*, ii; Trần Huy Liệu, "Những ngày cửa Khổng sân Trình," in *Hồi ký Trần Huy Liệu*, 12.

22. Interview with Nguyễn Đôn Phục in Lê Thanh, *Cuộc phỏng vấn các nhà văn Trần Trọng Kim, Nguyễn Văn Tố, Nguyễn Đôn Phúc, Ngô Văn Triện, Hoàng Ngọc Phách, Vũ Đình Long, Tú Mỡ, Đào Duy Anh* (Interviews with the writers Trần Trọng Kim, etc.), 54. The Five Classics, most of which date to the period before Confucius, include the *Book of Changes*, the *Book of History*, the *Book of Poetry*, the *Book of Rites*, and the *Spring and Autumn Annals*. The Four Books are the *Great Learning*, the *Doctrine of the Mean*, the *Analects*, and *Mencius*.

23. Ngô Đức Kế, "Luận về chánh học cùng tà thuyết Quốc văn, Kim Văn Kiều, Nguyễn Du" (A discussion of correct and heterodox teachings in the national literature, Kim Văn Kiều, Nguyễn Du [1924]), 33–34.

24. On French efforts to Confucianize the past, see Nola Cooke, "Colonial Political Myth and the Problem of the Other."

25. Neil Jamieson, *Understanding Vietnam*, 11 n. 13.

26. *Gia đình và xã hội* (The family and society), 31.

27. Marr, *Vietnamese Tradition on Trial*, 65.

28. Hà Tấn Phát, trans., *Chấn hưng phong tục* (Reform of mores), i. For more on this topic, see Cửu Kim Sơn and Văn Huê, *Đời chị em* (Life of young women), 14, and Trúc Khê, *Vấn đề cải cách lễ tục Việt Nam* (On the reform of rituals and customs), 26. Cửu Kim Sơn and Văn Huê assert that the practice of young men marrying older wives was most common in the north.

29. See, for example, the prescriptions in one highly influential primer: *Tam Tu Kinh*, 67–68.

30. My use of the term "Confucianism" reflects Vietnamese popular and scholarly usage. Vietnamese tend to refer to Confucianism as *đạo Khổng* (the Way of Confucius), *đạo Khổng Mạnh* (the way of Confucius and Mencius), *Nho giáo* (Nho teachings), *Nho học* (Nho studies), or *Khổng giáo* (Confucian teachings). Confucius is referred to as Khổng tử or, relatively rarely, as Khổng phu tử. Lionel Jensen has argued, significantly, that Jesuits introduced this latter term to China. See Lionel Jensen, *Manufacturing Confucianism*, chapter 1.

31. Some southerners (like Trần Hữu Độ) discussed Confucianism, but their writings had little impact on northern-centered debates. In contrast, southern writings on feminism and women's place in society, which did touch on Confucian arguments, had some effect on northern discourse. When the southerner Phan Văn Hùm published his massive study *Vương Dương Minh* (Wang Yangming) during World War II, communication between north and south was almost completely cut off. His book had no impact on northern intellectuals.

32. See Phạm Thế Ngữ, *Việt Nam văn học sử gian ước tân biên* (Short history of Vietnamese literature), 294–301.

33. Ngô Tất Tố, *Phê bình Nho giáo Trần Trọng Kim* (A criticism of Trần Trọng Kim's "Confucianism"), 11.

34. Trần Trọng Kim, *Việt Nam sử lược* (Brief history of Vietnam), x.

35. Trần Trọng Kim, *Nho giáo* (Confucianism), 724–725.

36. Ibid., ix.

37. Ibid., 722.

38. Ibid., vii. Nguyễn Bá Học had previously used this metaphor of a dilapidated house to describe Vietnam in a 1920 *Nam phong* article. See Marr, *Vietnamese Tradition on Trial*, 331.

39. Hoàng Đạo, *Mười điều tâm niệm* (Ten things to ponder), 15.

40. Trần Trọng Kim, *Nho giáo*, vii.

41. Ibid., xiv.

42. Ibid., xiv–xv.

43. Ibid., viii.

44. Ibid., 735.

45. Ibid.

46. Ibid., ix.

47. Ibid.

48. Ibid., xiii.

49. Ibid.

50. Ibid., xvi.

51. Bergson had enjoyed a vogue in China. Liang Shuming, for one, had used him in 1921 to explicate Confucianism. See Guy Alitto, *The Last Confucian*, 96–104. Trần Trọng Kim may have derived his interpretation from his reading of Liang Shuming, or he may have first encountered Bergson on his own (in French).

52. Henri Bergson, *La pensée et le mouvant*, 35–36. This book mostly brings together essays printed between 1903 and 1923. Note that the word *"conscience"* in French means both "consciousness" and "conscience."

53. Trần Trọng Kim, *Nho giáo*, xv.

54. Ibid., xvii.

55. These points were made at a conference at UCLA in 1999.

56. A sign of the importance of Đào Duy Anh's early work is that in 1944

Nguyễn Uyển Diêm wrote a book evaluating it. Diêm criticized Anh for his hastiness. See Nguyễn Uyển Diêm, *Khổng giáo với o. Đào Duy Anh* (Confucianism and Mr. Đào Duy Anh).

57. Đào Duy Anh, *Khổng giáo phê bình tiểu luận* (Short critique of Confucianism), 9–10.

58. Đào Duy Anh, *Việt Nam văn hóa sử cương* (Outline history of Vietnamese culture), viii. Vũ Ngọc Phan accorded the book a prominent place in his survey of intellectual life: see Vũ Ngọc Phan, *Nhà văn hiện đại*, vol. 1, 317–322.

59. Đào Duy Anh, *Việt Nam văn hóa*, 13.

60. Ibid., 13. Sartiaux (1876–?) was an archaeologist of Asia Minor as well as the writer of a book on civilization.

61. Ibid., 14–15.

62. Đào Duy Anh, *Khổng giáo*, 114–115.

63. Đào Duy Anh, *Việt Nam văn hóa*, 109.

64. Ibid., 142.

65. Ibid., 154.

66. Đào Duy Anh, *Khổng giáo*, 100–101.

67. Đào Duy Anh, *Việt Nam văn hóa*, 237.

68. Ibid., 114.

69. Ibid., 320–321.

70. Trương Tửu (1912[?]–1999) was an independent intellectual who was sometimes strikingly original. He also wrote, under the name Nguyễn Bách Khoa, *Nguyễn Du và truyện Kiều* (Nguyễn Du and the *Tale of Kiều*), an analysis of the changing reception of the *Tale of Kiều*; *Nhân loại tiến hóa sử* (The evolution of humanity); and *Nguồn gốc văn minh* (The roots of civilization). He participated in the famous Nhân Văn–Giai Phẩm affair in 1956, and after that time the government forbade him to publish books. He supposedly turned to Zen in his old age and lived in Hanoi until his death. In 1992 I asked to see him but was told that he still had "political problems" stemming from his 1956 actions.

71. Từ Lâm [Nguyễn Xuân Nghị], *Tân hiếu kinh* (The new filial piety), 7–8.

72. Phạm Thế Ngữ, *Việt Nam văn học sử*, vol. 3, 610.

73. Ibid., 613–614.

74. Ibid., 614.

75. To emphasize its respect for "tradition," the governor-general of Indochina established a program in the teaching of East Asian culture on 5 May 1942. See Vũ Đình Hòe, "Việc lập một nền cổ điển Á Đông ở Đông dương" (The establishment of an East Asian classical [program] in Indochina), *Thanh nghị*, 22 (1 October 1942), 2.

76. Trương Tửu [Nguyễn Bách Khoa], *Kinh thi Việt Nam* (Vietnamese classical odes), 80. This book was at the same time issue 53 (5 July 1945) of *Tạp chí văn học mới* (New literary journal). *Kinh thi Việt Nam* was first

printed in 1940 by the Hàn Thuyên publishing house, but I have not been able to compare the 1940 and 1945 copies.

77. On the *Odes*, Steven Van Zoeren writes: "The *Odes (Shi)*, or as it later came to be known, the *Classic of Odes (Shijing)* is on most modern accounts a collection of early songs and hymns, perhaps representing a repertoire of Zhou court musicians in the sixth or seventh century B.C.E. From an early date, it has been one of the centerpieces of the Confucian tradition, and at least since the time of Xunzi in the third century B.C.E., dignified with the title of "classic" (*jing*)." *Poetry and Personality*, 7.

78. Trương Tửu, *Kinh thi Việt Nam*, 23.

79. Ibid., 25.

80. Ibid.

81. Ibid., 87.

82. Ibid., 106.

83. Ibid., 183.

84. Ibid., 141. In his analysis, Trương Tửu cites Sigmund Freud. He also may have been influenced by an increased interest in sexuality among some Vietnamese, shown by the publication in the 1930s of "hygiene manuals" with sections on sex, love novels, and the import of French books on "normal" and "deviant" sexuality.

85. Ibid., 19.

86. Ibid., 22. *Linh hồn* is usually translated as "soul." In this context I have translated it as "soul force," partly to convey the full meaning of "*linh*" (magical power).

87. A notable attempt to portray Trương Tửu as a Trotskyist came after the Nhân Văn–Giai Phẩm literary affair in 1956, when the Communist Party was cracking down on perceived dissidents. See, for example, Văn Tân and Nguyễn Hồng Phong, *Chống quan điểm phi vô sản về văn nghệ và chính trị (nhận những ý kiến của ông Trương Tửu về văn nghệ và chính trị đã đặng trên báo Nhân văn và Giai phẩm mùa thu và mua đông)* (Opposing antiproletarian viewpoints on literature and art [found in Trương Tửu's opinions on literature and politics published in *Humanity* and *Works of Autumn and Winter*]). The label, however, seems singularly inapt. As Nguyễn Vỹ observed, in thought Trương Tửu was "completely independent." Nguyễn Vỹ, *Văn thi sĩ tiền chiến* (Writers of the prewar years), 198.

88. Lương Đức Thiệp, *Xã hội Việt Nam tiến hóa sử*, 458–459.

CHAPTER 4: PRINTING REVOLUTION, SPREADING COMMUNISM

1. Chánh Thi, "Rồi ba vào Đảng" (Then father entered the Party), 220. I have italicized words that would have been novel to Chánh Thi's father.

2. Huỳnh Kim Khánh, *Vietnamese Communism*, 337, 338.

3. Trần Đình Hượu, *Đến hiện đại từ truyền thống* (Approaching modernity through tradition), 131. He continues by arguing that "the scientific and philosophical content was abandoned or else was explained, carelessly, in a Confucian manner." Hượu's argument is a variant of Nguyen Khac Vien's, which stresses the continuities between Confucianism and Marxism in Vietnam. See Nguyen Khac Vien, "Confucianism and Marxism in Vietnam," 15–52.

4. Since Khánh published his book, scholars have been able to gain access to far more documents on the Vietnamese revolution than were once available. Some of this material is leading to serious revision of views, for example, on Hồ Chí Minh's role in the revolution and on the extent of communist and Việt Minh success by 1945.

5. Hue Tam Ho Tai's *Radicalism and the Origins of the Vietnamese Revolution* can be profitably read as a critique of Khánh's book.

6. See David Marr, *Vietnam 1945*, and Christopher E. Goscha, *Thailand and the Southeast Asian Networks of the Vietnamese Revolution, 1885–1954*.

7. Hans Van de Ven, *From Friend to Comrade*, esp. 55–56.

8. Vietnamese often refer to the two provinces of Nghệ An and Hà Tĩnh as Nghệ Tĩnh.

9. I was fortunate to be able to use the Revolutionary Museum's library in Hanoi. The museum has the richest collection of original Vietnamese propaganda outside that of the Communist Party itself. I also consulted French colonial records at the Centre des Archives d'Outre-Mer in Aix-en-Provence and at the Trung Tâm Lưu Trữ Quốc Gia–I (National Archive Center) in Hanoi.

10. Merleau-Ponty, quoted in Michael Yeo, "Perceiving/Reading the Other," 44.

11. It is worth mentioning, however, that while David Marr does not focus on the audience's interpretation of communist propaganda, he has conclusively shown that the Vietnamese uprisings of 1945 were not directed, marionette-like, from the center. Local groups calling themselves Việt Minh often interpreted directives (if they actually received them) in their own idiosyncratic ways. See Marr, *Vietnam 1945*, 402–472.

12. While much attention has been paid to the importance of South China in the development of Vietnamese communism, Christopher Goscha has underlined the importance of Southeast Asian bases as well. See his *Thailand and the Southeast Asian Networks*, esp. 1–113. On Thanh Niên's noncommunist origins, see Hoàng Nam Hùng, *Năm mươi năm cách mạng hải ngoại: hồi ký* (Fifty years of revolution from abroad), 134–135.

13. Ralph B. Smith, "The Foundation of the Indochinese Communist Party, 1929–1930," discusses the period up to unification of the parties in great

detail. Khổng Đức Thiêm, "Một số tư liệu về An Nam Cộng sản Đảng với việc thong nhất các lực lượng cách mạng ở Việt Nam năm 1930" (Some materials on the Annamese Communist Party and the unification of the revolutionary forces in Vietnam in 1930), brings some new material to bear on the different interpretations of the chronology of the founding of the party.

14. "Nghị quyết của trung ương" (Resolution from the center), 256, in Đảng Cộng sản Việt Nam, *Văn kiện Đảng toàn tập* (Complete collection of Party documents), vol. 1. The Annam Communist Party made identical criticisms of its rivals.

15. Khuất Duy Tiến, "Hồi ký về vô sản hóa" (Memoir on proletarianization), 354.

16. Trần Văn Cung was a native of Nghị Lộc (Nghệ An province) and a student at the Collège de Vinh. One of the earliest Vietnamese communists, he did not know who initially suggested the 1929 "proletarianization movement." Trần Văn Cung [Quốc Anh], "Vài mẩu chuyện về chi bộ cộng sản đầu tiên và Đông Dương Cộng sản Đảng" (Several parts of the story of the first communist cell and of the Indochinese Communist Party), 110. See also Khuất Duy Tiến, "Hồi ký về vô sản hóa," 131–132. Jailed after the Nghệ Tĩnh uprisings, Trần Văn Cung was amnestied in 1936. See P. V., "Trần Văn Cung và Hoàng Trọng Từ đã được ân xá" (Trần Văn Cung and Hoang Trọng Từ have been amnestied), *Tiếng dân*, 30 July 1936. Thanks to Peter Zinoman for showing me the *Tiếng dân* article.

17. In his account of "the revolutionary storm" in Guangzhou, Trần Văn Cung mentioned the Canton commune (1927) but not the Haifeng soviet (1927) in Guangzhou province. Trần Văn Cung [Quốc Anh], "Vài mẩu chuyện," 110, 108. See also "Các nhà cach mạng Việt Nam tham gia khởi nghĩa Quảng Châu" (Vietnamese revolutionaries who participated in the Guangzhou uprising), trans. Thanh Đạm, 72–75.

18. Qiang Zhai, *China and the Vietnam Wars, 1950–1975*, 11.

19. On this topic, see A. A. Xôcôlốp [Anatoli Sokolov], *Quốc tế Cộng sản và Việt Nam* (The Comintern and Vietnam). Sokolov's book is based on extensive use of Comintern archives. While some Russian scholars argue that Vietnamese first began studying in Moscow in 1923 or 1924, Sokolov believes, based on the documentation, that they first began arriving in 1925. The first three were "Phong Sơn" (real name: Nguyễn Thế Rục), "Tapkikhen," and "Ianô." Ibid., 57–58.

20. CAOM, Indochine, SPCE, c. 351, Rapport de Robert, le Commisaire Spécial de la Sûreté, No. 1733/C.S. Vinh, 25 September 1930.

21. See Phan Đình Phương, "Bước đầu tìm hiểu văn hóa dòng họ Nguyễn Năng ở Nghi Trường–Nghi Lộc" (Preliminary understandings of the

culture of the Nguyễn Năng lineage in Nghi Trường and Nghi Lộc), 331–332, and Nguyễn Sinh Quế and Nguyễn Sinh Tùng, "Văn hóa dòng họ Nguyễn sinh với quá trình phát triển trong cộng đồng dân cư vùng Kim Liên Nam Đàn–Nghệ Tĩnh" (The culture of the Nguyễn Sinh lineage and the development of the collective of inhabitants of the Kim Liên–Nam Đàn–Nghệ Tĩnh region), 255, both in *Văn hóa các dòng họ ở Nghệ An với sự nghiệp thực hiện chiến lược con người Việt Nam đầu thế kỷ XXI* (The culture of lineages in Nghệ An and the fulfillment of the strategy of the Vietnamese people at the beginning of the twenty-first century). For other examples of the importance of kin networks in politics, see Christopher Goscha, *Thailand and the Southeast Asian Networks*, 68–71, and Hy Van Luong, *Revolution in the Village*.

22. Hoàng Văn Hoan, *Giọt nước trong biển cả: hồi ký* (A drop in the ocean: a memoir), 3. Hoàng Văn Hoan was a high-ranking communist cadre for much of his career. Elected a member of the Central Committee of the Communist Party in 1951, he held a string of other high-level posts (e.g., in the Party and in the National Assembly). In 1976, Lê Duẩn forced him off the Party's Central Executive Committee. In 1979, Hoàng Văn Hoan fled from Vietnam to China.

23. CAOM, SPCE, c. 353, L. T. [Ly Thuy, i.e., Nguyễn Ái Quốc], "Critique de la 'Revolution.'"

24. "Nghị quyết của Trung Ương," in Đảng Cộng sản Việt Nam, *Văn kiện Đảng toàn tập*, vol. 1, 256–258.

25. "Đảng chương" (Party program, ca. 1928) of the New Vietnamese Revolutionary Party (Tân Việt Cách Mạng Đảng), in *Văn kiện Đảng toàn tập*, vol. 1, 156.

26. [Nguyễn] Sơn Trà, *Giai cấp là gì?* (What are classes?), 2.

27. Trần Huy Liệu, "Phấn đấu để trở nên một đảng viên cộng sản" (Striving to become a Communist Party member), 77.

28. *The ABC of Communism* was translated into French as early as 1925. On this book as a primer, see the account by early activists Trần Cung and Trịnh Đình Cửu, "Một vài nét về chi bộ đầu tiên của Đảng và về Đông Dương Cộng sản Đảng" (A few features of the first Party cells and of the Indochinese Communist Party), 108. Phạm Xanh writes that "many fighters (*chiến sĩ*) have affirmed that thanks to that book [*The ABC of Communism*], they came to communism" in the pre-1930 period. Phạm Xanh, *Nguyễn Ái Quốc với việc truyền bá chủ nghĩa Mác Lê-nin ở Việt Nam (1921–1930)* (Nguyễn Ái Quốc and the spread of Marxism-Leninism to Vietnam [1921–1930]), 181. Nguyễn Ái Quốc allegedly translated *The ABC of Communism*, *The Evolution of Humanity*, and *The Paris Commune* into Vietnamese while in Siam (1929), but no copies of his translations have survived.

29. Võ Bá Pha, *Staline nước Pháp đồng chí Maurice Thorez* (The Stalin of France: comrade Maurice Thorez), 19.

30. Numerous Sûreté reports of the 1930s mention commemoration of the "3Ls" and of May First. A political prisoner, San Hô, organized competitions on Poulo Condore (Côn Đảo) to celebrate the anniversary of the Paris Commune. San Hô, *Nhật ký tuyệt thực 9 ngày rưỡi: một cuộc tranh đấu của tù chính trị Côn Lôn* (Diary of a nine-and-a-half-day hunger strike: a struggle of the political prisoners on Côn Đảo), 1. While the Canton uprising was a disaster, it became symbolically important in the history of Chinese Communism. See S. Bernard Thomas, *"Proletarian Hegemony" in the Chinese Revolution and the Canton Commune of 1927*, 1. From their writings, one senses that the uprising deeply affected some Vietnamese revolutionaries, like Trần Văn Cung and Thiết Hùng, who participated in it. Trần Văn Cung, "Vài mẩu chuyện về chi bộ cộng sản," 108; Ban Nghiên cứu lịch sử Đảng trung ương, *Những sự kiện lịch sử Đảng* (Events in the history of the Party), 125–126.

31. Một người công nhân Hanoi (A Hanoi worker), "Ý kiến chung: nói về tình thế lao động" (General opinion: on the situation of labor), *Lao động*, 4 (1 November 1929), 4. This paper was probably printed in or around Hanoi. According to an official Communist Party chronology, an association with a slightly different name, the General Red Labor Association (Tổng Công Hội Đỏ Bắc Kỳ), was formed on 28 July 1929 in Hanoi. The newspaper *Lao động* served as its propaganda organ and the review *Cộng hội đỏ* (Red Labor Association) was its theoretical organ. This same source claims that General Red Labor Association led a number of strikes in Hải Phòng and right outside Hanoi in Yên Viên (Bắc Ninh). See also Ban Nghiên cứu lịch sử Đảng trung ương, *Những sự kiên lịch sử Đảng*, 153–154.

32. My analysis here draws inspiration from Takashi Shiraishi, *An Age in Motion*.

33. By way of comparison, in 1924 Đào Trinh Nhất used words like *"tư bản"* (capitalist) and *"nghề"*, *"nghề nghiệp"* (trade, profession) but not *"giai cấp"* (class) or *"công nhân"* (worker) to discuss Chinese economic activity in Vietnam. See Đào Trinh Nhất, *Thế lực Khách trú và vấn đề di dân vào Nam Kỳ* (The influence of the Chinese and the problem of immigration to Cochinchina).

34. *Búa liềm* (Hammer and sickle), 3 (1 November 1929), 4; *Búa liềm* 4 (15 November 1929).

35. The following call for improvement in laborers' working conditions uses such terms: "Khẩu hiệu tranh đấu" (Struggle slogans), *Búa liềm* 3 (1 November 1929), 3. Nguyễn Lương Hoàng states that the division between blue and brown shirts lasted until the August Revolution.

Nguyễn Lương Hoàng et al., *Ngành in Việt Nam* (Vietnamese printing), vol. 1, 67–68.

36. In 1935, Tuệ Châu and Hành Lâm argued that Vietnamese society was composed of nine classes: landlords, capitalists, petty bourgeoisie, petty merchants (*tiểu thương*), small farmers (*tiểu nông*), aristocratic workers (*thợ thuyền quý tộc*), very poor peasants (*bần nông*), poor farmhands (*cố nông*), and the proletariat. Tuệ Châu and Hành Lâm, "Mơ hồ, sai lầm, hay đeo mặt na?" (Unclear, wrong, or disguised?), *Đời mới* (New era), 3 (7 April 1935), 2. This article was mostly devoted to defining the meaning of "*bình dân*" (popular).

37. Phạm Văn Hảo, "Làm báo bí mật" (Producing secret newspapers), 123.

38. Ibid., 123–124.

39. Ibid.

40. Ibid.

41. Ibid., 126–127.

42. Ibid.

43. *Thanh niên* (Youth), 68 (7 November 1926).

44. Gareth Porter, "Proletariat and Peasantry in Early Vietnamese Communism," 333.

45. These claims come from a communist document translated from Russian into Vietnamese: "Phong trào cách mạng ở Đông Dương," 20 September 1930, in Đảng Cộng sản Việt Nam, *Văn kiện Đảng toàn tập*, vol. 1, 75.

46. CAOM, RST, d. 610, "Traduction d'un document à l'encre sympathique autographe de Nguyen Ai Quoc découvert le 14 Mai [1931] au cours de l'opération effectuée à Cholon."

47. Trần Huy Liệu, *Les Soviets du Nghe Tinh de 1930–31 au Vietnam*, argues that the Party was more or less in control. Good Western studies of the Nghệ Tĩnh uprising include Ngo Vinh Long, "The Indochinese Communist Party and Peasant Rebellion in Central Vietnam, 1930–1931"; Pierre Brocheux, "L'implantation du mouvement communiste en Indochine française"; and Martin Bernal, "The Nghe-Tinh Soviet Movement, 1930–1931." James Scott focuses less on the Party and more on how the violation of the peasants' moral economy was the motor for rebellion. See Scott, *The Moral Economy of the Peasant*. For revolutionary songs from Nghệ Tĩnh (collected far after the uprisings), see Nguyễn Đổng Chi and Ninh Viết Giao, *Hát giặm Nghệ Tĩnh* (Folk songs of Nghệ Tĩnh), vol. 2. This book is a revised and expanded version of *Hát dặm Nghệ Tĩnh*, first published in 1944. See also Lê Trọng Khánh and Lê Anh Trà, eds., *Xô viết Nghệ Tĩnh qua một số thơ văn* (The Nghệ Tĩnh soviets through literature).

48. Bernal, "The Nghe-Tinh Soviet Movement," 150.

49. Ibid., 152.

50. Ibid.

51. Annam regional committee of the Indochinese Communist Party, quoted in Bernal, "The Nghe-Tinh Soviet Movement," 160. The view that regional communists did not pay enough attention to the central leadership is confirmed in a postmortem written in 1933 by Hồ Nam (the pseudonym of Trần Văn Giàu), *Kỉ niệm Nghệ an bạo động (12 tháng 9 năm 1930)* (Anniversary of the Nghệ An revolt [12 September 1930]).

52. Central committee document, cited in Ban Chấp Hành Đảng Bộ Dảng Cộng sản Việt Nam tỉnh Hà Tĩnh, *Lịch sử Đảng bộ Hà Tĩnh* (History of the Hà Tĩnh province Party committee), 96–97.

53. Two sources are particularly helpful with regard to Nghệ Tĩnh revolutionary newspapers from this period: Quang Hưng and Quốc Anh, "Bước đầu tìm hiểu báo chí vô sản ở Nghệ An thời kỳ đầu cáchg mạng" (First steps in understanding proletarian newspapers in Nghệ An at the beginning of the revolution), and Nguyễn Thành, *Báo chí cách mạng Việt Nam.*

54. CAOM, GG, 7F d. 18 (1), "Rapport Annuel 1926–1927"; GG, 7F d. 18 (2), "Rapport Annuel 1927–28."

55. See Đào Duy Anh, *Nhớ nghĩ chiều hôm,* 35; on reading these books to understand Marxism, see, for example, Ninh Viết Giao and Hoc Phi, recorders, "Chỉ một con đường: hồi ký của Tôn Thị Quế" (Only one road to take: the memoir of Tôn Thị Quế), 8. Tôn Thị Quế was from Thanh Chương, central Vietnam, a key area in the Nghệ Tĩnh rebellions.

56. Trương Tửu, "Bốn mươi năm văn hóa Việt Nam, 1905–1945" (Forty years of Vietnamese culture, 1905–1945), *Văn mới,* 12[?] December 1945; Lê Thanh, "Vệ Thạch ông Đào Duy Anh," in Lê Thanh, *Cuộc phỏng vấn các nhà văn,* 161.

57. Quang Hưng and Quốc Anh, "Bước đầu tìm hiểu báo chí vô sản," 28. The authors note that many Nghệ An natives living in Siam sent publications back from that country.

58. Ibid., 27 n. 1.

59. T.N.T.T.V., "Cái nạn cộng sản" (The danger of communism), *Thanh Nghệ Tĩnh tân văn,* 8 August 1930, 1.

60. The three social bonds, a Confucian notion, are king-subject, father-son, and husband-wife. The five cardinal virtues are *nhân* (benevolence), *nghĩa* (righteousness), *lễ* (propriety), *trí* (knowledge), and *tín* (sincerity).

61. T.N.T.T.V., "Cái nạn cộng sản," 1.

62. But why would a peasant be moved by a song whose lyrics included "[He] set up the Third International / the foundation of our proletariat / providing leadership to the world / Brother Lenin has zealously sacrificed / Brother Liebknecht and sister Luxemburg are second to none"? See Tố Hữu, "Tình hình xã hội Việt Nam dưới ách áp bực của

thực dân và phong kiến qua thơ văn Xô Viết Nghệ Tĩnh" (Social conditions under the colonial and feudal yoke as seen through the literature of the Nghệ Tĩnh soviets), 82.

63. Bùi Thiết, *Vinh–Bến Thủy*, 106.

64. All three places had previous histories of labor organizing and strikes. See Trần Huy Liệu, Nguyễn Lương Bích, Văn Tạo, Hướng Tân, *Cách mạng cận đại Việt Nam* (The modern Revolution of Vietnam), vol. 4, 41–44. See also Ban Nghiên cứu lịch sử Đảng trung ương, *Những sự kiện lịch sử Đảng*, 138–140, 152–153, 165–168, 187–189, 189–190.

65. The following section is based on material found in the Revolutionary Museum (Hanoi) collection. These are only traces of messages from the past: the great majority of propaganda has been lost. For example, one French police agent knew of fifteen persons who printed tracts in their homes in the four villages of Nghệ An (Vo Liet, Ngoc Son, Xuan Truong, Thuong Tho) that he surveyed. See CAOM, SPCE, c. 351, Rapport du Robert, le Commissaire Special de la Sûreté, No. 1733/C.S. Vinh, 25 September 1930.

66. This paragraph is based on "Kỉ niệm ngày Quốc tế lao động mồng 1 tháng 5 năm 1930" (Celebrating International Workers Day on 1 May 1930), *Người lao khổ*, 1 May 1930. This article appeared, in slightly modified wording, as a posted leaflet, now in the collection of the Revolutionary Museum, Hanoi. Đảng Cộng sản Việt Nam, "Hợi anh em chị em thợ thuyền, dân cày, binh lính, thanh niên, học sinh . . ." (untitled, 1930). Note that I have preserved the idiosyncratic spelling of the original propaganda, which combines communist innovations (e.g., "f" for "ph") with Nghệ An localisms (e.g., lack of discrimination at times between *nặng* and *ngã* tones).

67. "Truyên cáo" (Proclamation), *Gương vô sản* 1 (1 July 1931), 1.

68. Ibid.

69. Ngo Vinh Long, "The Indochinese Communist Party," 29.

70. "Đế quốc chủ nghĩa fáp lại cho tụi cố-đạo rúc vào các xã thôn khuyến dụ quần chúng theo giáo 'gia-tô'" (French imperialism allows bands of missionaries to enter communes to exhort the masses to follow Christianity), *Tiến lên* 26 (17 December 1931), 1–2. This paper was published by the Nghệ An Party cell.

71. Propaganda leaflet, untitled, beginning with the words "Hỡi anh em chị em thợ thuyền, dân cày . . ." (Nghị Lộc village, Nghệ An, 1931). See also "Chết đói" (Starving to death) and "Thủ đoạn xỏ lá của đế quốc" (Trickery of the imperialists), *Gương vô sản* 4 (5 August 1931), both signed by "Nông Dân" (Peasant). Both stories use concrete examples of events in the vicinity to drive home large points and to get people to "struggle."

72. Nông Dân, "Thủ đoạn xỏ lá của đế quốc," 1.

73. "Chúng ta fải sửa soạn làm kỉ niệm" (We must prepare to celebrate the anniversary), *Chỉ đạo* 8 (17 August 1931), 2; "Trị chỉ trích (Chastise and find fault), *Tiến lên* 20 (September 1931).

74. Trung cảo cùng anh em chị em" (Frank advice to our brothers and sisters), *Tiến lên* 19 (20 August 1931), 5.

75. "Bức thư của cậu Học sinh gửi cho ông chủ bút báo Tiếng dân" (Letter from pupils to the editor of the newspaper *Tiếng dân*), *Xích sinh* 3 (15 January 1930), 5.

76. "Chúng tôi fải vạch mặt bọn fản đối tranh đấu" (We must expose those who oppose the struggle), *Chỉ đạo* 8 (17 August 1931), 5.

77. "Chúng ta fải sửa soạn làm kỉ niệm," *Chỉ đạo* 8 (17 August 1931), 2.

78. Hồ Nam (Trần Văn Giàu), a highly prominent southern communist, argued in 1932 that the peasant movement in Nghệ Tĩnh grew large because the proletariat "led" (*diù đắt*) the peasantry and because the party of the proletariat "commanded" (*chỉ uy*) the peasants. But he also argued that, "generally speaking, the proletarian class did not yet play a guiding role." Furthermore, he chastised those who neglected the importance of proletarians, saying that "there are few [proletarians], [but] not none, and furthermore, we should never forget the main responsibility in our revolution." Hồ Nam, *Kỉ niệm Nghệ an bạo động*, 16, 18, 27. In short, he blamed the proletariat of Nghệ Tĩnh for not playing its assigned role.

    Hồ Nam's pamphlet may have been written and published in Moscow; it begins with an account of the commemoration of the Nghệ An revolt at the "Stalin" school in Moscow.

79. Huynh Kim Khanh, *Vietnamese Communism*, 103.

80. Chánh Thi, quoted in Huynh Kim Khanh, *Vietnamese Communism*, 104.

81. See Comrade Nguyễn Phúc's story in Minh Huệ, *Ngọn cờ Bến Thủy: hồi ký xô viết Nghệ Tĩnh* (The flags of Bến Thủy: memoir of the Nghệ Tĩnh soviets), 56.

82. TTLTQG-II, TDNK, IIA45 195 (4), Cabinet du Gouverneur, "Rapport politique du mois d'Avril [1937]."

83. These figures come from a study carried out from 1967 to 1970 by the Historical Research Board of the provincial committee of Hà Tĩnh, quoted in Ban Chấp Hành Đảng bộ Đảng Cộng sản Việt Nam, *Lịch sử Đảng bộ Hà Tĩnh*, vol. 1, 116 n. 1. The study, with suspect accuracy (when were these figures collected?), also states that 5,563 pigs and 316 water buffalo were seized by troops.

84. Nguyen Khac Vien, *Vietnam: Une longue histoire*, 271–272. Vien states that his French sources grossly underestimate the true numbers. Note that some of the killed and arrested would have been noncommunist members of the Nationalist Party (Việt Nam Quốc Dân Đảng) as well as those incarcerated from other parts of Indochina.

85. Triệu Vân, *Chính phủ là gì* (What is government?), 31.

86. Mark Bradley, *Imagining Vietnam and America*, 42–44.

87. Khanh, *Vietnamese Communism*, 230.

88. Trần Huy Liễu and Văn Tạo, *Phong trào chống phát xít chống chiến tranh và các cuộc khởi nghĩa Bắc Sơn, Nam Kỳ Đô Lương* (The movements against fascism and war and the Bắc Sơn, Nam Kỳ, and Đô Lương uprisings), 24; Marr, *Vietnam 1945*, 162.

89. TTLTQG-II (Ho Chi Minh City), IIA45 306 (6), Gouvernement de la Cochinchine, Cabinet, No. 42-C/API, Saigon, 26 February 1942, "Preparation d'un nouveau mouvement insurrectionnel."

90. Khanh, *Vietnamese Communism*, 254; Trần Huy Liễu and Văn Tạo, *Phong trào chống phát xít*, 9, 21–25. Hà Huy Tập and Nguyễn Văn Cừ were Central Committee members; the former was a founding member of the Communist Party. Nguyễn Thị Minh Khai had been a representative to the Seventh Communist International. At the time of her arrest she was serving on the Saigon municipal committee of the Party.

91. In northern Annam, French police estimated that there were only one hundred Party members in Nghệ An and Thanh Hóa, and 1,100 mass followers, and that from Quảng Bình south to Phan Thiết (i.e., in the rest of Annam) there were less that one hundred more Party members. Liaison with communists in Cochinchina was irregular. In short, before the crackdown the party was not strong in the center. See TTLTQG-II, IIA45 232 (3), Service de Police en Annam, "Note sur l'activité révolutionnaire en Annam en cours du mois de janvier 1938," Huế, 29 January 1938.

92. Most Western scholars give the full name of the Việt Minh as "Việt Nam Độc Lập Đồng Minh Hội." David Marr, in his authoritative study *Vietnam 1945*, refers in his index to the Việt Nam Độc Lập Đồng Minh, but in one place in the text he refers to Việt Nam Độc Lập Đồng Minh (Hội). Phạm Hồng Tung notes that, while a variety of Western scholars use the longer term, almost all Vietnamese scholars refer to the organization as the Việt Nam Độc Lập Đồng Minh and that that is the term that should be used. A quick look at my own copies of Việt Minh newspapers and propaganda suggests that Tung is correct. For more on this terminological confusion, see Phạm Hồng Tung, "Tìm hiểu thêm về Mặt trận Việt Minh" (Understanding more about the Việt Minh front), 7–8.

93. Marr, *Vietnam 1945*, 168.

94. TTLTQG-II, IIA45 306 (6), Arnoux, Chef Local des Services de Police, "Projet de déclenchement d'un nouveau mouvement insurrectionnel. Nouvelles méthodes d'action," Saigon, le 17 septembre 1941. This source summarizes a meeting of the Communist Party in Tonkin at which delegates decided on this new approach.

95. Vũ Văn Hiền, "Tín ngưỡng" (Religious belief), *Thanh nghị* 33 (16 March 1943), 2.

96. Nguyễn Thế Mỹ, *Hai bà Trưng khởi nghĩa*. This book was also issue 41 of *Văn mới*, 25 August 1944. Pp. 187–201 discuss how nationalism appeared in various countries.

97. "Đề cương văn hóa Việt Nam" (Theses on Vietnamese culture) (1943), 15, 18, 19. The Communist Party also stated that it had to fight against the influences of Confucius, Mencius, Descartes, Bergson, Kant, and Nietzsche.

98. *Kinh nghiêm Việt Minh ở Việt Bắc* (The Việt Minh experience in Việt Bắc), 17, 18.

99. See, for example, "Nghề thuật ấn loát sách của người Nam Kỳ" (The southerner's art of publishing books), in *Nam kỳ kinh tế* (The economy of the south), 22; Tào Hoài, "Điều tra nhỏ: nghề làm giấy để in (A small investigation: using rice paper for printing), *Thanh nghị* 86 (7 October 1944), 7–8, 20. I believe that the Việt Minh produced some of its own paper in Việt Bắc. The Resistance produced some of its own paper in the post-1946 period. See *In bột* ("Flour" printing); *Phương pháp làm bột giang sản xuất giấy* (Method of making bamboo powder to produce paper).

100. Phạm Văn Hảo, "Làm báo bí mật," 126.

101. Figures and claims come from *Kinh nghiêm Việt Minh ở Việt Bắc*, 17.

102. [Nguyễn] Sơn Trà, *Giai cấp là gì*, 3.

103. Trần Huy Liệu, "Mặt trận dân chủ Đông dương" (The Indochinese democratic front), in *Hồi ký Trần Huy Liệu*, 200.

104. Thanks to David Chandler for pushing me to emphasize this point.

105. "Nhiệm vụ cần kíp phổ biến chính sách Việt Minh" (The urgent responsibility to popularize Việt Minh policy), *Hiệp lực* (Bắc Ninh), 2 (20 October 1943), 1.

106. Ibid.

107. Ibid. Capitalized text in original.

108. For the Vichy context, useful secondary sources are Phạm Thế Ngữ, *Việt Nam văn học sử*, vol. 3; N., "Regards sur notre action politique en Indochine"; Phạm Văn Hảo, "Làm báo bí mật"; Phạm Huy Thông, "La littérature vietnamienne depuis 1939." For rich archival sources in Vietnam on the topic, see, for example, TTLTQG-I, AMH, d. 3456; TTLTQG-II, TDNK, IIA45, d. 243.

109. See the brief mention in TTLTQG-II, TDNK, IIA45 315 (3). Le chef local des Services de Police, "Fête du Travail et de la Paix Social. Ier Mai 1941," Saigon, 30 April 1941.

110. Phong Châu, "Kỉ niệm ngày 14 tháng 7" (The anniversary of July 14), *Hồn Việt Nam* 2 (15 July 1942), 1. The Việt Minh may have adopted some of the Free French line, but I have found no evidence to support the

notion that Gaullists and the Việt Minh collaborated. Indeed, the Free French in China believed that the Việt Minh actively tried to hinder them from contacting people within Vietnam; see Ronald Spector, "'What the Local Annamites Are Thinking,'" 745.

111. See Philippe Devillers, *Histoire du Vietnam du 1940 à 1952*, 107, 110. In 1945 and after, however, the Việt Minh used assassination squads to kill opponents.

112. See, for example, "Lột mặt nạ đế quốc" (Unmask the imperialists), *Tự do* (Thanh Hóa) 4 (10 March 1941), 4. This article noted that the book *Les paroles du Maréchal* (Sayings of Maréchal Pétain) was selling briskly and that schools compelled pupils to read it.

   A February 1944 Việt Minh poster found in Yên Thế village (near Hanoi) warned Vietnamese that the Japanese wanted to bring parties like the Đại Việt, Phục Việt, and Quốc Xã into one group, the Việt Nam Phục Quốc Đồng Minh Hội, and also bring back Cường Để as a king. See TTLTQG-I, AMH, d. 3514, [Propaganda leaflet]: Việt Nam Độc Lập Đồng Minh (Việt Minh), "Hỡi Đồng Bào!"

113. Trần Huy Liệu discusses this change in "Từ 'tiếng suối reo,' 'Dòng sông công,' đến con 'Đường nghĩa'" (From "babbling brook" and "the common stream" to "righteous path"), in *Hồi ký Trần Huy Liệu*, 275.

114. "Hẩy [sic] phá nhà ngực! Mở xiềng tù tội!" (Destroy the prisons! Break the chains of imprisonment!), *Phá ngục*, 1 May 1940. This publication was the organ in central Vietnam of the Anti-Imperialist Popular United Front of Indochina (Mặt Trận Thống Nhứt Dân Tộc Phản Đế Đông Dương), presumably the same as one with a similar name (Mặt trận dân tộc phản đế Đông Dương) formed by the Indochinese Communist Party in November 1939. The article cited also exhorted Vietnamese to "study according to the spirit of sacrifice and struggle of the American proletariat."

115. *Kinh nghiêm Việt Minh ở Việt Bắc*, 16.

116. "Báo Quân Giải Phóng ra đời" (The birth of the newspaper *Liberation Army*), *Quân giải phóng* 1 (5 August 1945), 1. This newspaper cost money (30 *đồng*), unlike much propaganda.

117. TTLTQG-I, AMH, d. 3514, Délégation Spéciale de Hanoi, Le Commissaire de Police Lecomte à M. le Controleur de la Sûreté, Khâm Thuê, 7 July 1944; *Khởi nghĩa* 3 (4 April 1945), 3.

118. H. V., "Sinh hoạt tiểu tổ" (The life of a unit), *Mê Linh* 2 (15 August 1944 [?]), [3].

119. Ibid. Also see *Cộng sản sơ giải* (Summary of communism), i. Although printed after the August General Uprising, the book gives an interesting list of pointers for reading.

120. *Kinh nghiệm Việt Minh ở Việt Bắc*, 16–17.

121. *Việt Minh kêu gọi anh em binh lính đứng lên!* (The Việt Minh calls on soldiers to rise up!), 14.

122. Việt Kỉ, "Làm cho tổ chức hoạt động" (Making the organization work), *Đuổi giặc nước* 7 (10 June 1944), 2.

123. *Kinh nghiệm Việt Minh ở Việt Bắc*, 19.

124. Việt Con, "Phải làm gì lúc tung truyền đơn" (What must be done when circulating propaganda leaflets), *Đuổi giặc nước* 9 (15 August 1944), 1.

125. Ibid.

126. Phan Đan Quế, *Giai thoại và sấm ký Trạng Trình* (Stories and prophecies of Trạng Trình [Nguyễn Bỉnh Khiêm]), 97, 98.

127. "Dân chúng và cách mệnh" (The people and revolution), *Đuổi giặc nước* 11 (15 October 1944), 1.

128. Marr, *Vietnam 1945*, 2.

129. I have in mind here *Tài liệu tham khảo lịch sử cách mạng cận đại Việt Nam* (Research materials on the Vietnamese Revolution), vols. 9–12.

130. Tai, *Radicalism and the Origins of the Vietnamese Revolution*; Marr, *Vietnam 1945*; Goscha, *Thailand and the Southeast Asian Networks*; Peter Zinoman, *The Colonial Bastille*; Christoph Giebel, *Imagined Ancestries*; and Christopher Goscha and Bénoît de Treglodé, eds., *Vietnam since 1945*, are emblematic of this shift.

131. Gouvernement Général de l'Indochine, Direction des Affaires Politiques et de la Sûreté Générale, *Contribution à l'histoire des mouvements politiques de l'Indochine française, Documents—Vol. 5: La terreur rouge en Annam (1930–1931)*, [3].

132. Ty Thông Tin Hà Nội, *Tuyên truyền chỉ nam* (Guide to propagandizing), 65.

133. Ibid., 66.

134. X. Y. Z., "Chống thói ba hoa," in Ty Thông Tin Hà Nội, *Tuyên truyền chỉ nam*, 50.

135. Shiraishi, *Age in Motion*, 340.

136. Reynaldo Ileto, "Orators and the Crowd," 94.

137. Michael Williams, *Sickle and Crescent*, 27.

CHAPTER 5: FROM POPULAR VISIONS OF PARADISE TO THE BUDDHIST REVIVAL

1. The account of Nguyễn Kim Muôn is based on a series of documents found in CAOM, GG, 7 F59, files titled "Cambodge" and "Dao Phat Thich Ca."

2. Trần Văn Giáp, *Đạo lý Phật giáo với đạo lý Nho giáo ở nước ta* (Buddhism and Confucianism in our country), 3–4.

3. The history of Buddhism before the twentieth century has often been ill served by scholars, and its transformation in the twentieth century has

been little studied. For a learned and withering critique of many of the standard secondary texts in the study of pre-twentieth-century Vietnamese Buddhism, see Cuong Tu Nguyen, *Zen in Medieval Vietnam: A Study and Translation of the Thiền Uyển Tập Anh,* 22 n. 54. Studies of twentieth-century Vietnam usually ignore or distort Buddhism. Of those that touch on the topic, Trần Văn Giàu, *Sự phát triển của tư tưởng ở Việt Nam,* vol. 2, and Nguyễn Tài Thư et al., *Lịch sử Phật giáo Việt Nam* (The history of Vietnamese Buddhism), highlight critics of Buddhism. Trần Hồng Liên, *Đạo Phật trong cộng đồng người Việt ở Nam Bộ–Việt Nam* (The Way of the Buddha among the Vietnamese of the south of Vietnam), contains useful information, but for the post-1945 period, the author exaggerates the significance of American attempts to influence Buddhists. Contrast *50 năm chấn hưng Phật giáo* (Fifty years of the Buddhist revival), which contains useful information but no analysis.

Hue-Tam Ho Tai's *Millenarianism and Peasant Politics in Vietnam* focuses on the antecedents to and the rise of the Buddhist Hòa Hảo sect. An excellent article as well is Thien Do, "The Quest for Enlightenment and Cultural Identity."

The Vietnamese historian Hồng Chương has blamed French imperialism for opium shops, dance parlors, the spread of mystical idealism, and the Buddhist Revival. See Hồng Chương, "Đồng chí Hải Triều" (Comrade Hải Triều), 13.

4. Short Western-language treatments of the Buddhist Revival include Huynh Ba Yêt Duong, "Le mouvement de rénovation au Viet Nam," and parts of Alexander Woodside, *Community and Revolution in Vietnam.*
5. Mật Thể (Thường tọa), *Việt Nam Phật giáo sử lược* (A short history of Buddhism), 273.
6. Ibid., 262.
7. See CAOM, GG, 7 F22 (2), "Notes de la Sûreté concernant la situation politique indigène au 23 Mai 1923."
8. Nguyễn An Ninh, *Tôn giáo* (Religion), 57.
9. David Chappell, "From Dispute to Dual Cultivation," 164.
10. See Bruno Revertégat, *Le bouddhisme traditionnel au sud-Viêtnam,* 14–16.
11. Thiều Chửu, "Giảng nghĩa kinh Dược sư: mấy lời nói đầu" (Explaining the sutra of the Master of Healing [*Dược sư,* i.e., *Bhaisajayaguru sutra*]: some introductory remarks), i.
12. Nguyễn Lang, *Việt Nam Phật giáo sử luận* (History of Vietnamese Buddhism), vol. 2, 43; Phan Đại Doãn, in Nguyễn Tài Thư et al., *Lịch sử tư tưởng Việt Nam,* 399 and chapter 19.
13. Cuong Tu Nguyen, *Zen in Medieval Vietnam,* 54–55, 30.
14. Ibid., 86.
15. See Li Tana, *Nguyen Cochinchina,* 101–107; Philippe Papin, *Viet-Nam: parcours d'une nation,* 80–82, for brief looks at the variety of such beliefs.

16. Nguyễn Thế Anh, "The Vietnamization of the Cham Deity Po Nagar," 42–50. Po Nagar is referred to in Sino-Vietnamese as Thiên Y A Na Ngọc Diễn Phi. The following quotation by a Vietnamese writer of Khánh Hòa province, where the Po Nagar complex is found, shows the extent to which knowledge of the "Chamness" of this religious complex has been wiped out of the Vietnamese imagination: "Stupa of the lady— that is to say, stupa to worship Lady Thiên Y A Na, *in French* known as Poh Nagar." See Quách Tân, *Xứ trầm hương* (Land of aloe wood), 185; my emphasis.

17. Đoàn Trung Còn, *Phật học từ điển* (Buddhist dictionary), vol. 2, 136–137; vol. 3, 1476. Many other sites link the world of the text, the sacred geography of Buddhism, and the Vietnamese countryside together. Hương Sơn Tự (Perfume Mountain temple), for example, is named after the Perfumed Mountain, the highest peak in Jambudvipa (Nam Diêm Phù Đề) in the Himalayas. This mountain had the famous lake called Anavatapta that could quench all thirst and help one escape all suffering. See ibid., vol. 1, 136.

18. Nguyễn Lang, *Việt Nam Phật giáo sử luận*, vol. 2, 72.

19. In China, there are many versions of a *Nanhai Guanyin* (Guanyin of the southern seas), the title of a short novel that circulated in the late sixteenth century. See Glen Dudbridge, *The Legend of Miao-shan*, 51. The Vietnamese version in demotic script (Nôm) dates to the eighteenth or nineteenth century, if not before. It appears to be different from the versions described by Dudbridge.

20. On eleventh-century worship of Avalokitesvara, see *Đại Việt sử ký toàn thư*, comp. Ngô Sĩ Liên, vol. 1, 2:37a, 3:4b, 3:5a.

21. *Mời vào cửa Phật: lễ tụng, giáo lý, hành hóa* (Invitation to Buddhism: rites and teachings), i.

22. Nguyễn Lang, *Việt Nam Phật giáo sử luận*, vol. 2, 74–75.

23. Ibid., vol. 2, 75.

24. See, for example, Hàn Chính, "Phật giáo cần phải chấn hưng" (Buddhism needs to be reformed), *Quan Âm tạp chí* 11 (October 1940), 18–19.

25. Thiều Chửu, *Phật giáo với nhân gian* (Buddhism and the people), 2.

26. Nguyễn An Ninh, *Phê bình Phật giáo* (Critique of Buddhism), 44.

27. Mộng Vân, "Lễ Phật không bằng biết Phật" (Knowing Buddhist ritual is not the same as understanding the Buddha), *Quân Âm tạp chí* 10 (August 1940), 3.

28. Nguyễn Khắc Hiếu (Tản Đà), *Đài gương kinh* (Mirror of the classics), 49.

29. A sharp exception is the texts of Huỳnh Phú Sổ from 1939 onward.

30. Quoted in Cao Tự Thanh, *Nho giáo ở Gia Định* (Confucianism in Gia Dinh), 81. This book shows that a heterodox religious culture little

influenced by Confucianism permeated the south before the eighteenth century.

31. Sơn Nam, *Người Sài Gòn* (The people of Saigon), 46.

32. Ibid., 25. On the identification of Mariamman, thanks to Professor Michael Rabe of Xavier University, Chicago, and Philip Taylor.

33. There is even a report of human sacrifice. On the night of 2 December 1944, a follower of the Đạo Xen in Cần Thơ, saying that the spirits demanded a sacrifice, stabbed and then burned alive a beggar in a ritual watched by a reported one thousand persons. (It is worth noting, perhaps, that the area on the Cambodian side of the border with Vietnam, not too far from this area, is also reported to have seen human sacrifices in the nineteenth century.) On the 1944 sacrifice, see A. M. Savani, *Notes sur le Phat giao Hoa Hao*, 20. Li Tana has also noted the existence of human sacrifice in the central region of Vietnam from Quang Binh southward; see Li Tana, *Nguyen Cochinchina*, 132. Thanks to Li Tana for the citation to her book. On Cambodian sacrifices, see David Chandler, "Royally Sponsored Human Sacrifices in Nineteenth Century Cambodia," 119–135. It is impossible, of course, to deduce from such scattered information anything in general about religious practices in Vietnam as a whole. It is worth noting that the Lotus Sutra refers to self-immolation as "the supreme gift," but this would not seem to apply to the immolation of others.

34. See Sơn Nam, *Đất Gia Định xưa* (Gia Dinh in the past), Phố Hồ Chí Minh, 1984), esp. 51–68. Vietnamese authors often write as if Vietnamese were the first to settle the region; in fact, many Khmer and some Chinese predated them.

35. Vietnamese have often given landmarks two names: one in Sino-Vietnamese (e.g., Thất Sơn, or "Seven Mountains"), another in colloquial Vietnamese (e.g., Bảy Núi). Both terms have the same meaning, but the latter is more widely understood by all Vietnamese.

36. Hue-Tam Ho Tai, "Perfect World and Perfect Time," 156.

37. Cửu Long Giang, *Thất Sơn Hà Tiên* (From the Seven Mountains to Hà Tiên), 47.

38. CAOM, GG, 7F d. 59, Légation de la République Française au Siam, "Quatre bonzes suspects à la pagode [Wat] Sanammam," Bangkok, 5 June 1929.

39. Dật Sĩ and Nguyễn Văn Hầu, *Thất Sơn mầu nhiệm* (The wonders of Seven Mountains), 303, 306.

40. *Pháp âm* copied the name of a Chinese Buddhist journal, *Fayin*. A later Vietnamese periodical, *Hải triều âm* (Sound of the tides), took the name of a Chinese Buddhist periodical, *Hai chaoyin*. I located one issue of *Pháp âm* but no issues of *Phật hoá tân thanh niên*.

41. It was rare to find a newspaper with a press run over ten thousand. Most had runs of between five hundred and three thousand. Most tracts and books probably had five hundred to three thousand copies printed as well.

42. These included *Từ bi âm* (Sound of compassion) (Saigon), *Vĩ lâm Phật học* (Trà Vinh), *Viên âm* (Words of the Buddha) (Huế), *Niết bàn* (Nirvana), *Tiếng chuông sớm* (Sound of the early bell) (Hanoi?), *Duy tâm Phật học* (Buddhist idealism) (Trà Vinh), *Bác nhã âm* (Sound of wisdom) (Baria), *Bồ đề tạp chí* (Bodhi tree) (Sóc Trang), and *Phật học* (Buddhist studies) (Saigon).

43. I was not able to see copies of these last two newspapers, which are mentioned in Trần Văn Giàu, *Sự phát triển*, 237. No dates of publication are given.

44. Interest in Buddhism and Confucianism showed gender divisions. Hy Van Luong notes that in Sơn Dương village (northern Vietnam), the eligible men formed a literati association, while elderly women formed a Buddhist Association. Hy Van Luong, *Revolution in the Village*, 58.

45. Furthermore, authors of Buddhist texts often encouraged others to reprint their works. "Whoever has a good heart, who wants to print this sutra and distribute it does not need to request any permission from me as I give up [any rights to] the copyright," wrote one author. See *Địa Tạng kinh có âm nghĩa* (Transliteration of the *Ksitigarbha bodhisattva sutra*), 1.

46. Maurice Durand, *L'imagerie populaire vietnamienne*, xxi. This book has many plates of such images from the collection of the École française d'Extrême-Orient.

47. For example, see the instructions in Nam Kỳ Nghiên Cứu Phật Học Hội, *Kinh A Di Đà, Hồng Danh, Vu Long* (The *Amitabha* and *Ullambana* sutras), 59; Chùa Tam Bảo, Rạch Gía, *Niệm Phật qui tắc* (Methods for praying to the Buddha), 6; and the complaints about many monks' lack of reverence and ability in reading in *Phật thuyết A Di Đà Kinh* (Explaining the *Amitabha Sutra*), trans. Trần Quang Thuân, 4.

48. "Tỳ kheo-ni" (Bhikkhuni) writes that one has to ring the bell and beat the wooden fish when reciting sutras, but this view is not shared by all writers. See Tỳ kheo-ni (Thích nữ), *Kinh Vu lan bồn (diễn nghĩa)* (The *Ullambana Sutra* explained), 11. For precise definitions of the meanings of words used for reading and recitation in Buddhism, see Nguyễn Thuyết Phong, "La liturgie bouddhique du Vietnam et son répértoire," 44–55, 156–159.

49. Tỳ kheo-ni (Thích nữ), *Kinh Vu lan bồn (diễn nghĩa)*, 11. Many monks who championed the "Buddhist Revival" argued the contrary: that one had to understand the sutras first and then recite them.

50. Annam Phật Học Hội. *Nghi thức tụng niệm* (Correct rites for prayer), 5.

51. *Phật thuyết A Di Đà Kinh*, 4.

52. See the *dharani* and explanations for their use in Annam Phật Học Hội, *Nghi thức tụng niệm*, 5.

53. See Thiện Chiếu, *Tại sao tôi cám ơn đạo Phật* (Why I thank the Way of the Buddha), 9.

54. Viên Hoành "Lễ nghi" (Rituals), *Đông Pháp thời báo*, 22 October 1923, 1.

55. T. V., "Ảnh hưởng của bài Phật-giáo lược khảo" (The influence of the article on "an outline of Buddhism"), *Đông Pháp thời báo*, 23 January 1924, 1.

56. Thanh Từ (Thích), *Thiền sư Việt Nam* (Vietnamese Zen teachers), 516.

57. Nguên [*sic*] Mục Tiêu, "Nên chấn hưng Phật giáo ở nước nhà," 2.

58. Ibid.

59. Ibid.; Thiện Chiếu, untitled article in Tiên Lũ Đông Tư, comp., *Chấn hưng Phật giáo* (The Buddhist Revival), 19–20.

60. Nguyễn Khoa Tung, "Bàn về Phật học" (A discussion of Buddhist studies), *Pháp âm* 1 (1929), 8.

61. Tai Xu, quoted in Kenneth Ch'en, *Buddhism in China*, 456.

62. Nguyễn Khoa Tung, "Bàn về Phật học," *Pháp âm* 1 (1929), 8.

63. CAOM, GG, 7F d. 59, "Une interview de M. Chan promoteur de l'oeuvre de la renaissance du Bouddhisme," *L'opinion*, 16 December 1929.

64. Tương tế Phật Học Hội. *Statuts: Điều lệ* (Statutes), 22.

65. Lê Khánh Hòa, "Tự trần" (From this world of dust [?]), *Pháp âm* 1 (1929), 17–18.

66. Hội Nam Kỳ Nghiên Cứu Phật Học (Saigon), *Nghi thức tụng niệm của người tu tại gia* (Correct rites for believers praying at home), 2.

67. Anon., "Mục đích Từ Bi âm" (The goals of *Từ Bi âm*), *Từ Bi âm* 1 (1 January 1932), 4.

68. *Mời vào cửa Phật*, ii–iii.

69. Thiện Chiếu, untitled article, in Tiên Lũ Đông, comp., *Chấn hưng Phật giáo*.

70. Epigram signed "T. C." in *Phật học tổng yếu* (Fundamentals of Buddhism), trans. Thiện Chiếu, [i].

71. In a very different context, Richard Gombrich has made the stimulating argument that Sinhalese Buddhism is orthodox and has been for over 1,500 years. He states: "So long as Buddhists continue to treat their gods as a kind of supermen, able to grant favors to suppliants, but still ultimately of limited life and powers and subject to moral law, their beliefs are not syncretistic. Belief in gods like this is not logically (or otherwise) incompatible with Buddhist doctrine." See Richard Gombrich, *Precept and Practice*, 49. But this view of an unchanging Theravada tradition has recently come under attack: see Anne Blackburn, *Buddhist Learning and Textual Practice in Eighteenth-Century Lankan Monastic Culture*, chapter 1.

72. See Hàn Chính, "Phật giáo cần phải chấn hưng" (Buddhism must be revived), *Quan Âm tạp chí* 11 (October 1940), 19.

73. On the early Marxist critique of Buddhism, see Shawn McHale, "Imagining Human Liberation."

74. Bửu Tín, "Trong cuộc trường kỳ chù a sắc-tứ Tam Bảo (Hà Tiên)" (The instructional sessions at the royally decreed [?] "Three Jewels" temple), *Phật học,* 13 October 1936, 1015. The movement even came to the attention of persons who were not very sympathetic to the revival, like the Marxist scholar Đào Duy Anh. See Đào Duy Anh, *Nhớ nghĩ chiều hôm,* 188.

75. Mật Thể, *Việt Nam Phật giáo sử lược,* 270. Đoàn Trung Còn explains this theory as follows: "[For] every Buddha who comes into existence and establishes the Way, the Way of the Dharma is from that point divided into three consecutive eras: Chánh Pháp [True Dharma], Tượng Pháp [Imitation Dharma], and Mạt Pháp [Destruction of the Dharma]. In the era of True Dharma, those who lead a religious life reach enlightenment [as an arhat or bodhisattva, for example] easily. In the Imitation Dharma period, people who lead a religious life have difficulty reaching enlightenment. By the era of the Destruction of the Dharma, far removed from the Buddha, wicked people are many and so very few people lead a religious life and achieve enlightenment." Đoàn Trung Còn, *Phật học từ điển,* vol. 2, 289. Cf. Hue-Tam Ho Tai, "Perfect World and Perfect Time," 164.

76. The phrase is from David Ownby, "Chinese Millenarian Traditions," 1513.

77. In CAOM, GG, 7F d. 59, see the following sources: Cochinchine, Service de la Sûreté, "Rensignements ... provenant du chef de la brigade mobile de Mytho," Saigon, 2 May 1928; Service de la Sûreté, "Note confidentielle No. 1866/S," Saigon, 2 June 1928; "Note confidentielle No. 1645/S," Saigon, 9 June 1928.

78. CAOM, GG, 7F d. 22 (2), "Notes de Sûreté concernant la situation politique indigène au 25 mai 1923."

79. Revolutionaries took advantage of the general tolerance of Buddhists. For example, Nguyễn Ái Quốc's *Đường kách mệnh* (Revolutionary road) circulated in An Giang province disguised as a Buddhist sutra, the *Đạo Nam kinh.* See Phạm Xanh, *Nguyễn Ái Quốc với việc truyền bá chủ nghĩa Mác-Lê Nin ở Việt Nam,* 140.

80. In Vietnam, Quan Âm is often called "Phật Bà Quan Âm," or the female Buddha Guanyin (the Goddess of Mercy). People pray to her in case of misfortune.

81. On eleventh-century discussion of Avalokitesvara, see *Đại Việt sử ký toàn thư,* vol. 1, 2:37a, 3:4b, 3:5a.

82. See Hội Phật Giáo Quan Âm Tịnh Độ, *Lễ luật* (Regulations). One of the

main purposes of this association was to allow male and female believers to gather on days of religious ceremonies to read the sutras together.

83. *Pháp môn Tịnh Độ* (The dharma-gate to the Pure Land), 1. Note: *quấc độ* is the southern spelling of *quốc độ*.

84. Ibid. This is the Vietnamese pronunciation of "Nammo Amitabha Buddha."

85. Tỷ-kheo-ni [Bhikkuni] (Thích-nữ), *Kinh Vu lan bồn (diễn nghĩa)*, 11.

86. Chùa Tam Bảo Rạch Giá, *Niệm Phật quy tắc*, 1.

87. Huỳnh Kim Long, *Vọng cổ Phật nhập Niết bàn* (*Vọng cổ* song on the Buddha entering Nirvana).

88. Mật Thể (Thích), *Lời yêu cầu của một đoàn-thể thanh niên tăng già về cấn đề cải tổ sơn môn Huế* (Request of a collectivity of youth and monks on the reorganization of the *sơn môn* of Huế), 5.

89. Mật Thể, *Việt Nam Phật giáo sử lược*, 273.

90. Trần Văn Giàu, quoted in Trinh Van Thao, *Vietnam du confucianisme au communisme*, 265.

CONCLUSION

1. For an example of the revival of interest in Confucianism, see Phan Đại Doãn, ed., *Một số vấn đề về nho giáo Việt Nam*; for assertions that Confucianism can help create a new modernity, see Nguyễn Tài Thư, *Nho học và Nho học ở Việt Nam* (The teaching of the scholars and the teaching of the scholars in Vietnam), 178, 198–199.

2. Trần Đức Thảo, "Sur l'Indochine," 878.

3. Ibid., 881.

4. Đào Duy Anh, *Khổng giáo phê bình tiểu luận*, 151.

5. Trần Đức Thảo, "Sur l'Indochine," 882.

6. Hoài Thanh and Hoài Chân, *Thi nhân Việt Nam*, 11.

7. Tố Liên, "Tăng-Già muốn nâng cao trình độ thời phải nhiệt liệt tham gia vào việc Bình dân Học Vụ" (If the Buddhist order wants to heighten the [populace's] level [of knowledge], it should enthusiastically participate in the campaign for Popular Education), *Diệu Am nguyệt san* 2 (25 June 1946), 7.

8. Võ Nguyên Giáp speech in *Trang sử mới*, 23.

9. Anderson, *Imagined Communities*, 114.

10. On this issue, Goscha, *Thailand and the Southeast Asian Networks of the Vietnamese Revolution*, is key.

BIBLIOGRAPHY

Research for this book was carried out at the Centre des Archives d'Outre-Mer, Aix-en-Provence; the Bibliothèque nationale, Paris; the library of the Institut nationale des Langues et Civilisations Orientales, Paris; the Library of Congress, Washington, D.C.; the Social Sciences Library, Ho Chi Minh City; the Bảo Tàng Lịch Sử Cách Mạng (Revolutionary Museum), Hanoi; the Thư Viện Quốc Gia (National Library), Hanoi; the Trung Tâm Lưu Trữ Quốc Gia–I (National Archives Center–I), Hanoi; the Trung Tâm Lưu Trữ Quốc Gia–II (National Archives Center–II), Ho Chi Minh City, and Cornell University Library.

ARCHIVAL SOURCES

The book relies on the following archival record groups. Some record groups are known under both French and Vietnamese names, and I have included both names below when I knew them. Abbreviations preceding names are those used in the notes.

CAOM   Centre des Archives d'Outre-Mer (Aix-en-Provence, France)
Affaires Politiques
Commission Guernut
DSE   Gouvernement Général, Direction des Services Économiques
GF   Indochine, Gouvernement de Fait
GG   Gouvernement Général
INF   Indochine, Nouveau Fonds
Papiers Decoux
Papiers Moutet
Papiers Révertégat
RST   Résidence Supérieure au Tonkin
SLOTFOM   Service de Liaison des Originaires des Territoires d'Outre-Mer
SPCE   Indochine, Service de Protection du Corps Expéditionnaire

TTLTQG-I   Trung Tâm Lưu Trữ Quốc Gia–I (National Archives Center–I) (Hanoi, Vietnam)
AMH   Archives de la Mairie—Hanoi
DABI   Département des Archives et Bibliothèques de l'Indochine / Sở Lưu Trữ Thư Viện Đông Dương

RND   Résidence de Nam Dinh
RST   Résidence Supérieure au Tonkin

TTLTQG-II   Trung Tâm Lưu Trữ Quốc Gia–II (National Archives Center–II) (Ho Chi Minh City, Vietnam)
RSA   Résidence Supérieure en Annam
TDBNV   Tòa Đại Biểu Nam Việt
TDNK   Gouvernement de la Cochinchine / Thống Đốc Nam Kỳ

Cornell University Libraries (Ithaca, N.Y.)
Gaston Liebert Papers

INTERVIEWS

Hoàng Xuân Hãn, Paris, 1991
Tô Hòai, Hanoi, 1992
Kim Cương Tử, Hanoi, 1992
Nguyễn Đình Đầu, Ho Chi Minh City, 1992

NEWSPAPERS AND PERIODICALS CONSULTED

Legal Periodicals

Chính nghĩa (Just cause) (Hanoi), 1946
Cloche fêlée (Saigon), 1924
Đàn bà (Women) (Hanoi), 1939, 1940
Dân chúng (The masses), 1939
Diệu am nguyệt san (Monthly magazine of the wonderful temple), 1946
Đời mới (New era) (Hanoi), 1935
Đông Pháp thời báo (Indochina times) (Saigon), 1923–1924
Écho annamite (Annamite echo) (Saigon)
Journal officiel de l'Indochine française (Hanoi), 1927–1943
Lao động (Labor) (Hanoi), 1939
Ngày mới (New day) (Hanoi), 1935, 1939
Ngày nay (Today) (Hanoi), 1939
Ngo báo (Noon report) (Hanoi), 1930
Nữ giới chung (Women's bell) (Saigon), 1918
Pháp âm (The sound of the dharma) (Saigon), 1929–1932
Phật học (Buddhist learning)
Phụ nữ tân văn (Women's news) (Saigon), 1929–1934
Quan Âm tạp chí (Guanyin magazine) (Hanoi), 1940
Thần chung (Morning bell) (Saigon), 1929

Thanh Nghệ Tĩnh tân văn (News of Thanh Hóa, Nghệ An, and Hà Tĩnh provinces) (Vinh), 1931
Thanh nghị (Refined opinion) (Hanoi), 1942–1945
Tiếng dân (Voice of the people) (Hue), 1936
Tin tức (News) (Hanoi), 1938
Tri tân (Modern understanding) (Hanoi), 1941–1942
Từ bi âm (Voice of compassion) (Saigon)
Văn mới (New literature) (Hanoi), 1945

Clandestine Periodicals in the Collection of the Revolutionary Museum, Hanoi

Note: The Revolutionary Museum usually had only a few issues of each periodical.

Báo cờ vô sản (Proletarian flag), 1931
Báo đỏ (Red news), 1931
Báo học sinh (Student paper)
Búa liềm (Hammer and sickle) (Canton?), 1929
Bước tới (Step forward) (Hà Tĩnh), 1930
Chỉ đạo (Pointing the way) (Trung Kỳ), 1931
Cờ giải phóng (Liberation flag)
Con đường sống (Path of life), 1931
Công nông binh (Workers, peasants, soldiers) (Trung Kỳ), 1931
Đời mới (New era), 1935
Đuổi giặc nước (Chase out the invaders) (Thanh Hóa), 1944
Gương vô sản (Proletarian example) (Anh Sơn, Nghệ An province), 1931
Hiệp lực (Join forces) (Bắc Ninh), 1943
Hồn lao động (Soul of labor) (Thanh Hóa), 1934
Hồn nước (Soul of the country), 1930
Hồn nước (Soul of the country), 1945
Hồn Việt Nam (Soul of Vietnam), 1942
Kháng địch (Resist the enemy), 1945
Khởi nghĩa (Uprising) (Ba Đình region), 1945
Lao động (Labor) (Hanoi?), 1929
Mê Linh (Phúc Anh), 1944
Người lao khổ (Toilers) (Trung Kỳ), 1930
Phá ngục (Destroy our prisons), 1941
Quân giải phóng (Liberation army) (Việt Bắc), 1945
Tấc đất (Plot of ground), 1945
Thân Ái (Fraternity) (Siam), 1930
Thanh niên (Youth) (Canton), 1925
Tiến lên (Advance) (Nghệ An), 1931–1932
Tin tranh đấu Bắc Kỳ (News of struggle in the north)

Tự do (Freedom) (Thanh Hóa), 1941
Việt Nam độc lập (Vietnam independence), 1945
Việt Nam lao động báo (Vietnamese labor newspaper) (Marseille), 1929
Xích sinh (Students in chains) (Nghệ An), 1930

BOOKS, TRACTS, AND ARTICLES

Alitto, Guy. *The Last Confucian: Liang Shu-ming and the Chinese Dilemma of Modernity*. Second edition. Berkeley: University of California Press, 1986.

Allen, James Smith. *In the Public Eye: A History of Reading in Modern France, 1800–1940*. Princeton, N.J.: Princeton University Press, 1991.

Anderson, Benedict. *Imagined Communities: Reflection on the Origin and Spread of Nationalism*. Revised edition. London: Verso, 1991.

Annam Phật Học Hội (Huế). *Nghi thức tụng niệm* (Correct rites for prayer). Hue: Phật Học Hội, [1939?].

Ba Xuyên. "Phê bình sách Vương Dương Minh của ông Phan văn Hùm" (Evaluating Phan Văn Hùm's book on Wang Yangming). *Tập kỷ yếu Hội Khuyến Học / Bulletin de la Société d'Enseignment Mutuel* (Saigon), 1949:6–25.

Bắc Kỳ Phật giáo. *A Di Đà kinh* (Amitabha or Sukhavati-vyuha sutra). [Hanoi]: Bắc Kỳ Phật Giáo, 1940.

Ban Chấp Hành Đảng Bộ Đảng Cộng sản Việt Nam tỉnh Hà Tĩnh. *Lịch sử Đảng bộ Hà Tĩnh* (History of the Hà Tĩnh province Party committee). Hanoi: NXB Chính Trị Quốc Gia, 1993.

Ban Nghiên Cứu Lịch Sử Đảng Trung Ương. *Những sự kiện lịch sử Đảng* (Events in the history of the Party). Vol. 1. Hanoi: NXB Sự Thật, 1976.

Bằng Giang. *Văn học quốc ngữ ở Nam Kỳ 1865–1930* (Southern literature in romanized script, 1865–1930). Ho Chi Minh City: NXB Trẻ, 1992.

Beau, Paul. *Situation de l'Indochine de 1902 à 1907*. Vol. 1. Saigon: Imprimerie commerciale Marcellin Rey, 1908.

Bell, Catherine. "'A Precious Raft to Save the World': The Interaction of Scriptural Traditions and Printing in a Chinese Morality Book." *Late Imperial China* 17:1 (1996), 158–200.

Bergson, Henri. *La pensée et le mouvant*. Paris: Libraire Félix Alcan, 1934.

Bernal, Martin. "The Nghe-Tinh Soviet Movement." *Past and Present* 92:148–168.

Berry, Mary Elizabeth. "Public Life in Authoritarian Japan." *Daedelus* 127:3 (Summer 1998), 133–165.

Bibliothèque nationale (France). *Catalogue du fonds indochinois de la bibliothèque nationale*, vol. 1: *Livres vietnamiens imprimés en quoc ngu*. By Christiane Rageau. Paris: Bibliothèque nationale, 1979.

Bình Nguyên Lộc. "Thời vàng son của nghề xuất bản tại Sài Gòn" (The golden age of publishing in Saigon). *Tân văn* (New literary review), 16/17 (September–October 1969): 12–19.

Bissachère, M. de la. *État actuel du Tunkin, de la Cochinchine, et des royaumes de Cambodge, Laos, et Lac Tho.* Vol. 2. Reprint of the 1812 edition. Westhead, Hants., England: Gregg International, 1971.

Blackburn, Anne. *Buddhist Learning and Textual Practice in Eighteenth-Century Lankan Monastic Culture.* Princeton, N.J.: Princeton University Press, 2001.

Boudarel, Georges. *Cent fleurs écloses dans la nuit du Vietnam.* Paris: Jacques Bertoin, 1991.

Bouinais, A., and A. Paulus. *L'Indochine française contemporaine: Cochinchine, Cambodge, Tonkin, Annam.* Paris: Challamel ainé, 1885.

Bradley, Mark. *Imagining Vietnam and America: The Making of Postcolonial Vietnam, 1919–1950.* Chapel Hill: University of North Carolina Press, 2000.

Brocheux, Pierre. "L'implantation du mouvement communiste en Indochine française: le cas du Nghe-Tinh (1930–1931)." *Revue d'histoire moderne et contemporaine* 24 (January–March 1977): 49–77.

———. "La question de l'indépendance dans l'opinion vietnamienne de 1939 à 1945." Paper presented at the conference "Les problemes de la décolonisation de l'empire français (1936–1956)," l'Institut du temps présent, 4–5 October 1984.

———. "Vietnam: le grand tournant de 1930." *Histoire* 69 (1984): 109–115.

Brocheux, Pierre, and Daniel Hémery. *Indochine: la colonisation ambiguë 1858–1954.* Paris: La Découverte, 1995.

Brooks, Jeffrey. *When Russia Leaned to Read: Literacy and Popular Literature, 1861–1917.* Princeton, N.J.: Princeton University Press, 1985.

Bùi Giáng, comp. *Giảng luận về Tản Đà Ng.[uyễn] Khắc Hiếu* (Explanatory essay on Tản Đà [Nguyễn Khắc Hiếu]). [Saigon?]: Tân Việt, 1959.

Bùi Thiết. *Vinh–Bến Thủy.* Hanoi: NXB Văn Hóa, 1984.

Bulletin administratif de la Cochinchine. Saigon: Nguyễn Văn Của, 1941.

Bulletin administratif du Tonkin.

Bửu Tín. "Trong cuộc trường kỳ chùa sắc-tứ Tam Bảo (Hà Tiên)" (The instructional sessions at the royally decreed [?] "Three Jewels" temple). *Phật học* (Buddhist learning), 13 October 1936, 1015–1019.

"Các nhà Cách mạng Việt Nam tham gia khởi nghĩa Quảng Châu" (Vietnamese revolutionaries who participated in the Guangzhou uprising). Translated from the Chinese by Thanh Đạm. *Nghiên cứu lịch sử* (Historical research), 253 (November–December 1990): 72–75.

Calhoun, Craig, ed. *Habermas and the Public Sphere.* Cambridge, Mass.: MIT Press, 1992.

Cao Tự Thanh. *Nho giáo ở Gia Định* (Confucianism in Gia Định). Ho Chi Minh City: NXB Thành phố Hồ Chí Minh, 1996.

Chabas, J. "Le contrôle de l'opinion publique en Indochine depuis 1940." *La revue indochinoise juridique et économique* 16 (1941): 595–640.

———. "Le régime de la presse en Indochine." Part 1. *La revue indochinoise juridique et économique* 8 (1938): 668–703.

———. "Le régime de la presse en Indochine." Part 2. *La revue indochinoise juridique et économique* 9 (1939): 106–138.

Chandler, David. "Royally Sponsored Human Sacrifices in Nineteenth Century Cambodia." In David Chandler, *Facing the Cambodian Past: Selected Essays 1971–1994*. Chiang Mai: Silkworm Books, 1996.

Chánh Thi. "Rồi ba vào Đảng" (Then father entered the Party). In *Ngọn đuốc* (The torch). Hanoi: NXB Văn Học, 1980.

Chappell, David. "From Dispute to Dual Cultivation: Pure Land Responses to Ch'an Critics." In Peter Gregory, ed., *Traditions of Meditation in Chinese Buddhism*. Honolulu: University of Hawai'i Press, 1986.

Chartier, Roger. *The Cultural Origins of the French Revolution*. Durham and London: Duke University Press, 1991.

———. "Le monde comme representation." *Annales: Économies, Sociétés, Civilisations*, November–December 1989, 1505–1520.

———. *Les usages de l'imprimé*. Paris: Fayard, 1989.

Ch'en, Kenneth. *Buddhism in China: A Historical Survey*. Princeton, N.J.: Princeton University Press, 1964.

Chesneaux, P. "Enquête sur l'analphabétisme en milieu rural dans une province du Nord-Annam." *Bulletin général de l'instruction publique*, April 1938, 267–278.

Chow, Kai Wing. "Writing for Success: Printing, Examinations, and Intellectual Change in Late Ming China." *Late Imperial China* 17:1 (June 1996), 120–157.

Chùa Hoa thành phố Hồ Chí Minh (Chinese temples of Ho Chi Minh City). Ho Chi Minh City: NXB Thành phố Hồ Chí Minh, 1992.

Chùa Tam Bảo, Rạch Gía. *Niệm Phật qui tắc* (Methods for praying to the Buddha). Saigon: Nhà In Xưa Nay, 1933.

Clanchy, Michael. *From Memory to Written Record: England, 1066–1307*. Cambridge: Cambridge University Press, 1979.

Code Annamite. Second edition, translated by P.-L.-F. Philastre. Paris: Ernest Leroux, 1909.

Comaroff, Jean. *Body of Power, Spirit of Resistance*. Chicago: University of Chicago Press, 1985.

Cộng sản sơ giải (Summary of communism). Loại Sách Mac-xít. [Saigon]: NXB Hà Huy Tập, [1947].

Cooke, Nola. "Colonial Political Myth and the Problem of the Other: French and Vietnamese in the Protectorate of Annam." Ph.D. dissertation, Australian National University, 1991.

Cribb, Robert. "Introduction: The Late Colonial State in Indonesia." In Robert Cribb, ed., *The Late Colonial State in Indonesia: Political and Economic Foundations of the Netherlands East Indies, 1880–1942*. Leiden: KITLV Press, 1994.

Cuong Tu Nguyen. *Zen in Medieval Vietnam: A Study and Translation of the Thiền Uyển Tập Anh*. Honolulu: University of Hawai'i Press, 1997.

Cưu Kim Sơn and Vân Huê. *Đời chị em* (Life of young women). Hanoi: Dân Chúng, 1938.

Cửu Long Giang. *Thất Sơn Hà Tiên* (From the Seven Mountains to Hà Tiên). Saigon: Imprimerie de Đức Lưu Phương, 1935.

Đại Việt sử ký toàn thư (Complete historical annals of Dai Viet). Compiled by Ngô Sĩ Liên. Vietnamese translation and reprint of 1697 edition. Hanoi: Khoa Học Xã Hội, 1983.

Đại Việt sử ký tục biên (Historical annals of Dai Viet: continuation [1676–1789]). Trans. Ngô Thế Long and Nguyễn Kim Hưng; ed. Nguyễn Đổng Chi. Hanoi: Khoa Học Xã Hội, 1991.

Đảng Cộng sản Việt Nam. *Văn kiện Đảng toàn tập* (Complete collection of Party documents). Vol. 1. Hanoi: NXB Chính Trị Quốc Gia, 1999.

Đặng Thai Mai. "The Anxieties of a Vietnamese Student in the Twenties." In *Vietnamese Intellectuals at a Historic Turning Point.* Hanoi: Foreign Languages Publishing House, 1989.

———. *Hồi ký thời kỳ thanh thiếu niên* (Memoirs of my youth). Hanoi: NXB Tác Phẩm Mới, 1985.

———. *Văn thơ cách mạng đầu thế kỷ XX (1900–1925)* (Revolutionary prose and poetry from the beginning of the twentieth century [1900–1925]). Hanoi: NXB Văn Học, 1974.

Đào Duy Anh. *Khổng giáo phê bình tiểu luận* (Short critique of Confucianism). Hue: Quan Hải Tùng Thư, 1938.

———. *Lịch sử Việt Nam* (History of Vietnam). Vol. 2. Hanoi: Xây Dựng, 1955.

———. *Nhớ nghĩ chiều hôm* (Evening meditations). Ho Chi Minh City: Tuổi trẻ, 1989.

———. *Tôn giáo* (Religion). Hue: Quan Hải Tùng Thư, 1929.

———. *Việt Nam văn hóa sử cương* (Historical outline of Vietnamese culture). Reprint of 1938 edition. Paris: Đông Nam Á, 1985.

Đào Trinh Nhất. *Thế lực Khách trú và vấn đề di dân vào Nam Kỳ* (The influence of the Chinese and the problem of immigration to Cochinchina). Hanoi: Nhà In Thụy Ký, 1924.

Darnton, Robert. "A Police Inspector Sorts His Files: An Anatomy of the Republic of Letters." In Robert Darnton, *The Great Cat Massacre and Other Episodes in French Cultural History.* New York: Vintage, 1985.

Dật Sĩ and Nguyễn Văn Hầu. *Thất Sơn mầu nhiệm* (The wonders of Seven Mountains). Saigon: Liên Chính XB, 1955.

"Đề cương về văn hóa Việt Nam" (Theses on Vietnamese culture). In Nguyễn Phúc et al., *Một chặn đường văn hóa* (A cultural transition). [Hanoi]: NXB Tác Phẩm Mới, 1985.

"Để làm 'sang giá và 'sang gia' tác phẩm văn học (phỏng vấn nhà nghiên cứu phê bình văn học Hoàng Ngọc Hiền)" (Making literary works "limpid" and "illustrious": an interview with the literary scholar Hoàng Ngọc Hiến). *Sông Hương* 5 (September–October 1992): 64–66.

Devillers, Philippe. *Histoire du Vietnam du 1940 à 1952*. Paris: Éditions du Seuil, 1952.

Địa Tạng kinh có âm nghĩa (Transliteration of the *Ksitigarbha bodhisattva sutra*). Bến Tre–Trà Vinh: Temple Long Khanh, 1930.

Direction Générale de l'Instruction Publique. *Les manuels scolaires et les publications de la Direction Générale de l'Instruction Publique*. Hanoi: IDEO, 1931.

Đòan Trung Còn. *Phật học từ điển* (Buddhist dictionary). Three volumes. Reprint. 1963. N.p., n.d.

Donnison, F. S. V. *British Military Administration in the Far East 1943–46*. London: Her Majesty's Stationery Office, 1956.

Duara, Prasenjit. "Bifurcating Linear History: Nation and Histories in China and India." *Positions: East Asia Cultural Critique* 1:3 (Winter 1993), 779–804.

Đức Huỳnh Giáo Chủ (Huỳnh Phú Sổ). *Sấm giảng thi văn toàn bộ* (Prophecies, poetry, and prose: collected works). Reprint of 1965 edition. Santa Fe Springs, Calif.: Văn Phòng Phật Giáo Hải Ngoại, 1984.

Dudbridge, Glen. *The Legend of Miao-shan*. London: Ithaca Press, 1978.

Duiker, William. *The Rise of Nationalism in Vietnam, 1900–1941*. Ithaca, N.Y.: Cornell University Press, 1976.

Dumarest, André. *La formation de classes sociales en pays annamite*. Lyon: P. Ferreol, 1935.

Duncan, John B. "Uses of Confucianism in Modern Korea." In Benjamin A. Elman, John B. Duncan, and Hermann Ooms, eds. *Rethinking Confucianism: Past and Present in China, Japan, Korea, and Vietnam*. Los Angeles: UCLA Asia Pacific Monograph Series, 2002.

Durand, Maurice. *L'imagerie populaire vietnamienne*. Paris: École française d'Extrême-Orient, 1960.

Eisenstein, Elizabeth. *The Printing Press as an Agent of Change: Communications and Cultural Transformations in Early Modern Europe*. Cambridge: Cambridge University Press, 1980.

Elman, Benjamin. *From Philosophy to Philology: Intellectual and Social Aspects of Change in Late Imperial China*. Cambridge, Mass.: Harvard University Press, 1984.

Elman, Benjamin, Hermann Ooms, and John Duncan, eds. *Rethinking Confucianism: Past and Present in China, Japan, Korea, and Vietnam*. Los Angeles: UCLA Asia Pacific Monograph Series, 2002.

Farge, Arlette. *Le gout de l'archive*. Paris: Éditions du Seuil, 1989.

Fitzgerald, John. *Awakening China: Politics, Culture, and Class in the Nationalist Revolution*. Stanford, Calif.: Stanford University Press, 1996.

Foster, Ann. "Secret Police Cooperation and the Roots of Anti-Communism in Interwar East Asia." *Journal of American–East Asian Relations* 4:4 (Winter 1995), 331–350.

Gabriel-Robinet, L. *La censure.* Paris: Hachette, 1965.

Galan, F. W. *Historic Structures: The Prague School Project, 1928–1946.* Austin: University of Texas Press, 1985.

Geertz, Clifford. "Local Knowledge: Fact and Law in Comparative Perspective." In Clifford Geertz, *Local Knowledge: Further Essays in Interpretive Anthropology.* New York: Basic Books, 1983.

Gellner, Ernest. *Nations and Nationalism.* Ithaca, N.Y.: Cornell University Press, 1983.

Gia đình và xã hội (The family and society). Hue: Imprimerie Tiếng Dân, 1929.

Giebel, Christoph. *Imagined Ancestries: Historical Engineering in Viet Nam. The Case of Ton Duc Thang.* Seattle: University of Washington Press, 2004.

Gluck, Carol. "The Past in the Present." In Andrew Gordon, ed., *Postwar Japan as History.* Berkeley: University of California Press, 1993.

Gombrich, Richard. *Precept and Practice: Traditional Buddhism in the Rural Highlands of Ceylon.* Oxford: Clarendon Press, 1971.

Goody, Jack. *The Domestication of the Savage Mind.* Cambridge: Cambridge University Press, 1977.

———. *The Interface between the Written and the Oral.* Cambridge: Cambridge University Press, 1987.

Goscha, Christopher E. *Thailand and the Southeast Asian Networks of the Vietnamese Revolution, 1884–1954.* Nordic Institute of Asian Studies monograph series no. 79. Surrey, England: Curzon Press, 1999.

———. "Vietnamese Revolutionaries in the Early Spread of Communism to Peninsular Southeast Asia: Towards a Regional Perspective." Conference paper, EUROSEAS (Hamburg), September 1998.

Goscha, Christopher E., and Bénoît de Treglodé, eds. *Vietnam since 1945: The State, Its Margins and Constructions of the Past.* Paris: Les Indes savantes, 2003.

Gouvernement Général de l'Indochine. *Les administrations et les services publics indochinois.* Second revised and augmented edition. Hanoi: Imprimerie Mac Dinh Tu, 1931.

———. *Recueil général de la législation et de la réglementation de l'Indochine: Supplément de 1926–1927.* [Hanoi?]: Service de législation et d'administration du Gouverneur Général, 1930.

Gouvernement Général de l'Indochine. Direction des Affaires Politiques et de la Sûreté Générale. *Contribution à l'histoire des mouvements politiques de l'Indochine française*, vol. 5: *La Terreur Rouge en Annam.* Hanoi: IDEO, [1933?].

Gouvernement Général de l'Indochine. Direction des Affaires Économiques. Service de la Statistique Générale. *Annuaire statistique de l'Indochine.* Hanoi: IDEO, 1938.

———. *Annuaire statistique de l'Indochine.* Hanoi: IDEO, 1945.

Groff, David. "The Dynamics of Collaboration and the Rule of Law in French West Africa: The Case of Kwame Kangah of Assikasso (Côte d'Ivoire), 1898–1922." In Kristin Mann and Richard Roberts, eds., *Law in Colonial Africa*. Portsmouth, N.H.: Heinemann, 1991.

Guillemot, François. "Viet-nam 1945–1946: l'élimination de l'opposition nationaliste et anticolonialiste dans le nord du pays: au coeur de la fracture vietnamienne." In Christopher Goscha and Bénoît de Treglodé, eds., *Vietnam since 1945: The State, Its Margins and Constructions of the Past*. Paris: Les Indes savantes, 2003.

Hà Tấn Phát, trans. *Chấn hưng phong tục* (Reform of mores). Cholon: Cao Binh, 1933.

Habermas, Jürgen. *The Structural Transformation of the Public Sphere: An Inquiry into a Category of Bourgeois Society*. Cambridge, Mass.: MIT Press, 1989.

Halbwachs, Maurice. *On Collective Memory*. Edited, translated, and with an introduction by Lewis Coser. Chicago: University of Chicago Press, 1992.

Harootunian, Harry. "Disciplinizing Native Knowledge and Producing Place: Yanagita Kunio, Origuchi Shinobu, Takata Yasuma." In J. Thomas Rimer, ed., *Culture and Identity: Japanese Intellectuals during the Interwar Years*. Princeton, N.J.: Princeton University Press, 1990.

———. *Things Seen and Unseen: Discourse and Ideology in Tokugawa Nativism*. Chicago: University of Chicago Press, 1988.

Héméry, Daniel. "Journalisme révolutionnaire et système de la presse au Vietnam dans les années 1930." *Cahiers du CURSA* (Amiens), 8 (1978): 55–85.

———. *Révolutionnaires vietnamiens et pouvoir colonial en Indochine: communistes, trotskystes, nationalists à Saigon de 1932 à 1937*. Paris: F. Maspero, 1975.

Hồ Nam [Trần Văn Giàu]. *Kỉ niệm Nghệ an bạo đông (12 tháng 9 năm 1930)* (Anniversary of the Nghệ An revolt [12 September 1930]). N.p., 1932.

Hoa Bằng. "Kỹ thuật ấn loát của ta thời xưa," *Nghiên cứu lịch sử* (Historical research), 133 (July–August 1970).

Hoài Thanh and Hoài Chân. *Thi nhân Việt Nam (1932–1941)* (Vietnamese poets, 1932–1941). Reprint of 1942 edition. Paris: Đông Nam Á, 1985.

Hoàng Đạo. *Mười điều tâm niệm* (Ten things to ponder). Saigon: Khai Trí, n.d. [1938].

Hoàng Lê. "Vài nét về công việc sưu tầm thư tịch Hán Nôm trong lịch sử" (Aspects of the collection of Chinese and Nôm books in history). In Viện Nghiên cứu Hán Nôm, *Nghiên cứu Hán Nôm* (Researches on Chinese and Nôm). Hanoi: Ủy Bản Khoa Học Xã Hội, 1984.

Hoàng Nam Hùng. *Năm mươi năm cách mạng hải ngoại: hồi ký* (Fifty years of revolution from abroad: a memoir). Saigon: Phạm Giật Đức, 1960.

Hoàng Văn Hoan. *Giọt nước trong biển cả: hồi ký* (A drop in the ocean: a memoir). Reprint of the Beijing edition. [Portland, Oregon?]: Nhóm Tìm Hiểu Lịch Sử, 1991.

Hội Khai trí Thanh Niên. *Điều lệ Hội Khai trí thanh niên và nhà thơ viện nơi làng Khánh An* (Statutes of the Association for the Development of the Intellect and for the library of Khánh An village). Sa Đéc: Nhà In Duy Xuân, 1926.

Hội Nam Kỳ Nghiên Cứu Phật Học (Saigon). *Nghi thức tụng niệm của người tu tại gia* (Correct rites for believers praying at home). Saigon: Hội Nam Kỳ Nghiên Cứu Phật Học, 1936.

Hội Phật Giáo Quan Âm Tịnh Độ. *Lễ luật* (Regulations). Long Xuyên: Nhà In Hậu Giang, 1940.

Hội Truyền Bá Học Quốc Ngữ (Hanoi). *Mấy điều cần thiết các giáo viên của Hội nên biết* (Some necessary things that the association's instructors should know). Hanoi: Hội Truyền Bá Học Quốc Ngữ, 1942.

Hồng Chương. "Đồng chí Hải Triều" (Comrade Hải Triều). In Hồng Chương, ed., *Hải Triều tác phẩm* (The works of Hải Triều). Ho Chi Minh City: NXB Thành phố Hồ Chí Minh, 1987.

Hong The Cong [Hà Huy Tập]. "Troisième anniversaire de l'unification du Parti communiste indochinois." *Cahiers du bolchévisme* 10:5 (1 March 1933), 274–283.

Hughes, Thomas Parke. "Technological Momentum." In Merritt Roe Smith and Leo Marx, eds., *Does Technology Drive History?: The Dilemma of Technological Determinism.* Cambridge, Mass.: MIT Press, 1994.

Huynh Ba Yêt Duong. "Le mouvement de rénovation au Viet Nam." *Duong moi / La voie nouvelle* 4 (1985): 94–112.

Huynh Kim Khanh. *Vietnamese Communism, 1925–1945.* Ithaca, N.Y.: Cornell University Press, 1982.

Huỳnh Kim Long. *Vọng cổ Phật nhập Niết bàn* (Vọng cổ song on the Buddha entering Nirvana). Saigon: Bảo Tôn, [1935].

Huỳnh Lứa. *Lịch sử khai phá vùng đất Nam Bộ* (A history of the opening up of the south). Ho Chi Minh City: NXB Thành phố Hồ Chí Minh, 1987.

Huỳnh Văn Tòng. *Báo chí Việt Nam từ khởi đầu đến 1930* (Vietnamese newspapers from their origins to 1930). Saigon: Trí Đăng, 1970.

Hy Van Luong. *Revolution in the Village: Tradition and Transformation in North Vietnam, 1925–1988.* Honolulu: University of Hawai'i Press, 1992.

Ileto, Reynaldo Clemena. "Orators and the Crowd: Philippine Independence Politics 1910–1914." In Peter W. Stanley, ed., *Reappraising an Empire: New Perspectives on Philippine-American History.* Cambridge, Mass.: Committee on American–East Asian Relations, 1984.

———. *Pasyon and Revolution.* Quezon City: Ateneo de Manila Press, 1979.

———. "Rizal and the Underside of Philippine History." In David Wyatt and Alexander Woodside, eds., *Moral Order and the Question of Change.* New Haven, Conn.: Yale University Southeast Asian Studies, 1982.

In bột ("Flour" printing). Liên Khu 5: Sở Thông Tin Liên Khu 5, [194?].

Iser, Wolfgang. "The Reading Process: A Phenomenological Approach." In Jane Tompkins, ed., *Reader-Response Criticism: From Formalism to Post-Structuralism.* Baltimore: Johns Hopkins University Press, 1980.

Jamieson, Neil. *Understanding Vietnam.* Berkeley: University of California Press, 1993.

Jensen, Lionel. *Manufacturing Confucianism: Chinese Traditions and Universal Civilizations.* Durham, N.C.: Duke University Press, 1997.

Johns, Adrian. *The Nature of the Book: Print and Knowledge in the Making.* Chicago: University of Chicago Press, 1998.

Johnson, David, ed. *Popular Culture in Late Imperial China.* Berkeley: University of California Press, 1985.

Journal officiel de l'Indochine. 1908.

Judge, Joan. *Print and Politics: "Shibao" and the Culture of Reform in Late Qing China.* Stanford, Calif.: Stanford University Press, 1996.

Khổng Đức Thiêm. "Một số tư liệu về An Nam Cộng sản Đảng với việc thong nhất các lực lượng cách mạng ở Việt Nam năm 1930" (Some materials on the Annamese Communist Party and the unification of the revolutionary forces in Vietnam in 1930). *Nghiên cứu lịch sử* (Historical research), 297:3/4 (1998), 68–77.

Khuất Duy Tiến. "Hồi ký về vô sản hóa" (Memoir on proletarianization). In *Ngọn đuốc: hồi ký* (The torch: memoirs). Hanoi: NXB Văn Học, 1980.

Kinh nghiệm Việt Minh ở Việt Bắc (The Việt Minh experience in Việt Bắc). Việt Bắc: Việt Minh XB, 1944.

Landes, Joan. *Women and the Public Sphere in the Age of the French Revolution.* Ithaca, N.Y., and London: Cornell Univeristy Press, 1988.

Lanessan, Jean Louis de. *L'Indochine française* (French Indochina). Paris: Alcun, 1889.

Le Goff, Jacques. *Histoire et mémoire.* Paris: Gallimard, 1988.

Lê Hương. *Việt kiều ở Kampuchea* (Vietnamese in Cambodia). Saigon: Trí Đăng, 1971.

Lê Hữu Mỹ. *Hương lửa* (Conjugal happiness). Hanoi: Lạc Hồng, 1936.

Lê Thanh. *Cuộc phỏng vấn các nhà văn Trần Trọng Kim, Nguyễn Văn Tố, Nguyễn Đôn Phúc, Ngô Văn Triện, Hoàng Ngọc Phách, Vũ Đình Long, Tú Mỡ, Đào Duy Anh* (Interviews with the writers Trần Trọng Kim, etc.). Hanoi: NXB Đời Mới, [1942?].

Lê Trọng Khánh and Lê Anh Trà, eds. *Xô viết Nghệ Tĩnh qua một số thơ văn* (The Nghệ Tĩnh soviets through literature). Hanoi: Sự Thật, 1959.

Lê Trung Ngọc (Mme.). *Nữ lưu phận sự* (Female duties). Hanoi: published by the author, 1936.

Leach, Edmund. *Political Systems of Highland Burma.* London: Athlone Press, 1964 [1954].

Li Tana. *Nguyen Cochinchina: Southern Vietnam in the Seventeenth and Eighteenth Century.* Ithaca, N.Y.: Southeast Asia Program, 1998.

Litolff, Henri, comp. *Recueil des textes concernant le régime de la presse en Indochine.* Hanoi: IDEO, 1939.

Liu, Lydia H. *Translingual Practice: Literature, National Culture, and Translated Modernity—China, 1900–1937.* Stanford, Calif.: Stanford University Press, 1995.

Lương Đức Thiệp. *Xã hội Việt Nam tiến hóa sử* (History of the evolution of Vietnamese society). Saigon: Liên Hiệp, 1950 [1944].

Luong, Hy Van. *Revolution in the Village: Tradition and Transformation in North Vietnam, 1925–1988.* Honolulu, University of Hawai'i Press, 1992.

Lưu Văn Ngôn. *Nhưng phương pháp giáo hóa dân quê* (Methods of educating rural people). Hanoi: Lê Cường, 1937.

MacIntyre, Alisdair. *After Virtue: A Study in Moral Theory.* Notre Dame, In.: University of Notre Dame Press, 1981.

Mak Phouen. "La frontière entre le Cambodge et le Vietnam du XVIIe siècle à l'instauration du protectorat français presenté à travers les chroniques royales khmères." In P. B. Lafont, ed., *Les frontières du Vietnam: Histoire des frontières de la péninsule indochinoise.* Paris: Harmattan, 1989.

Mamdani, Mahmood. *Citizen and Subject: Contemporary Africa and the Legacy of Late Colonialism.* Princeton, N.J.: Princeton University Press, 1996.

Marr, David. *Vietnam 1945: The Quest for Power.* Berkeley: University of California Press, 1995.

———. *Vietnamese Anticolonialism, 1885–1925.* Berkeley: University of California Press, 1971.

———. *Vietnamese Tradition on Trial, 1920–1945.* Berkeley: University of California Press, 1981.

Martin, Henri-Jean. "Culture écrite et culture orale: culture savante et culture populaire." In Henri-Jean Martin, *Le livre français sous l'Ancien régime.* Paris: Promodis, 1987.

Mật Thể (Thích). *Lời yêu cầu của một đoàn-thể thanh niên tăng già về cấn đề cải tổ sơn môn Huế* (Request of a collectivity of youth and monks on the reorganization of the *sơn môn* of Huế). Hue: Imprimerie Mirador, 1940.

Mật Thể (Thường tọa). *Việt Nam Phật giáo sử lược* (A short history of Buddhism). Hanoi: Tân Việt, 1944.

McHale, Shawn. "Imagining Human Liberation: Vietnamese Buddhists and the Marxist Critique of Religion, 1920–1939." *Social Compass* 42:3 (1995).

———. "Mapping a 'Confucian' Past: Vietnam and the Transition to Modernity." In Benjamin Elman, Hermann Ooms, and John Duncan, eds., *Rethinking Confucianism: Past and Present in China, Japan, Korea, and Vietnam.* Los Angeles: UCLA Asia Pacific Monograph Series, 2002.

———. "Printing and Power: Debates over Women's Place in Vietnamese Society, 1918–1934." In Keith Weller Taylor and John Whitmore, eds.,

Essays into Vietnamese Pasts. Ithaca, N.Y.: Cornell Southeast Asia Program, 1995.

———. "Printing, Power, and the Transformation of Vietnamese Culture, 1920–1945." Ph.D. dissertation, Cornell University, 1995.

———. "Texts and Bodies: Refashioning the Disturbing Past of Tran Vietnam (1225–1400)." *Journal of the Economic and Social History of the Orient* (Leiden), November 1999, 494–518.

Milner, Anthony. *The Invention of Politics in Colonial Malaya: Contesting Nationalism and the Expansion of the Public Sphere.* Cambridge: Cambridge University Press, 1994.

Minh Huệ. *Ngọn cờ Bến Thủy: hồi ký xô viết Nghệ Tĩnh* (The flags of Bến Thủy: memoir of the Nghệ Tĩnh soviets). Hanoi: NXB Thanh Niên, 1975.

Mời vào cửa Phật: lễ tụng, giáo lý, hành hóa (Invitation to Buddhism: rites and teachings). Hanoi: Đuốc Tuệ, 1938.

Moriya, Katsuhisa. "Urban Networks and Information Networks." In Chie Nakane and Sinzaburo Oishi, eds., *Tokugawa Japan: The Social and Economic Antecedents of Modern Japan.* Tokyo: University of Tokyo Press, 1991.

Morlat, Patrice. *La repression coloniale en Indochine (1908–1940).* Paris: Harmattan, 1990.

Mỹ Ngọc [Ngô Huy Vỏ (*sic*)]. *Aí tình khoa học* (The science of love). Cần Thơ: Imprimerie Trần Văn, 1934.

N. "Regards sur notre action politique en Indochine." *Les temps modernes* 2 (March 1947): 1113–1149.

Nam Cao. "Nhật ký và thư từ" (Diary and correspondence). In *Cách mạng—kháng chiến và đời song văn học, 1945–1954* (Revolution, resistance war, and literary life), vol. 2. Hanoi: Tác Phẩm Mới, 1985.

Nam kỳ kinh tế (The economy of the south). Saigon: Nam My Van Đoan, 1942.

Nam Kỳ Nghiên Cứu Phật Học Hội. *Kinh A Di Đà, Hồng Danh, Vu Long* (The *Amitabha* and *Ullambana* sutras). Saigon: Nam Kỳ Nghiên Cứu Phật Học Hội, 1934.

50 [nam mươi] năm chấn hưng Phật giáo (Fifty years of the Buddhist Revival). Reprint. Sepulveda, Calif.: Phật Học Viện Quốc Tế, 1987.

Ngô Đức Kế. "Luận về chánh học cùng tà thuyết Quốc văn, Kim Văn Kiều, Nguyễn Du" (A discussion of correct and heterodox teachings in the national literature, Kim Văn Kiều, Nguyễn Du [1924]). In Th. S. Tr. N. K., comp., *Những áng văn hay* (Fine literary works). Hanoi: Nam Kỳ Thư Quán, [1931?].

Ngô Hà. "Lược sử báo chí thành phố" (Brief history of the city's newspapers). In Trần Văn Giàu, Trần Bạch Đằng, and Nguyễn Công Bình, eds., *Địa chí văn hóa thành phố Hồ Chí Minh* (Geography and culture of Ho Chi Minh City), vol. 2. Ho Chi Minh City: NXB Thành phố Hồ Chí Minh, 1988.

Ngô Tất Tố. *Phê bình Nho giáo* (Critique of [Trần Trọng Kim's] Confucianism). Hanoi: Mai Lĩnh, 1940.

Ngo Vinh Long. "The Indochinese Communist Party and Peasant Rebellion in Central Vietnam, 1930–1931." *Bulletin of Concerned Asian Scholars* 10:4 (October–December 1978), 15–34.

Ngọc Giao. "Hồi ký văn học: Chủ nhà in, nhà xuất bản Tân Dân Ông Vũ Đình Long" (Literary memoir: Vũ Đình Long, head of Tân Dân print shop and publishing house). *Tạp chí văn học* 1 (1991): 58–61.

Ngọn cờ Giải phóng (rút những bài đã đặng trong báo "Cờ giải phóng" và tạp chí "Cộng sản" xuất bản hồi bí mật) (Liberation flag [excerpted from essays previously published in the newspaper *Liberation Flag* and the review *Communism* published in the clandestine period]). Hanoi: NXB Sự Thật, 1974.

Nguên [*sic*] Mục Tiêu. "Nên chấn hưng Phật giáo ở nước nhà" (We should revive Buddhism in our country). In Tiên Lu Đông Tự, comp., *Chấn hưng Phật giáo* (The Buddhist revival). Hanoi: Long Quang Ấn Quán, 1927.

Nguyễn An Nhân and Lê Trúc Hiên. *Nam nữ bí mật chỉ nam* (Guide to men and women's secrets). Hanoi: Nhật Nam Thư Quán, 1932.

Nguyễn An Ninh. *Phê bình Phật giáo* (Critique of Buddhism). Mỹ Tho: Đông Phương Thư Xã, 1938.

———. *Tôn giáo* (Religion). Saigon: Bảo Tôn, 1932.

Nguyễn Bách Khoa. *Nguyễn Du và truyện Kiều* (Nguyen Du and the *Tale of Kieu*). Hanoi: Hàn Thuyên, 1942.

———. *Văn chương truyện Kiều* (Literature and the *Tale of Kieu*). Reprint. Hanoi: Thế Giới, 1953.

Nguyễn Đình Đầu. *Chế độ công điền công thổ trong lịch sử khan hoang lập ấp ở Nam Kỳ Lục Tỉnh* (The public landholding system in the history of land clearing and settlement in the six provinces of the south). Hanoi: Hội Sử Học Việt Nam, 1992.

Nguyễn Đổng Chi and Ninh Viết Giao. *Hát giặm Nghệ Tĩnh* (Folk songs of Nghệ Tĩnh). Revised version of 1944 edition. Vol. 2. Hanoi: NXB Sử Học, 1962.

Nguyễn Đức Bạch and Nguyễn Đoàn Tuân. "Vài nét về tình hình phân bố tài liệu Hán Nôm ở 4 huyện phía Bắc ngoài thành" (Several features of the distribution of Chinese and Nôm materials in four districts north of Hanoi). *Tạp chí Hán Nôm* 1 (1988): 96–98.

Nguyễn Huệ Chi. "Lời giới thiệu" (Introduction). In Nguyễn Huệ Chi, ed., *Tuyển tập Hoàng Ngọc Phách* (Selected works of Hoàng Ngọc Phách). Hanoi: NXB Văn Học, 1989.

Nguyễn Hữu Đang and Nguyễn Đình Thi. *Một văn hóa mới* (A new culture). Hanoi: Hội Văn Hóa Cứu Quốc Việt Nam Trong Mặt Trận Việt Minh, 1945.

Nguyễn Khắc Hiếu [Tản Đà]. *Đài gương kinh* (Mirror of the classics). Hanoi: Nghiêm Hàm, 1925.

Nguyen Khac Vien. "Confucianism and Marxism in Vietnam." In Nguyen Khac Viên, *Tradition and Revolution in Vietnam*. Berkeley, Calif.: Indochina Resource Center, 1974.

———. *Vietnam: Une longue histoire*. Hanoi: Éditions en langues étrangères, 1987.

Nguyễn Lang. *Việt Nam Phật giáo sử luận* (History of Vietnamese Buddhism). Vol. 2. Hanoi: Văn Học, 1992 [1978].

Nguyễn Lộc. *Văn học Việt Nam nửa cuối thế kỷ XVIII nửa đầu thế kỷ XIX* (Vietnamese literature from the second half of the eighteenth century to the beginning of the nineteenth century). Reprint edition. Ho Chi Minh City: NXB Đại Học và Giáo Dục Chuyện Nghiệp, 1992.

Nguyễn Lương Hoàng et al. *Ngành in Việt Nam* (Vietnamese printing). Vol. 1. Hanoi: Liên Hiệp Các Xí Nghiệp In Việt Nam XB, 1987.

Nguyễn Ngọc Thiên, Nguyễn Thị Kiều Anh, and Phạm Hồng Toàn, eds. *Tuyển tập phê bình, nghiên cứu văn học Việt Nam (1900–1945)* (Selected works of literary criticism and research). Five volumes. Hanoi: NXB Văn Học, 1997.

Nguyễn Q. Thắng. *Huỳnh Thúc Kháng tác phẩm* (Huỳnh Thúc Kháng: collected works). Ho Chi Minh City: NXB Thành Phố Hồ Chí Minh, 1992.

Nguyễn Quang. "Nghề ấn loát ở Việt Nam" (Printing in Vietnam). *Văn hóa nguyệt san* (Monthly review of culture), 5:25 (1957), 885–889.

Nguyễn Tài Thư. *Nho học và Nho học ở Việt Nam* (The teaching of the scholars and the teaching of the scholars in Vietnam). Hanoi: Khoa Học Xã Hội, 1997.

Nguyễn Tài Thư et al. *Lịch sử Phật giáo Việt Nam* (History of Vietnamese Buddhism). Hanoi: NXB Khoa Học Xã Hội, 1988.

———. *Lịch sử tư tưởng Việt Nam* (History of Vietnamese thought). Hanoi: Khoa Học Xã Hội, 1992.

Nguyễn Thành. *Báo chí cách mạng Việt Nam 1925–1945* (Vietnamese revolutionary newspapers, 1925–1945). Hanoi: NXB Khoa Học Xã Hội, 1984.

———. "Nguyễn Mậu Kiến với sự nghiệp văn hóa—xã hội và giáo dục ở quê hưởng" (Nguyễn Mậu Kiến's educational and sociocultural accomplishments in his native village). *Nghiên cứu lịch sử* (Historical research), 262 (1992): 18–21.

Nguyễn Thế Anh. "The Vietnamization of the Cham Deity Po Nagar." In Keith Weller Taylor and John Whitmore, eds., *Essays into Vietnamese Pasts*. Ithaca, N.Y.: Cornell Southeast Asia Program, 1995.

Nguyễn Thế Mỹ. *Hai bà Trưng khởi nghĩa* (The Trưng sisters' revolt). Hanoi: Hàn Thuyên, [1944].

Nguyễn Thị Dương. "Hải Học Đường và việc in sách đầu thế kỷ XIX" (The Sea of Learning Hall and the printing of books at the beginning of the nineteenth century), *Nghiên cứu lịch sử* (Historical research), 303 (March–April 1999): 59–63.

Nguyễn Thị Thập. *Từ đất Tiên Giang* (From Tiên Giang). As told to Doan Gioi. Ho Chi Minh City: NXB Văn Nghệ Thành phố Hồ Chí Minh, 1986.

Nguyễn Thuyết Phong. "La liturgie bouddhique du Vietnam et son répértoire." *Vietnam Forum* 2 (Summer–Fall 1983): 44–55, 156–159.

Nguyễn Tiến Lãng. "Tựa" (Introduction). In Nguyễn Xuân Nghị [Từ Lâm], *Tân hiếu kinh* (The new classic of filial piety). Hanoi: Quốc Học Thư Xã, [1944].

Nguyễn Trần. "Nam kỳ văn hoc năm vừa qua" (Southern literature in the past year). In *Xuân Tây Đô: Tập kỷ yếu Khuyên học Cantho* (Spring in the Western capital: Bulletin of the Can Tho Society for the Encouragement of Studies). Saigon: Nhà In Xưa Nay, 1944.

Nguyen Tu Cuong. *Zen in Medieval Vietnam: A Study and Translation of the Thien Uyen Tap Anh.* A Kuroda Institute book. Honolulu: University of Hawai'i Press, 1997.

Nguyễn Uyển Diêm. *Khổng giáo với o. Đào Duy Anh* (Confucianism and Mr. Đào Duy Anh). Hanoi: Đại Học Thư Xã, 1944.

Nguyễn Văn An and Trịnh Như Luân. *Giải phóng và độc lập* (Liberation and independence). Hanoi: Việt Nam Văn Đoàn, 1945.

Nguyễn Văn Xuân. *Phong trào Duy Tân biên khảo* (Research on the modernization movement). Saigon: Lá Bối, 1970.

Nguyễn Vỹ. *Tuân, chàng trai nước Việt* (Tuân, young man of Vietnam). Two volumes. Saigon: published by the author, 1970.

Nhà Xuất Bản Á Châu (Asia Publishers). *Thể lệ bán sách và mục lục những sách đã in* (Guidelines on selling books and list of published books). Hanoi: Á Châu, 1942.

Nhượng Tống. *Hỗ trợ thảo luận* (A discussion of mutual aid). Hanoi: published by the author, 1945.

———. *Nguyễn Thái Học (1902–1930).* Hanoi: Việt Nam Thư Xã XB (cơ quan tuyền truyên Trung ương của Việt Nam Quốc Dân Đảng Hội XB), 1945.

Ninh Viết Giao and Hoc Phi, recorders. "Chỉ một con đường: hồi ký của Tôn Thị Quế" (Only one road to take: the memoir of Tôn Thị Quế). In *Cô giáo Sa đéc* (The schoolmistress of Sa Dec). Hanoi: NXB Phụ Nữ, 1981.

Nosco, Peter. *Remembering Paradise: Nativism and Nostalgia in Eighteenth Century Japan.* Cambridge, Mass.: Council on East Asian Studies, 1990.

Ong, Walter. *Orality and Literacy: The Technologizing of the Word.* New York: Methuen, 1982.

Osterhammel, Jürgen. *Colonialism: A Theoretical Overview.* Princeton, N.J.: Markus Wiener, 1997.

Ownby, David. "Chinese Millienarian Traditions: The Formative Age." *American Historical Review* 104:5 (December 1999), 1513–1530.

Papin, Philippe. "Hanoi et ses territoires." *Bulletin de l'École française d'Éxtrême-Orient* 82 (1995): 201–230.

————. *Viet-Nam: parcours d'une nation.* Paris: La documentation française, 1999.

Paroles du Maréchal. Hanoi: IDEO, 1941.

Pasquel-Rageau, Christiane. "L'imprimerie au Vietnam de l'impression xylographique traditionelle à la revolution du quôc ngu (XIIIe–XIXe siècles)." *Revue française d'histoire du livre* 43, n.s. (April–May–June 1984): 299–312.

Pelley, Patricia. "Writing Revolution: The New History in Post-Colonial Vietnam." Ph.D. dissertation, Cornell University, 1993.

Peycam, Phillipe. "Intellectuals and Political Commitment in Vietnam: The Emergence of the Public Sphere in Saigon (1916–1928)." Ph.D. dissertation, SOAS, 1999.

Phạm Hồng Tung. "Tìm hiểu thêm về Mặt trận Việt Minh" (Understanding more about the Việt Minh front), *Nghiên cứu lịch sử* (Historical research), 309 (March–April 2000): 3–11.

Phạm Huy Thông. "La littérature vietnamienne depuis 1939." *La pensée* 22 (January–February 1949): 20–26.

————. "The Sound of the Flute on the Black River: Tiếng Dịch Sông Ô." *Vietnam Forum* 3 (Winter–Spring 1984): 127–130.

Phạm Ngọc Khuê. *Óc khoa học* (The scientific mind). Hanoi: n.p., 1943.

Phạm Thế Ngữ. *Việt Nam văn học sử gian ước tân biên* (Short history of Vietnamese literature). Vol. 3. S.L.: Đại Nam, n.d.

Phạm Văn Hảo. "Làm báo bí mật" (Producing secret newspapers). In Chánh Thi et al., *Lên đường thắng lợi* (The road to victory). Hanoi: NXB Văn Học, 1960.

Phạm Xanh. *Nguyễn Ái Quốc với việc truyền bá chủ nghĩa Mác Lê-nin ở Việt Nam (1921–1930)* (Nguyễn Ái Quốc and the spread of Marxism-Leninism to Vietnam [1921–1930]). Hanoi: NXB Thông Tin và Lý Luận, 1990.

Phan Bội Châu. "Vấn đề báo chí" (On newspapers). In *Phan Bội Châu: thời kỳ ở Huế (1926–1940)* (Phan Bội Châu: his time in Huế [1926–1940]). Hue: NXB Văn Hóa, 1987.

Phan Châu Trinh. *Bài diễn thuyết đạo đức, luân lý Đông Tây* (Address on Eastern and Western philosophy and morality). Saigon: Xưa Nay, 1926.

Phan Đại Doãn. *Làng Việt Nam một số vấn đề kinh tế xã hội* (The Vietnamese village: a number of economic and social topics). Hanoi: NXB Khoa Học Xã Hội, 1992.

————, ed. *Một số vấn đề về nho giáo Việt Nam* (Some topics in Vietnamese Confucianism). Hanoi: Chính Trị Quốc Gia, 1998.

Phan Đan Quế. *Giai thoại và sấm ký Trạng Trình* (Stories and prophecies of Trạng Trình [Nguyễn Bỉnh Khiêm]). [Hanoi?]: NXB Văn Học, 2000.

Phan Huy Chú. *Lịch triều hiến chương loại chí* (Classified survey of the institutions of successive courts). Hanoi: Khoa Học Xã Hội, 1992.

Phan Kế Bính. *Việt Nam phong tục* (Vietnamese mores). N.p.: Sông Mới, 1983.

Phan Văn Hùm. *Ngồi tu Khám lớn* (In Khám Lớn prison). Saigon: NXB Dân Tộc, 1957 [1929].

Pháp môn Tịnh Độ (The dharma-gate to the Pure Land). Cần Thơ: An Hà, 1936.

Phật học tổng yếu (Fundamentals of Buddhism). Trans. by Thiện Chiếu. Saigon: Đức Lưu Phương, 1929.

Phật thuyết A Di Đà Kinh (Amitabha sutra). Translated by Trần Quang Thuân. Saigon: 1928.

Phương pháp làm bột giang sản xuất giấy (Method of making bamboo powder to produce paper). Liên Khu X: Nhà In Vệ Quốc Liên Khu X, 1949.

Porter, Gareth. "Proletariat and Peasantry in Early Vietnamese Communism." *Asian Thought and Society* 1:3 (December 1976), 333–346.

Qúach Tân. *Xứ trầm hương* (Land of aloe wood). Reprint of 1969 edition. Nha Trang [?]: NXB Thông Tin và NXB Tổng Hợp Khánh Hòa, 1992.

Quang Hưng and Quốc Anh. "Bước đầu tìm hiểu báo chí vô sản ở Nghệ An thời kỳ đầu cáchg mạng" (First steps in understanding proletarian newspapers in Nghệ An at the beginning of the revolution). *Nghiên cứu lịch sử* (Historical research), 175 (July–August 1977): 27–36.

Rawski, Evelyn. *Education and Popular Literacy in Ch'ing China.* Ann Arbor: University of Michigan Press, 1979.

Revertégat, Bruno. *Le bouddhisme traditionnel au sud-Viêtnam.* Vichy: Wallon, 1974.

Roberts, Richard, and Kristin Mann. "Law in Colonial Africa." In Richard Roberts and Kristin Mann, eds., *Law in Colonial Africa.* Portsmouth, N.H.: Heinemann, 1991.

Roff, William. *The Origins of Malay Nationalism.* Kuala Lumpur and Singapore: University of Malaya Press, 1967.

Rogers, Susan, ed. *Telling Lives, Telling History: Autobiography and the Historical Imagination in Modern Indonesia.* Berkeley and Los Angeles: University of California Press, 1995.

Sabatié, Léon. *La censure.* Paris: A. Pedone, 1908.

Sahlins, Peter. *Forest Rites: The War of the Demoiselles in Nineteenth-Century France.* Cambridge, Mass.: Harvard University Press, 1994.

San Hô. *Nhật ký tuyệt thực 9 ngày rưỡi: một cuộc tranh đấu của tù chính trị Côn Lôn* (Diary of a nine-and-a-half-day hunger strike: a struggle of the political prisoners on Côn Lôn [Poulo Condore]). Hanoi: Editions Sự Thực, 1939.

Savani, A. M. *Notes sur le Phat giao Hoa Hao.* Typescript, December 1951.

Scott, James. *Domination and the Arts of Resistance: Hidden Transcripts.* New Haven, Conn.: Yale University Press, 1990.

———. *The Moral Economy of the Peasantry: Rebellion and Subsistence in Southeast Asia.* New Haven, Conn.: Yale University Press, 1976.

———. *Seeing like a State: How Certain Schemes to Improve the Human Condition Have Failed.* New Haven, Conn.: Yale University Press, 1998.

Shiraishi, Masaya. "State, Villagers, and Vagabonds: Vietnamese Rural Society and the Phan Ba Vanh Rebellion." *Senri Ethnological Studies* 13 (1984): 345–400.

Shiraishi Takashi. *An Age in Motion: Popular Radicalism in Java, 1912–1926.* Ithaca, N.Y.: Cornell University Press, 1990.

Smith, Ralph B. "The Foundation of the Indochinese Communist Party, 1929–1930." *Modern Asian Studies* 32:4 (October 1998), 778–805.

Sơn Nam. *Đất Gia Định xưa* (Gia Định in the past). Ho Chi Minh City: NXB Thành phố Hồ Chí Minh, 1984.

———. *Người Sài Gòn* (The people of Saigon). Ho Chi Minh City: NXB Trẻ, 1990.

Sơn Trà [Nguyễn Sơn Trà]. *Giai cấp là gì?* (What are classes?). Tourane: Tư Tưởng Mới, 1938.

Spector, Ronald. "'What the Local Annamites Are Thinking': American Views of Vietnamese in China, 1942–1945." *Southeast Asia* (Carbondale, Ill.) 3:2 (Spring 1974), 741–751.

Strand, David. *Rickshaw Beijing.* Berkeley: University of California Press, 1989.

Suleiman, Susan. "Introduction: Varieties of Audience-Oriented Criticism." In Susan Suleiman and Inge Crosman, eds., *The Reader in the Text: Essays on Audience and Interpretation.* Princeton, N.J.: Princeton University Press, 1980.

Tai, Hue Tam Ho. *Millenarianism and Peasant Politics in Vietnam.* Cambridge, Mass.: Harvard University Press, 1983.

———. "Perfect World and Perfect Time: Maitreya in Vietnam." In Alan Sponberg and Helen Hardacre, eds., *Maitreya, the Future Buddha.* Cambridge: Cambridge University Press, 1988.

———. *Radicalism and the Origins of the Vietnamese Revolution.* Cambridge, Mass.: Harvard University Press, 1992.

Tam Tu Kinh ou le livre des phrases de trois caractères. Translated by Abel des Michels. Paris: Ernest Leroux, 1882.

Tambiah, Stanley. *The Buddhist Saints of the Forest and the Cult of Amulets: A Study in Charisma, Hagiography, Sectarianism, and Millennial Buddhism.* Cambridge: Cambridge University Press, 1984.

Tavernier, Emile. *Le régime de la presse au Tonkin.* Hanoi: Long Quan, n.d.

Taylor, Keith Weller. "Authority and Legitimacy in Eleventh Century Vietnam." *Vietnam Forum* 12 (1986): 26–59.

———. "Surface Orientations in Vietnam: Beyond Histories of Nation and Region." *Journal of Asian Studies* 57:4 (November 1998), 949–978.

Thái Bach. *Thi văn quốc cấm thời thuộc Pháp* (Forbidden literature from the French colonial period). Reprint of 1969 edition. Taipei: Cơ Sở Xuất Bản Đại Nam, 1984.

Thái Phỉ. *Một nền giáo dục Việt Nam mới* (A new Vietnamese education). Hanoi: Đời Mới, [1941].

Thanh Châu. "Hồi ký văn học: mười năm với tuần báo *Tiểu thuyết thứ bảy*" (Literary memoir: ten years with the weekly newspaper *Saturday Novel*). *Tạp chí văn học* 2 (1991): 79–82, 86.

Thanh Lãng. *Bảng lược đồ văn học Việt Nam* (Outline of Vietnamese literature). [Saigon]: Trình Bầy, [1967?].

———. *13 [mười ba] năm tranh luận văn học (1932–1945)* (Thirteen years of literary debates). Three volumes. Ho Chi Minh City: NXB Văn Học, 1995.

———. *Văn chương chữ Nôm trong Bộ khởi thảo văn học sử Việt Nam* (Nôm literature in the history of Vietnamese literature). N.p.: N.p., 1957.

Thanh Từ (Thích). *Thiền sư Việt Nam* (Vietnamese Zen teachers). Second edition, revised. Ho Chi Minh City: Hội Phật Giáo Thành phố Hồ Chí Minh, 1992.

Thiện Chiếu. *Tại sao tôi cám ơn đạo Phật* (Why I thank the Way of the Buddha). Mỹ Tho: Nam Cường, 1937.

Thien Do. "The Quest for Enlightenment and Cultural Identity: Buddhism in Contemporary Vietnam." In Ian Harris, ed., *Buddhism and Politics in 20th-Century Asia*. London: Pinto/Cassell, 1999.

Thiều Chửu. "Giảng nghĩa kinh Dược sư: mấy lời nói đầu" (Explaining the *Bhaisajyaguru sutra*: some introductory remarks). In Thái Hư Pháp Sư, *Giảng nghĩa kinh Dược sư* (Explaining the *Bhaisajyaguru sutra*). Hanoi: Đuốc Tuệ, 1941.

———. *Phật giáo với nhân gian* (Buddhism and the people). Hanoi: Đuốc Tuệ, 1936.

Thiệu Hùng. *Con đường trụ lạc: tiểu thuyết* (The road to decadence: a novel). Hanoi: NXB Trác Vỹ, 1940.

Thiếu Sơn. *Câu chuyện văn học* (Literary conversations). Hanoi: Công Lực, [1944].

Thomas, S. Bernard. *"Proletarian Hegemony" in the Chinese Revolution and the Canton Commune of 1927*. Ann Arbor: Center for Chinese Studies, University of Michigan, 1975.

Thượng Chi [Phạm Quỳnh]. "Đọc sách có cảm" (Feelings on reading). *Nam phong* 149 (April 1930): 307–310.

Tiên Lũ Đông Tự, comp. *Chấn hưng Phật giáo* (The Buddhist Revival). Hanoi: Long Quang Ấn Quán, 1927.

Tin Đức Thư Xã (Imprimerie—Librairie). *Catalogue, septembre 1933*. Saigon: Tin Đức Thư Xã XB, 1933.

Tố Hữu. "Tình hình xã hội Việt Nam dưới ách áp bực của thực dân và phong kiến qua thơ văn Xô Viết Nghệ Tĩnh" (Social conditions under the colonial and feudal yoke as seen through the literature of the Nghệ Tĩnh soviets). In Lê Trọng Khánh and Lê Anh Trà, *Xô viết Nghệ Tĩnh qua một số thơ văn* (The Nghệ Tĩnh soviets as seen through literature). Hanoi: Sự Thật, 1959.

Trần Bá Dệ, Nguyễn Ngọc Cơ, and Nguyễn Đình Lê. *Lịch sử Việt Nam 1930–45* (History of Vietnam, 1930–1945). Hanoi: Trường Đại Học Sư Phạm Hà Nội 1, 1992.

Trần Cung and Trịnh Đình Cửu. "Một vài nét về chi bộ đầu tiên của Đảng và về Đông Dương Cộng sản Đảng" (A few features of the first Party cells and of the Indochinese Communist Party). In *Ngọn đuốc* (The flame). Hanoi: NXB Văn Học, 1960.

Trần Đình Hượu. *Đến hiện đại từ truyền thống* (Approaching modernity through tradition). Hanoi: NXB Văn Hóa và Thông Tin, 1995.

Trần Đức Thảo. "Sur l'Indochine." *Les temps modernes* 1:5 (February 1946), 878–900.

Trần Hồng Liên. *Đạo Phật trong công đồng người Việt ở Nam Bộ–Việt Nam* (The Way of the Buddha among the Vietnamese of the south of Vietnam). Hanoi: NXB Khoa Học Xã Hội, 1995.

———. "Vài nét về Phật giáo thời Nguyễn (1802–1862)" (Several features of Buddhism under the Nguyễn). In Viện Khoa Học Xã Hội, *Những vấn đề văn hóa–xã hội thời Nguyễn* (Some cultural and social issues of the Nguyễn dynasty). Ho Chi Minh City: NXB Khoa Học Xã Hội, 1992.

Trần Hữu Độ. *Triết học của vô sản* (The philosophy of the proletariat). [Saigon?]: Tân Văn Hóa Tùng Thơ, 1937.

Trần Huy Liệu. *Hồi ký Trần Huy Liệu* (Memoirs of Trần Huy Liệu). Compiled by Phạm Như Thơm. Hanoi: NXB Khao Học Xã Hội, 1991.

———. *Một bầu tâm sự* (A heartfelt concern). Saigon: Cương Học Thư Xã, 1927.

———. "Phấn đấu để trở nên một đảng viên cộng sản" (Striving to become a Communist Party member). *Nghiên cứu lịch sử* (Historical research), 11 (February 1960): 77–90.

———. *Les Soviets du Nghe Tinh de 1930–31 au Vietnam.* Hanoi: Éditions en langues étrangères, 1960.

Trần Huy Liệu et al. *Tài liệu tham khảo lịch sử Cách mạng Cận đại Việt Nam* (Materials for research on the modern Vietnamese revolution). Vol. 3. Hanoi: NXB Văn Sử Địa, 1958.

Trần Huy Liệu and Nguyễn Khắc Đạm. *Xã hội Việt Nam thời Pháp Nhật* (Vietnamese society in the Franco-Japanese period). Hanoi: NXB Văn Sử Địa, 1957.

Trần Huy Liệu, Nguyễn Lương Bích, Văn Tạo, and Hướng Tân. *Cách mạng cận đại Việt Nam* (The modern revolution of Vietnam). Vol. 4. Hanoi: Ban Nghiên Cứu Văn Sử Địa, 1956.

Trần Huy Liệu and Văn Tạo. *Phong trào chống phát xít chống chiến tranh và các cuộc khởi nghĩa Bắc Sơn, Nam Kỳ Đô Lương* (The movements against fascism and

war and the Bắc Sơn, Nam Kỳ, and Đô Lương uprisings). Hanoi: Văn Sử
Địa, 1957.

———. Tổng khởi nghĩa tháng tám (The August General Uprising). Hanoi:
NXB Văn Sử Địa, 1957.

Trần Kim. *Nữ huấn: sách dạy con gái những phép trau mình* (Teachings for females:
a book to teach etiquette to girls). Can Tho: Imprimerie de l'Ouest, 1932.

Trần Nghĩa. "Bước đầu tìm hiểu các kho sách Hán Nôm và lịch sử thư mục
học Hán Nôm" (Toward a preliminary understanding of the Han-Nôm
repositories and the history of Han-Nôm catalogs), *Tạp chí Hán Nôm* 2:5
(1988), 3–20.

Trần Quốc Vượng. "Dân gian và bác học" (The people and the learned). In
Trần Quốc Vượng, *Trong cõi* (In the world). Garden Grove, Calif.: NXB
Trăm Hoa, 1993.

Trần Trọng Kim. *Nho giáo* (Confucianism). Ho Chi Minh City: NXB Thành
phố Hồ Chí Minh, 1992 [1929–1930].

———. *Việt Nam sử lược* (Brief history of Vietnam). Saigon: Bộ Giáo Dục,
1971 [1920].

Trần Văn Cung [Quốc Anh]. "Vài mẩu chuyện về chi bộ cộng sản đầu tiên
và Đông Dương Cộng sản Đảng" (Several parts of the story of the first
communist cell and of the Indochinese Communist Party). In *Bước ngoặt vĩ
đại của lịch sử catch mạng Việt Nam* (Great turning points in the history of the
Vietnamese Revolution). Hanoi: Ban Nghiên Cứu Lịch Sử Đảng [1961].

Trần Văn Giáp. *Đạo lý Phật giáo với đạo lý Nho giáo ở nước ta* (Buddhism and
Confucianism in our country). Hanoi: Phật Giáo Hội, 1935.

Trần Văn Giáp et al. *Lược truyện các tác giả Việt Nam* (Biographical sketches of
Vietnamese authors). Vol. 1. Hanoi: NXB Khoa Học Xã Hội, 1971.

Trần Văn Giàu. *Sự phát triển của tư tưởng ở Việt Nam từ thời kỳ XIX đến Cách
Mạng Tháng Tám* (The development of thought in Vietnam from the nineteenth century to the August Revolution). Hanoi: Khoa Học Xã Hội,
1973.

Trần Văn Giàu, Trần Bạch Đằng, and Nguyễn Công Bình, eds. *Địa chí văn hóa
thành phố Hồ Chí Minh* (Geography and culture of Ho Chi Minh City). Vol.
1. Ho Chi Minh City: NXB Thành phố Hồ Chí Minh, 1988.

Trang sử mới (A new page in history). Hanoi: Lê Văn Tân, 1945.

Triệu Vân. *Chính phủ là gì?* (What is government?). Tourane: Tư Tưởng Mới,
1938.

Trinh Van Thao. *Vietnam du confucianisme au communisme*. Paris: Harmattan,
1990.

Trúc Khê. *Vấn đề cải cách lễ tục Việt Nam* (Problem of the reform of ceremonies and customs). Hanoi: Lê Cương XB, 1943.

Trương Tửu. *Kinh thi Việt Nam* (Vietnamese classical odes). Reprint of 1940
edition. Hanoi: Hàn Thuyên, 1945.

Tsuboi, Yoshiharu. "Politique et confucianisme dans le Vietnam du XIXe siècle: le cas de l'Empereur Tu Duc (1847–1883)." In Yuzo Mizoguchi and Léon Vandermeesch, eds., *Confucianisme et sociétés asiatiques*. Paris: Harmattan, 1991.

Tự Do. *Fragments journalistiques.* Saigon: Imprimerie de l'Union, 1926.

Từ Lâm [Nguyễn Xuân Nghị]. *Lược khảo về mỹ thuật Việt Nam* (Short study of Vietnamese fine arts). Hanoi: Quốc Học Thư Xã, 1942.

————. *Tân hiếu kinh* (The new filial piety). Hanoi: Quốc Học Thư Xã, [1944].

"Tư liệu về Mặt Trận Việt Minh." *Nghiên cứu lịch sử* (Historical research), 255 (March–April 1991): 42–49.

Tương tế Phật Học Hội. *Statuts: Điều lệ.* Soctrang: Imprimerie Ly Cong Quan, 1934.

Tỷ-kheo-ni [Bhikkuni] (Thích-nữ). *Kinh Vu lan bồn (diễn nghĩa)* (The *Ullambana Sutra* explained). Saigon: Tin Đức Thư Xã, [1932].

Ty Thông Tin Hà Nội. *Tuyên truyền chí nam* (Propagandizing guide). Hanoi: Ty Thông Tin Hà Nội XB, 1950.

Van de Ven, Hans. *From Friend to Comrade: The Founding of the Chinese Communist Party, 1920–1927.* Berkeley: University of California Press, 1991.

Văn hóa các dòng họ ở Nghệ An với sự nghiệp thực hiện chiến lược con người Việt Nam đầu thế kỷ XXI (The culture of lineages in Nghệ An and the fulfillment of the strategy of the Vietnamese people at the beginning of the twenty-first century). [Nghệ An]: NXB Nghệ An, 1997.

Văn Tân and Nguyễn Hồng Phong. *Chống quan điểm phi vô sản về văn nghệ và chính trị (nhận những ý kiến của ông Trương Tửu về văn nghệ và chính trị đã đặng trên báo Nhân văn và Giai phẩm mùa thu và mua đông)* (Opposing antiproletarian viewpoints on literature and art [found in Trương Tửu's opinions on literature and politics published in *Humanity* and *Works of Autumn and Winter*]). Hanoi: Sự Thật, 1957.

Van Zoeren, Steven. *Poetry and Personality: Reading, Exegesis, and Hermeneutics in Traditional China.* Stanford, Calif.: Stanford University Press, 1991.

Viện Nghiên Cứu Hán-Nôm, *Nghiên cứu Hán-Nôm* (Studies of Chinese and Demotic script). Hanoi: Nhà In Khoa Học Xã Hội, 1984.

Việt Minh kêu gợi anh em binh lính đứng lên! (The Việt Minh calls on soldiers to rise up!). [Việt Bắc?]: Việt Minh XB, 1943.

Việt Nam giệt [sic] *giặc dốt* (Vietnam eradicates ignorance). Hanoi: Bình Dân Học Vụ, 1951.

Việt Tha and Lê Văn Thử. *Hội kín Nguyễn An Ninh* (The Nguyễn An Ninh secret society). Cholon: NXB Mê Linh, 1961 [1949].

Vietnamese Traditional Medicine. Hanoi: Thế Giới, 1993.

Viollis, Andrée [Ardenne de Tizac, Andrée Francoise Caroline d']. *Indochine S.O.S.* Reprint ed., Paris: Les Éditeurs français réunis, 1949.

Võ Bá Pha. *Staline nước Pháp đồng chí Maurice Thorez* (The Stalin of France: comrade Maurice Thorez). Saigon: Tân Văn Hóa Tòng Thơ, 1938.

Vũ Đình Chi (Tam Lang). "Tựa" (Introduction). In Thiệu Hùng, *Con đường truy lạc: tiểu thuyết* (The road to decadence: a novel). Hanoi: NXB Trác Vỹ, 1940.

Vũ Ngọc Phan. *Ca dao Việt Nam* (Vietnamese folk songs). Hanoi: NXB Khoa Học Xã Hội, 1978.

———. *Nhà văn hiện đại* (Modern writers). Hanoi: NXB Khoa Học Xã Hội, 1989 [1942].

Vũ Văn Sạch, Vũ Thị Minh Hương, and Phillipe Papin, comps. *Văn thơ Đông Kinh Nghĩa Thục / Prose et poésies du Đông Kinh Nghĩa Thục* (Prose and poetry of the Tonkin Free School). [Hanoi]: Cục Lưu Trữ Nhà Nước Việt Nam and Viện Viễn Đông Bác Cổ Pháp, 1997.

Werth, Léon. *Cochinchine*. Paris: F. Rieder, 1926.

Williams, Michael. *Sickle and Crescent: The Communist Revolt of 1926 in Banten*. Ithaca, N.Y.: Southeast Asia Program, 1982.

Winichakul, Thongchai. *Siam Mapped: A History of the Geo-Body of a Nation*. Honolulu: University of Hawai'i Press, 1994.

Wolters, Oliver. *History, Culture and Region in Southeast Asian Perspectives*. Singapore: ISEAS, 1982.

———. "On Telling a Story of Vietnam in the Thirteenth and Fourteenth Centuries." *Journal of Southeast Asian Studies* 26:1 (1995), 63–74.

———. "What Else Might Ngo Si Lien Mean? A Matter of Distinctions in the Fifteenth Century." In Anthony Reid, ed., *Sojourners and Settlers: Histories of Southeast Asia and the Chinese*. Sydney: Allen and Unwin, 1995.

Woodside, Alexander. *Community and Revolution in Modern Vietnam*. New York: Houghton Mifflin, 1976.

———. "The Development of Social Organizations in Vietnamese Cities in the Late Colonial Period." *Pacific Affairs* 44:1 (Spring 1971), 39–64.

———. "History, Structure and Revolution in Vietnam." *International Political Science Review / Revue Internationale des Sciences Politiques* 10:2 (1989), 143–157.

———. "Preface to the Paperback Edition." In Alexander Woodside, *Vietnam and the Chinese Model: A Comparative Study of Vietnamese and Chinese Government in the First Half of the Nineteenth Century*. Second edition. Cambridge, Mass.: Harvard University Press, 1988.

———. "Territorial Order and Collective-Identity Tensions in Confucian Asia: China, Vietnam, Korea." *Daedelus* 127:3 (Summer 1998), 191–220.

———. *Vietnam and the Chinese Model: A Comparative Study of Vietnamese and Chinese Government in the First Half of the Nineteenth Century*. Cambridge, Mass.: Harvard University Press, 1971. Second edition, 1988.

Woodside, Alexander, and David Wyatt, eds. *Moral Order and the Question of Change: Essays on Southeast Asian Thought*. New Haven, Conn.: Yale Southeast Asian Studies, 1982.

Xôcôlôp, A. A. [Anatoli Sokolov]. *Quốc tế Cộng sản và Việt Nam* (The Comintern and Vietnam). Hanoi: Chính Trị Quốc Gia, 1999.

Xuân Diệu. "Apport de la poésie française dans la poésie vietnamienne moderne." *Vietnam Forum* 5 (Winter–Spring 1985): 146–163.

Yeo, Michael. "Perceiving/Reading the Other: Ethical Dimensions." In Thomas Busch and Shaun Gallagher, *Merleau-Ponty, Hermeneutics and Postmodernism*. Albany, N.Y.: SUNY Press, 1992.

Young, Crawford. *The African Colonial State in Comparative Perspective*. New Haven, Conn.: Yale University Press, 1994.

Zhai, Qiang. *China and the Vietnam Wars, 1950–1975*. Chapel Hill: University of North Carolina Press, 2000.

Zinoman, Peter. *The Colonial Bastille: A History of Imprisonment in Vietnam, 1862–1940*. Berkeley: University of California Press, 2001.

———. "The History of the Modern Prison and the Case of Indochina." In Vicente Rafael, ed., *Figures of Criminality in Indonesia, the Philippines, and Colonial Vietnam*. Ithaca, N.Y.: Southeast Asia Program, 1999.

ABOUT THE AUTHOR

Shawn Frederick McHale is associate professor of history and international affairs at George Washington University, where he teaches courses on Southeast Asia and colonialism. Born in Southeast Asia, he was educated at Swarthmore College, the University of Hawai'i, and Cornell University. His works have appeared in *Social Compass* and the *Journal of Asian Studies*. This is his first book.

Production Notes for McHale/PRINT AND POWER

Cover and interior designed by April Leidig-Higgins in Monotype Garamond.

Composition by Asco Typesetters

Printing and binding by The Maple-Vail Book Manufacturing Group

Printed on 60# Text White Opaque, 440 ppi